KEYSTONE Finish Line

Literature

Acknowledgments

Cover and title page: www.shutterstock.com/connel; Page 42: David Stirba; Page 140: www.shutterstock.com/la tuan anh; Page 146: Library of Congress, Prints and Photographs Division, LC-USZ62-132047; Page 163: *cabin,* image used under Creative Common from RhythmicQuietude at en.wikipedia; *pond,* image used under Creative Commons from ptwo; Page 181: Library of Congress, Prints and Photographs Division, LC-USZ62-819; Page 185: courtesy of NASA; Page 219: Library of Congress, Prints and Photographs Division, LC-USZ62-117121; Page 239: courtesy of NASA

ISBN 978-0-8454-7598-0

Contents

Welcome to Keystone Finish Line Literature

An important purpose of school is to prepare you for what you need to know and be able to do in order to be ready for college and careers. With that focus in mind, some of the most important skills you can master are comprehension and critical thinking skills. Reading and responding to both fiction literature and nonfiction literature helps you to hone these skills.

These skills and more are addressed in the Keystone Literature Exam, an end-of-course assessment given no later than grade 11. The test is used to measure how well you have mastered goals set within two modules: fiction literature and nonfiction literature. Within these two modules, you will be assessed on your ability to read for meaning and to analyze and interpret what you have read. The Keystone Literature Exam is aligned to the Pennsylvania Keystone Course Standards, Curriculum Frameworks, and Assessment Anchors/Eligible Content. The Assessment Anchors are a set of subtopics that help clarify what essential skills you should learn in a literature course so you will be ready to do the work expected of you in college and a career. The anchors are further divided into standards that specify eligible content; they provide a guide to help teachers prepare you for the Keystone Literature Exam.

This book is divided into two modules and four units, which parallel the breakdown of the assessment anchors. Each unit covers all the anchors within that area of literature. Within each unit are lessons that review the main concepts and skills related to that anchor.

The question types provide practice with the kinds on questions on the Keystone Literature Exam. On the test, multiple-choice items have four possible answers. Each correct answer is worth 1 point.

The Keystone Literature Exam also has written-response questions. Each constructed response question takes 10 minutes to complete and is scored on a 0–3 scale. An answer that merits a score of 3 provides a clear and accurate response that uses relevant and specific information from the passage.

This book was written to help you get ready for the Keystone Literature Exam. The lessons in this book will help you improve your skills in vocabulary, reading, and writing. You will read nonfiction literature, such as speeches, argumentative essays, articles, and biographies, as well as stories, plays, and poems.

The lessons in this book are in three parts:

- The first part of the lesson introduces the reading skill you are going to study and explains what it is and how you use it.

- The second part of the lesson is called Guided Practice. You will get more than just practice here; you will get help. You will read a passage and answer questions. After each question, you will find an explanation of the correct answer. So you will answer questions and find out right away if you are right. You will also learn why one answer is right and the others are not.

- The third part is called It's Your Turn. This time you will read a passage and answer the questions on your own. You will answer multiple-choice questions, and you will write some answers.

Module 1
Fiction

Unit 1
Reading for Meaning

This unit will help you sharpen the skills you need to comprehend what you are reading. You will review vocabulary words, including affixes, synonyms, and antonyms. Gaining meaning from context is another skill you will review. Comprehension skills will also be assessed. You will read passages and then be asked to determine the main idea and important supporting details. Authors write for various purposes, and it is important to determine why an author has chosen to write in a particular form and style.

Vocabulary is the key to reading and writing. The more words you understand, or are able to figure out, the easier it is to make sense of what you read. The easiest way to increase your vocabulary is by reading. When you come across unfamiliar words, you can look in a dictionary to find out what they mean. However, it is often possible to figure out their meaning from the text itself.

Synonyms and Antonyms

One of the most useful ways to improve your reading vocabulary is to identify and use **synonyms** (words that mean the same or nearly the same as a given word) and **antonyms** (words that mean the opposite of a given word).

The right to vote is the most <u>fundamental</u> right in a democracy. (*synonym for* basic)

After two tense hours on the tennis court, Lelia <u>vanquished</u> her opponent. (*synonym for* defeated)

The detective had never encountered such a <u>challenging</u> problem. (*antonym of* simple)

She remained <u>taciturn</u> despite our efforts to draw her into the conversation. (*antonym of* talkative)

Read this sentence.

> *Cal impressed us with his <u>profound</u> knowledge of the music of the 1970s.*

Which word is a synonym for <u>profound</u> as used in this sentence?

A   deep

B   secret

C   glittering

D   restrained

The phrase "impressed us" gives you a clue. It tells you that Cal demonstrated his knowledge to other people. Therefore, it could not have been *secret* or *restrained*, and *glittering* makes no sense in this context. Choice A is the correct answer.

Read this sentence.

> *After living all her life in rainy Oregon, Elana was uncomfortable in Arizona's <u>arid</u> climate.*

Which word is an antonym for <u>arid</u> as used in this sentence?

A   dry

B   wet

C   cold

D   changeable

The sentence contrasts the <u>arid</u> climate of Arizona with the rainy place where Elana had been living. You can conclude, therefore, that <u>arid</u> is a synonym for *dry* and thus an antonym of *wet*, choice B.

Read this sentence.

> *Blue mass was the only <u>physic</u> in the doctor's kit, but it did seem to make Greta feel better.*

Which word is a synonym for <u>physic</u>?

A   body

B   science

C   medicine

D   possibility

You might encounter the word <u>physic</u> used this way in a text from the 1800s or earlier. You might think it could mean *body* or *science* from its relation to similar words that you know, but since it made Greta feel better, you can conclude that it's a synonym for what we today would call *medicine,* choice C.

Read this sentence.

> *Greg was pleasantly surprised at the <u>leniency</u> of the penalty he received.*

Which word is an antonym for <u>leniency</u> in this sentence?

A   bravery

B   argument

C   harshness

D   suitability

You can infer from this sentence that Greg was expecting a severe penalty for what he had done because he was "pleasantly surprised" when the opposite occurred. It's easy to conclude that <u>leniency</u> is an antonym for *harshness,* choice C.

Affixes

Affixes—prefixes and suffixes—change the meaning of a word. If you know the meanings of prefixes, suffixes, and root words, you can figure out the meaning of the whole word.

Prefixes are word parts that are added to the beginning of the word. For example, the prefix *il-* means "not." If a word begins with the prefix *il-*, the word becomes an antonym of what the root word actually means. If you are told that a certain act is *illegal,* you can conclude that it's in violation of the law, the opposite of *legal.*

Some Standard Prefixes

Prefix	Meaning	Example
anti-	against, opposite of	antisocial
auto-	self	autodirective
co-	together	cosponsor
contra-	against	contradict
dis-	not, opposite of	disengage
il-	not	illiterate
in-, im-	in, into, or not	impossible
inter-	between, among	intervene
micro-	small	microcomputer
mid-	middle	midterm
mis-	bad or wrong	misunderstand
non-	not	nonsmoking
pre-	before	preheat
post-	after	postscript
re-	back, again	reinhabit
quad-	four	quadrangle
sub-	under, of less importance	subset
trans-	through, over, across	transport
uni-	one	universe

Read this sentence.

> *At the <u>preconcert</u> reception Carissa was thrilled to meet members of her favorite band.*

The prefix *pre-* helps the reader know that <u>preconcert</u> means

  A   one concert.

  B   a bad concert.

  C   after the concert.

  D   before the concert.

To answer this question, you need to know the meaning of the prefix *pre-*. Think of other words that begin with *pre-*, such as *preview* or *pretest*. Both words have the sense of something that happens *before* something else. So the best answer is that the reception happened before the concert, choice D.

Read this sentence.

> *The main character's tendency to avoid confrontation makes him a kind of <u>antihero</u>.*

The prefix *anti-* is an indication that the character is

  A   a small hero.

  B   against a hero.

  C   repeatedly a hero.

  D   the opposite of a hero.

The prefix *anti-* can mean either "against" or "the opposite of." The sense of this sentence, which apparently describes a character in a book or a movie, is that he avoids confrontation. That suggests that he is not "against" anything, but that he acts in a way that is opposite to how we usually think of heroes in stories. The correct answer is choice D.

Suffixes are word parts added to the end of a word. Many suffixes change a word to a different part of speech. Recognizing these changes can help you figure out the meanings of new words.

Some Common Suffixes

Suffix	Meaning	Part of Speech Changes	Examples
-able, -ible	able to, tending to do or be	verb or noun to adjective	breakable; horrible
-ance, -ence	state, condition, or action	verb to noun	continuance; residence
-en	to cause to be, made of	adjective to verb, noun to adjective	lighten; wooden
-ful	full of, able to	noun to adjective	plentiful; wonderful
-ic	of, relating to	noun to adjective	romantic
-ion	act, condition of	verb to noun	satisfaction
-ish	having the quality of	noun to adjective	childish
-ist	one who is or who does something	(none)	artist
-less	without	noun to adjective	thoughtless
-ly	like, in the manner of, tending to be	adjective or noun to adverb	foolishly; heavenly
-ment	the act of or result of	verb to noun	encouragement
-ness	the state or quality of	adjective to noun	darkness
-ous	full of, tending toward	noun to adjective	hazardous
-ship	condition, state of	(none)	relationship
-tion, -ation	the act of	verb to noun	reaction

Read this sentence.

> *Putting up the rain canopy wisely prevented a <u>disastrous</u> start to the camping trip.*

In this sentence, the word <u>disastrous</u> means

    A like a disaster.

    B relating to a disaster.

    C tending toward disaster.

    D the consequence of a disaster.

> You know the meaning of the noun *disaster.* The suffix *-ous* changes a noun to an adjective, meaning "full of" or "tending toward." Leaving a rain canopy off a tent while camping can create a situation that is full of or *tends toward disaster,* choice C.

Read this sentence.

> *Stephani's belief that the dealer practiced <u>deception</u> led her to hire a lawyer.*

What does the word <u>deception</u> mean in this sentence?

    A without deceiving

    B an act of deceiving

    C able to be deceived

    D a person who deceives

> You can tell that the word *deception* has to do with deceiving, or trickery. The suffix *-tion,* meaning "the act of," changes the verb, *deceive,* to the noun, *deception.* You can guess that the word means "an act of deceiving," so choice B is correct.

Read this sentence.

> The <u>disbandment</u> of the team was a shock to its many supporters as well as to the players.

In this sentence, the word <u>disbandment</u> means that the team was

A broken up.

B not confident.

C weakened by injury.

D left without a leader.

Here both a prefix and a suffix have been added to the root word *band,* making the noun <u>disbandment</u>. The root *band* means "group." The prefix *dis-* means "not" or "opposite of," and the suffix *-ment* means "the act or result of." So <u>disbandment</u> means "the act of being made not a group," and choice A is the correct answer.

Words in Context

You have a much larger vocabulary than you may think! It includes not only the many words you use when you speak or write (your active vocabulary), but also the many more words you understand when you listen or read (your passive vocabulary). Even if you don't know a word, you can often figure out its meaning from **context clues** in the sentence or paragraph.

Read this sentence.

> *Despite his notoriety for reckless violence, he had a civil, courteous* <u>demeanor</u>.

What does the word <u>demeanor</u> mean as used in the sentence?

A face

B manner

C fascination

D understanding

You may know the word <u>demeanor</u>, but if you don't, you can figure it out from context clues. The subject is known to be reckless and violent, but his <u>demeanor</u> appears civil and courteous. It is a good guess that the word means "the way a person looks and acts," which makes choice B, "manner," the correct answer.

Read this sentence.

> *She could not easily afford expensive clothing, but tonight she wore splendid* <u>raiment</u> *suggestive of a duchess.*

What does the word <u>raiment</u> mean as used in the sentence?

A music

B flowers

C clothing

D weather

Sometimes a sentence actually defines a word. <u>Raiment</u> is an uncommon word today, but the sentence tells you it was something "splendid" that the subject wore even though she could "not easily afford expensive clothing." <u>Raiment</u> means "clothing," choice C.

Read these sentences.

> *The flagon on the table was empty. Inspector Granger sniffed it suspiciously as though it might lately have held poisoned wine.*

In the first sentence, the word flagon means

   A   box.

   B   bottle.

   C   banner.

   D   balcony.

Sometimes another sentence in the paragraph provides an explanation of what a word means. The explanatory sentence tells you that the flagon "might lately have held poisoned wine." You can figure out that flagon means "a container for liquids." The correct answer is choice B.

Read these sentences.

> *Melanie was a narcissist, Amber decided that first day. She seemed to spend half her time primping in front of a mirror.*

As used in the sentence, a narcissist is a person who

   A   admires herself excessively.

   B   is overly shy among strangers.

   C   disrespects other people's privacy.

   D   pretends she knows more than she does.

A clue to the meaning of a word may also be found in an example or a description. A person who seems "to spend half her time primping in front of a mirror" is probably overly concerned about the way she looks. You can infer that a narcissist is someone filled with self-admiration, choice A.

Words with Multiple Meanings

Often as you read you come across words that may have more than one meaning. Being able to understand different levels of meanings for words makes you a stronger reader and can also make your reading more enjoyable.

Take the word innocent, for example. In an article about a criminal trial in a court of law, the word innocent would mean "not guilty of a crime." In a religious context, innocent can mean "without knowledge of evil." And in poet William Blake's collection, *Songs of Innocence and Experience,* the word innocent connotes "without experience of the world."

A word may have different shades of meaning, such as innocent in the example above. It may be a **homograph**—a word that is spelled the same as another word but has a different meaning and may even be pronounced differently, as in the sentence, "Don't desert your companions in the desert." Or it may be a word that itself has several distinct meanings, or that may be used as different parts of speech, such as the word court.

The young woman had not expected the man to court her so ardently. *(verb: pay loving attention to)*

"See you in court," the lawyer muttered. *(noun: place where justice is administered)*

The referee ordered Kevin off the court. *(noun: place marked off for a game)*

Being an American, I arrived at the palace innocent of court manners. *(adjective: relating to the household of a king or queen)*

GUIDED PRACTICE

Read this sentence.

Anthony checked two bags at the airport.

As used in this sentence, what does the word checked mean?

A held back

B in a pattern of squares

C looked over and corrected

D left or taken for safekeeping

A dictionary gives many definitions of the word checked, both as a verb and as an adjective. In this sentence, it is plainly a verb, and it is something one does with personal property to keep it safe. You can conclude that the correct answer is choice D.

Read this sentence.

> Arianna understood that they would have to scale the rock if she was going to continue the hike.

What does the word scale mean in this sentence?

   A   to go upward

   B   to remove outer layers

   C   a series of steps or degrees, from lowest to highest

   D   an instrument for measuring or comparing weights

Scale is a word with literally dozens of meanings, as a noun, verb, and adjective. The context tells you that in this sentence it is a verb, not a noun (choices C and D). Is it more likely that hikers have to remove outer layers from a rock, as they would from a fish before cooking it, or that they have to climb it? Choice A is the answer you want.

Read this sentence.

> The closet appeared compact, but it held a lot of storage space.

What does the word compact mean in this sentence?

   A   small

   B   to compress

   C   closely packed together

   D   a small case containing make-up

Is the word COM•pact, or com•PACT? The word can be pronounced either way, and it can have several different meanings depending on which syllable is accented. The context tells you that compact in this sentence is an adjective, describing a space. The sense of the sentence shows you that the word is com•PACT, and that choice A is the correct answer.

Denotation and Connotation

There can be many shades of difference among synonyms. For example, if you earned your living telling jokes, would you rather be called a comedian or a clown? Both words name someone who makes you laugh. But you think of a comedian as an actor, while a clown may suggest a fool or an awkward person.

The difference is between denotation and connotation. The **denotation** of a word is its dictionary definition. The **connotations** of a word are the associations your feelings and imagination have with it. Connotations can be important whether you're reading poetry or listening to a political speech because they can complicate meaning or plant suggestions in your mind.

GUIDED PRACTICE

Read these sentences.

> *"He won't change his mind. He's the most <u>bullheaded</u> person I've ever met."*

What characteristic is being suggested by the use of the word <u>bullheaded</u>?

    A strength

    B firmness

    C consistency

    D stubbornness

There are several adjectives that can describe a person who won't change his mind. Some of these synonyms have positive connotations, such as *firm* or *consistent*. The word <u>bullheaded</u>, however, suggests someone who is entirely closed off to other people's reasons, someone as mindlessly stubborn as an animal. The correct answer is choice D.

Read this sentence.

> *Ellen was <u>beaming</u> as she ascended the stage to receive her reward.*

What word is being suggested by the use of the word <u>beaming</u>?

A pride

B conceit

C kindness

D confidence

The word <u>beaming</u> denotes "shining with light." Of course, the sentence is not meant to suggest that she was literally shining, but rather that she was "lit from within" by what she was feeling. Pride can have the negative connotation of conceit, but here it suggests only the positive feeling of a job well done. Choice A is the correct answer.

IT'S YOUR TURN

Read this passage from Jane Austen's novel *Pride and Prejudice* and answer the questions.

Elizabeth listened in silence, but was not convinced; their behavior at the assembly had not been calculated to please in general; and with more quickness of observation and less <u>pliancy</u> of temper than her sister, and with a judgment too <u>unassailed</u> by any attention to herself, she was very little disposed to approve them. They were in fact very fine ladies; not deficient in good humor when they were pleased, nor in the power of making themselves agreeable when they chose it, but <u>proud</u> and conceited. They were rather handsome, had been educated in one of the first private <u>seminaries</u> in town, had a fortune of twenty thousand pounds, were in the habit of spending more than they ought, and of associating with people of rank, and were therefore in every respect entitled to think well of themselves, and meanly of others. They were of a respectable family in the north of England; a circumstance more deeply impressed on their memories than that their brother's fortune and their own had been acquired by trade.

Mr. Bingley inherited property to the amount of nearly a hundred thousand <u>pounds</u> from his father, who had intended to purchase an estate, but did not live to do it. Mr. Bingley intended it likewise, and sometimes made choice of his county; but as he was now provided with a good house and the liberty of a manor, it was <u>doubtful</u> to many of those who best knew the easiness of his temper, whether he might not spend the remainder of his days at Netherfield, and leave the next generation to purchase.

1 Which word is an antonym of <u>proud</u> as used in this passage?

   A   foolish

   B   humble

   C   agreeable

   D   unpleasant

2 Read the sentence from the passage.

> *"Elizabeth listened in silence, but was not convinced; their behavior at the assembly had not been calculated to please in general; and with more quickness of observation and less <u>pliancy</u> of temper than her sister, and with a judgment too <u>unassailed</u> by any attention to herself, she was very little disposed to approve them."*

By the word <u>pliancy</u>, how does Austen suggest that Elizabeth is different from her sister?

   A   She talks less than her sister does.

   B   She is less critical of others than her sister is.

   C   She gets angry less often than her sister does.

   D   She is less influenced by others than her sister is.

3 The prefix *un-* helps the reader know that <u>unassailed</u> means

   A   not attacked.

   B   wrongly attacked.

   C   repeatedly attacked.

   D   attacked among others.

4 Which word is a synonym for <u>seminaries</u>?

   A   schools

   B   gardens

   C   burial grounds

   D   religious establishments

5 As used in this passage, the word <u>pounds</u> means

  A hits hard and heavily.

  B enclosures for animals.

  C English units of money.

  D makes a loud, booming noise.

6 The suffix -*ful* added to the root *doubt* changes the meaning of the word to

  A without a doubt.

  B to cause to doubt.

  C able to be doubted.

  D the condition of doubting.

Main Idea and Details

L.F.1.3.1, L.F.1.3.2

Every book, every poem, every chapter has a single idea that expresses, "What's it about?" It is essential when you read to understand the **main idea.** For example, this sentence could describe the main idea of *The Curious Incident of the Dog in the Night-Time,* by Mark Haddon: "An autistic teen conquers his fears and difficulties and uncovers secrets about his family when he investigates the killing of a neighbor's dog." In addition to the main idea, you must also understand the important **supporting details.** For example, in *The Curious Incident,* if you don't understand why Chris Boone thinks the way he does and are unfamiliar with the fictional detective Sherlock Holmes, a lot of the book will remain a mystery to you—including the title.

Once you understand the main idea and supporting details of any reading passage, you can write an effective **summary** of the passage. A summary is an extended answer to the question "What's it about?"—a brief statement of those essential ideas that leaves out the unimportant details and shows that you understand the essence of what you have read.

GUIDED PRACTICE

Read the beginning of Herman Melville's novel *Moby Dick* and answer the questions.

Chapter 1

Loomings

Call me Ishmael. Some years ago—never mind how long precisely—having little or no money in my purse, and nothing particular to interest me on shore, I thought I would sail about a little and see the watery part of the world. It is a way I have of driving off the spleen and regulating the circulation. Whenever I find myself growing grim about the mouth; whenever it is a damp, drizzly November in my soul; whenever I find myself involuntarily pausing before coffin warehouses, and bringing up the rear of every funeral I meet; and especially whenever my hypos[1] get such an upper hand of me, that it requires a strong moral principle to prevent me from deliberately stepping into the street, and methodically knocking

---

[1]**hypos:** stimulations of the nerves

Unit 1 Reading for Meaning

people's hats off—then, I account it high time to get to sea as soon as I can. This is my substitute for pistol and ball. With a philosophical flourish Cato[2] throws himself upon his sword; I quietly take to the ship. There is nothing surprising in this. If they but knew it, almost all men in their degree, some time or other, cherish very nearly the same feelings towards the ocean with me.

There now is your insular city of the Manhattoes,[3] belted round by wharves as Indian isles by coral reefs—commerce surrounds it with her surf. Right and left, the streets take you waterward. Its extreme downtown is the battery, where that noble mole is washed by waves, and cooled by breezes, which a few hours previous were out of sight of land. Look at the crowds of water-gazers there.

Circumambulate the city of a dreamy Sabbath afternoon. Go from Corlears Hook to Coenties Slip, and from thence, by Whitehall, northward. What do you see?—Posted like silent sentinels all around the town, stand thousands upon thousands of mortal men fixed in ocean reveries. Some leaning against the spiles; some seated upon the pier-heads; some looking over the bulwarks of ships from China; some high aloft in the rigging, as if striving to get a still better seaward peep. But these are all landsmen; of week days pent up in lath and plaster—tied to counters, nailed to benches, clinched to desks. How then is this? Are the green fields gone? What do they here?

But look! here come more crowds, pacing straight for the water, and seemingly bound for a dive. Strange! Nothing will content them but the extremest limit of the land; loitering under the shady lee of yonder warehouses will not suffice. No. They must get just as nigh the water as they possibly can without falling in. And there they stand—miles of them—leagues. Inlanders all, they come from lanes and alleys, streets and avenues,—north, east, south, and west. Yet here they all unite. Tell me, does the magnetic virtue of the needles of the compasses of all those ships attract them thither…?

Now, when I say that I am in the habit of going to sea whenever I begin to grow hazy about the eyes, and begin to be over conscious of my lungs, I do not mean to have it inferred that I ever go to sea as a passenger. For to go as a passenger you must needs have a purse, and a purse is but a rag unless you have something in it. Besides, passengers get sea-sick—grow quarrelsome—don't sleep of nights—do not enjoy themselves much, as a general thing;—no, I never go as a passenger; nor, though I am something of a salt, do I ever go to sea as a Commodore, or a Captain, or a Cook. I abandon the glory and distinction of such offices to those who like them. For my part, I abominate all honorable respectable toils, trials, and tribulations of every kind whatsoever. It is quite as much as I can do to take care of myself, without taking care of ships, barques, brigs,

---

[2]**Cato:** an ancient Roman noted for his rectitude and honor
[3]**city of the Manhattoes:** New York

schooners, and what not. And as for going as cook—though I confess there is considerable glory in that, a cook being a sort of officer on ship-board—yet, somehow, I never fancied broiling fowls;—though once broiled, judiciously buttered, and judgmatically salted and peppered, there is no one who will speak more respectfully, not to say reverentially, of a broiled fowl than I will....

No, when I go to sea, I go as a simple sailor, right before the mast, plumb down into the forecastle,[4] aloft there to the royal mast-head. True, they rather order me about some, and make me jump from spar to spar, like a grasshopper in a May meadow. And at first, this sort of thing is unpleasant enough. It touches one's sense of honor, particularly if you come of an old established family in the land.... And more than all, if just previous to putting your hand into the tar-pot, you have been lording it as a country schoolmaster, making the tallest boys stand in awe of you. The transition is a keen one, I assure you, from the schoolmaster to a sailor, and requires a strong decoction of Seneca and the Stoics[5] to enable you to grin and bear it. But even this wears off in time.

Based on information in the passage, why does Ishmael decide to go to sea?

A   He is bored with teaching school.

B   It's his way of working off tension.

C   He is running away from the police.

D   Every path he takes seems to lead to water.

Even if you have never read *Moby Dick,* you probably know it's about a sea voyage in pursuit of a whale. In this opening passage, the main character explains what draws him to the sea. That's what the passage is *about.* He explains, "It is a way I have of driving off the spleen and regulating the circulation." If this 19th-century language seems obscure, Ishmael provides supporting details that explain what he means—he speaks of a "November in my soul," he finds himself picking fights in the street, and his reference to "pistol and ball" refers to thoughts of suicide. Choice B is the correct answer.

---

[4]**before the mast...forecastle:** describing the part of a ship where the common sailors sleep
[5]**Seneca, Stoics:** an ancient Roman philosopher and others, who believed that living rightly and not giving in to emotions made a person free and immune to misfortune

Unit 1 Reading for Meaning

What is the main idea of paragraphs 2–4?

   A   New York City is a busy seaport.

   B   People are naturally drawn to the ocean.

   C   Office workers secretly dream of a sailor's life.

   D   Most of the world is ocean, and all land areas are like islands.

> In these paragraphs, Melville expands on Ishmael's desire to go to sea. He describes people in New York, rich and poor, standing in great crowds near the water's edge watching the ocean and the ships. Choice A is too narrow to be the main idea of the passage—it's about more than that. Choice D is too broad—the passage is about less than that. Choice C is irrelevant—Melville isn't expressing that idea at all. The correct answer is choice B.

Read the incomplete summary of the passage.

- *Ishmael explains why he likes to go to sea.*

- *Ishmael describes New Yorkers gazing at the water.*

- *Ishmael describes the fascination of landsmen toward the ocean.*

- _____

Which sentence **best** completes the summary?

   A   Ishmael describes the hard life of a sailor.

   B   Ishmael contrasts the jobs of sailor and schoolteacher.

   C   Ishmael explains why he goes to sea as a common sailor.

   D   Ishmael tells why he likes eating chickens better than cooking them.

> A summary should contain only the main ideas and the most important supporting details. In the last two paragraphs of this passage, Ishmael explains why he ships as a sailor, not as a passenger, officer, or cook. Choices A, B, and D are details that support the point Ishmael (and Melville) is making in these paragraphs—his decision to embark on a sea voyage. Choice C helps explain that decision, and it is the answer you want.

Now read a passage from Chapter 2 of *Moby Dick* and answer the questions.

Ishmael has arrived in New Bedford, Massachusetts, and is waiting for a boat that will take him to Nantucket Island.

Now having a night, a day, and still another night following before me in New Bedford, ere I could embark for my destined port, it became a matter of concernment where I was to eat and sleep meanwhile. It was a very dubious-looking, nay, a very dark and dismal night, bitingly cold and cheerless. I knew no one in the place. With anxious grapnels[1] I had sounded my pocket, and only brought up a few pieces of silver,— So, wherever you go, Ishmael, said I to myself, as I stood in the middle of a dreary street shouldering my bag, and comparing the gloom towards the north with the darkness towards the south—wherever in your wisdom you may conclude to lodge for the night, my dear Ishmael, be sure to inquire the price, and don't be too particular.

With halting steps I paced the streets, and passed the sign of 'The Crossed Harpoons'—but it looked too expensive and jolly there. Further on, from the bright red windows of the 'Sword-Fish Inn', there came such fervent rays, that it seemed to have melted the packed snow and ice from before the house, for everywhere else the congealed frost lay 10 inches thick in a hard, asphaltic pavement,— rather weary for me, when I struck my foot against the flinty projections, because from hard, remorseless service the soles of my boots were in a most miserable plight. Too expensive and jolly, again thought I, pausing one moment to watch the broad glare in the street, and hear the sounds of the tinkling glasses within. But go on, Ishmael, said I at last; don't you hear? get away from before the door; your patched boots are stopping the way. So on I went. I now by instinct followed the streets that took me waterward, for there, doubtless, were the cheapest, if not the cheeriest inns….

Moving on, I at last came to a dim sort of light not far from the docks, and heard a forlorn creaking in the air; and looking up, saw a swinging sign over the door with a white painting upon it, faintly representing a tall straight jet of misty spray, and these words underneath—'The Spouter-Inn:—Peter Coffin.'

Coffin?—Spouter?—Rather ominous in that particular connexion, thought I. But it is a common name in Nantucket, they say, and I suppose this Peter here is an emigrant from there. As the light looked so dim, and the place, for the time, looked quiet enough, and the dilapidated little wooden house itself looked as if it might have been carted here from the ruins of some burnt district, and as the swinging sign had a poverty-stricken sort of creak to it, I thought that here was the very spot for cheap lodgings, and the best of pea coffee.

---

[1]**grapnels:** literally a kind of anchor; here referring to his fingers

Which of these sentences **best** expresses the main idea of the passage?

   A   Ishmael is too poor to afford the best inns.

   B   Ishmael is looking for a place to eat and sleep.

   C   Ishmael explains why he wants to ship from Nantucket.

   D   Ishmael reflects on the kind of lodgings available for sailors.

> What is the main thing that this passage is about? The first sentence of the passage effectively summarizes the rest: It is cold; Ishmael needs a place to stay for two nights, and he has little money. The rest of the passage describes his search for an inn with many details, but all are in support of the main idea, choice B.

Write a summary of the passage. Include only the main ideas and most important supporting details.

_____

_____

_____

_____

_____

_____

_____

> A question such as this one on a test has no single correct answer as a multiple-choice question does. Instead, it asks you for a **constructed response** to the question—an answer in your own words. Constructed-response questions are scored according to a **rubric**—a set of guidelines such as this one:

3 POINTS

- The response provides a clear, complete, and accurate answer to the task.
- The response provides relevant and specific information from the passage.

2 POINTS

- The response provides a partial answer to the task.
- The response provides limited information from the passage and may include inaccuracies.

1 POINT

- The response provides a minimal answer to the task.
- The response provides little or no information from the passage and may include inaccuracies *OR*, the response relates minimally to the task.

0 POINTS

- The response is totally incorrect or irrelevant or contains insufficient information to demonstrate comprehension.

One way to identify the ideas that belong in a summary is to identify the sentence in each paragraph that carries the main idea. Here is an example of a summary that might earn a score of 3:

Ishmael is looking for an inn where he can eat and sleep until his ship sails. He decides that the cheery-looking inns are probably too expensive. He heads for the water, where he thinks he can find places he can afford. At "The Spouter-Inn" he hesitates because the innkeeper's name is Coffin, but he decides that it looks shabby enough to be cheap and so he goes in.

Read this passage and answer the questions.

from **Frankenstein**

by Mary Shelley

Chapter 4

From this day natural philosophy[1], and particularly chemistry, in the most comprehensive sense of the term, became nearly my sole occupation…. As I applied so closely, it may be easily conceived that my progress was rapid. My ardor was indeed the astonishment of the students, and my proficiency that of the masters…. Two years passed in this manner, during which I paid no visit to Geneva, but was engaged, heart and soul, in the pursuit of some discoveries, which I hoped to make. None but those who have experienced them can conceive of the enticements of science. In other studies you go as far as others have gone before you, and there is nothing more to know; but in a scientific pursuit there is continual food for discovery and wonder. A mind of moderate capacity, which closely pursues one study, must infallibly arrive at great proficiency in that study; and I, who continually sought the attainment of one object of pursuit, and was solely wrapped up in this, improved so rapidly that, at the end of two years, I made some discoveries in the improvement of some chemical instruments which procured me great esteem and admiration at the university. When I had arrived at this point, and had become as well acquainted with the theory and practice of natural philosophy as depended on the lessons of any of the professors at Ingolstadt, my residence there being no longer conducive to my improvement, I thought of returning to my friends and my native town, when an incident happened that protracted my stay.

One of the phenomena which had peculiarly attracted my attention was the structure of the human frame, and, indeed, any animal endued with life. Whence, I often asked myself, did the principle of life proceed? It was a bold question, and one which has ever been considered as a mystery; yet with how many things are we upon the brink of becoming acquainted, if cowardice or carelessness did not restrain our inquiries. I revolved these circumstances in my mind, and determined thenceforth to apply myself more particularly to those branches of natural philosophy which relate to physiology[2]. Unless I had been animated by an almost supernatural enthusiasm, my application to this study would have been irksome, and almost intolerable. To examine the causes of life, we must first have recourse to death. I became acquainted with the science of anatomy: but this was not sufficient; I must also observe the natural decay and corruption of the human body. In my education my father had taken the greatest precautions that my mind should be impressed with no supernatural horrors. I do not ever remember to have trembled at a tale of superstition, or to have feared the apparition of a spirit. Darkness had no effect upon my fancy; and a churchyard was to me merely the receptacle of bodies deprived of life, which, from being the seat of beauty and strength, had become food for the worm. Now I was led to examine the cause and progress of this decay, and forced to spend days and nights in vaults and

---

[1]**natural philosophy:** science
[2]**physiology:** the study of the structure of living thing

charnel-houses.[3] My attention was fixed upon every object the most insupportable to the delicacy of the human feelings. I saw how the fine form of man was degraded and wasted; I beheld the corruption of death succeed to the blooming cheek of life; I saw how the worm inherited the wonders of the eye and brain. I paused, examining and analyzing all the minutia of causation, as exemplified in the change from life to death, and death to life, until from the midst of this darkness a sudden light broke in upon me—a light so brilliant and wondrous, yet so simple, that while I became dizzy with the immensity of the prospect which it illustrated, I was surprised, that among so many men of genius who had directed their inquiries towards the same science, that I alone should be reserved to discover so astonishing a secret.

Remember, I am not recording the vision of a madman. The sun does not more certainly shine in the heavens, than that which I now affirm is true. Some miracle might have produced it, yet the stages of the discovery were distinct and probable. After days and nights of incredible labor and fatigue, I succeeded in discovering the cause of generation and life; nay, more, I became myself capable of bestowing animation upon lifeless matter.

The astonishment which I had at first experienced on this discovery soon gave place to delight and rapture. After so much time spent in painful labor, to arrive at once at the summit of my desires was the most gratifying consummation of my toils. But this discovery was so great and overwhelming that all the steps by which I had been progressively led to it were obliterated, and I beheld only the result. What had been the study and desires of the wisest men since the creation of the world was now within my grasp. Not that, like a magic scene, it all opened upon me at once: the information I had obtained was of a nature rather to direct my endeavors so soon as I should point them towards the object of my search, than to exhibit that object already accomplished....

I see by your eagerness, and the wonder and hope which your eyes express, my friend, that you expect to be informed of the secret with which I am acquainted; that cannot be: listen patiently until the end of my story, and you will easily perceive why I am reserved upon that subject. I will not lead you on, unguarded and ardent as I then was, to your destruction and infallible misery. Learn from me, if not by my precepts, at least by my example, how dangerous is the acquirement of knowledge, and how much happier that man is who believes his native town to be the world, than he who aspires to become greater than his nature will allow.

When I found so astonishing a power placed within my hands, I hesitated a long time concerning the manner in which I should employ it. Although I possessed the capacity of bestowing animation, yet to prepare a frame for the reception of it, with all its intricacies of fibers, muscles, and veins, still remained a work of inconceivable difficulty and labor. I doubted at first whether I should attempt the creation of a being like myself, or one of simpler organization; but my imagination was too much exalted by my first success to permit me to doubt of my ability to give life to an animal as complex and wonderful as man. The materials at present within my command hardly appeared adequate to so arduous an undertaking; but I doubted not that I should ultimately succeed. I prepared myself for a multitude of reverses; my operations might be incessantly baffled, and at last my work be imperfect: yet, when I considered the improvement which every day takes place in science and mechanics, I was encouraged to hope my present attempts would at least lay the foundations of future success. Nor could I consider the magnitude and complexity of my plan as

---

[3]**vaults and charnel-houses:** tombs and buildings where the bones of the dead are kept

any argument of its impracticability. It was with these feelings that I began the creation of a human being. As the minuteness of the parts formed a great hindrance to my speed, I resolved, contrary to my first intention, to make the being of a gigantic stature; that is to say, about eight feet in height, and proportionably large. After having formed this determination, and having spent some months in successfully collecting and arranging my materials, I began.

No one can conceive the variety of feelings which bore me onwards, like a hurricane, in the first enthusiasm of success. Life and death appeared to me ideal bounds, which I should first break through, and pour a torrent of light into our dark world. A new species would bless me as its creator and source; many happy and excellent natures would owe their being to me. No father could claim the gratitude of his child so completely as I should deserve theirs. Pursuing these reflections, I thought, that if I could bestow animation upon lifeless matter, I might in process of time (although I now found it impossible) renew life where death had apparently devoted the body to corruption.

These thoughts supported my spirits, while I pursued my undertaking with unremitting ardor. My cheek had grown pale with study, and my person had become emaciated with confinement. Sometimes, on the very brink of certainty, I failed; yet still I clung to the hope which the next day or the next hour might realize. One secret which I alone possessed was the hope to which I had dedicated myself; and the moon gazed on my midnight labors, while, with unrelaxed and breathless eagerness, I pursued nature to her hiding-places. Who shall conceive the horrors of my secret toil, as I dabbled among the unhallowed damps of the grave, or tortured the living animal to animate the lifeless clay? My limbs now tremble and my eyes swim with the remembrance; but then a resistless, and almost frantic, impulse urged me forward; I seemed to have lost all soul or sensation but for this one pursuit. It was indeed but a passing trance that only made me feel with renewed acuteness so soon as, the unnatural stimulus ceasing to operate, I had returned to my old habits. I collected bones from charnel houses; and disturbed, with profane fingers, the tremendous secrets of the human frame. In a solitary chamber, or rather cell, at the top of the house, and separated from all the other apartments by a gallery and staircase, I kept my workshop of filthy creation: my eyeballs were starting from their sockets in attending to the details of my employment. The dissecting room and the slaughterhouse furnished many of my materials; and often did my human nature turn with loathing from my occupation, whilst, still urged on by an eagerness which perpetually increased, I brought my work near to a conclusion.

1 What is the **main** thing that happens in this excerpt?

   A Frankenstein's long hours in the laboratory drive him mad.

   B Frankenstein becomes the best scientist in his university class.

   C Frankenstein believes that he can create life from nonliving matter.

   D Frankenstein works at building a living man from parts of dead bodies.

2 Based on information in the passage, why does Frankenstein become preoccupied with death?

   A   He is trying to overcome superstitions about ghosts.

   B   He can't understand why people are afraid of dying.

   C   He sees the study of death as a key to understanding life.

   D   He thinks it is the best way to learn about human anatomy.

3 Which of these sentences expresses the main idea of paragraph 4?

   A   "The astonishment which I had at first experienced on this discovery soon gave place to delight and rapture."

   B   "After so much time spent in painful labor, to arrive at once at the summit of my desires was the most gratifying consummation of my toils."

   C   "But this discovery was so great and overwhelming that all the steps by which I had been progressively led to it were obliterated, and I beheld only the result."

   D   "What had been the study and desires of the wisest men since the creation of the world was now within my grasp."

4 Based on information in the passage, why does Frankenstein choose to make his creation unnaturally large?

   A   He believes that "bigger is better."

   B   He wants people to be awed by his creation.

   C   He grows impatient with the smallness of human body parts.

   D   He finds that the body parts of large people are the best preserved.

5 Read the incomplete summary of the passage.

- *Frankenstein becomes obsessed with the study of science.*
- *Frankenstein comes to believe that he can discover the secret of life.*
- *Frankenstein attempts to create life from inanimate matter.*
- _____

Which sentence **best** completes the summary?

A   Frankenstein brings his creation to life.

B   Frankenstein works hard to accomplish his goal.

C   Frankenstein comes to question whether he is sane.

D   Frankenstein reveals the secret of how he created life.

Author's Purpose

L.F.1.1.1, L.F.1.1.2

Authors have various purposes in mind when they write. Think of the different reasons an author might have for writing an account of foreign travel, a politician's campaign biography, a cookbook, a newspaper editorial, or a journal entry.

Of course, literary authors are writing mainly to entertain their readers. But just what are they doing to keep you turning the pages? One passage may be written to make you laugh. Another may be written to make you cry. Yet a third might have the purpose of making you think. And all those passages might be part of the same work. When you read literature, it's important to be able to discover the author's purpose for writing. By recognizing the author's purpose or purposes, you are better able to critically analyze and assess the meaning of a selection.

GUIDED PRACTICE

Read this poem and answer the questions.

No!

by Thomas Hood

No sun—no moon!

No morn—no noon—

No dawn—no dusk—no proper time of day—

No sky—no earthly view—

5 No distance looking blue—

No road—no street—no "t'other side the way"—

No end to any Row—

No indications where the Crescents go—

No top to any steeple—

10 No recognitions of familiar people—

No courtesies for showing 'em—

No knowing 'em—

No traveling at all—no locomotion,

No inkling of the way—no notion—

15   "No go"—by land or ocean—

No mail—no post—

No news from any foreign coast—

No Park—no Ring—no afternoon gentility—

No company—no nobility—

20   No warmth, no cheerfulness, no healthful ease

No comfortable feel in any member—

No shade, no shine, no butterflies, no bees

No fruits, no flowers, no leaves, no birds—

NOVEMBER!

What is the author's purpose in writing the poem?

  A   to describe the climate of his city

  B   to express unhappiness about his life

  C   to complain humorously about the weather

  D   to comment on the way people behave in bad weather

Thomas Hood lived in London in the mid-1800s, in a climate notorious for chilling autumn fog compounded by air pollution. He "sets up" his readers by setting a dismal, morose scene emphasized by the repeated word "no." But he concludes with a pun, which is usually meant to make people laugh, and at the same time showing that he is only griping about the weather. The correct answer is choice C.

How does the repetition of the word *no* communicate an idea in the poem?

   A   It suggests the futility of life.

   B   It establishes the speaker's negative feeling.

   C   It shows the speaker's thoughts about his city.

   D   It conveys the speaker's feelings about other people.

> The **speaker** in a poem is the narrative voice that conveys the poet's feelings. In "No!" the speaker's repetition of that word gives the feeling of one door after another being slammed in one's face. How would you feel if you heard that word directed at you any time you were feeling cheerful about something? Choice B is the correct answer.

The last word of the poem reveals the author's purpose by

   A   making a joke.

   B   shocking the reader.

   C   making a plea for cheerfulness.

   D   creating an abrupt change of tone.

> This question calls on you to explain or analyze how a sample of the text supports the author's purpose. The final line of the poem—the final word— does shock the reader, in a nice way, and it does completely change the tone of the poem from sadness to a kind of good-natured grumpiness. But both of these factors are only in support of Hood's main purpose—to make you chuckle with recognition about something we all like to do: complain about the weather, which we can't do anything to change. Choice A is the answer you want.

Now read another description of November weather in London—the opening paragraphs of the novel *Bleak House,* by Charles Dickens—and answer the questions.

Chapter 1—In Chancery

LONDON. Michaelmas Term[1] lately over, and the Lord Chancellor sitting in Lincoln's Inn Hall. Implacable November weather. As much mud in the streets as if the waters had but newly retired from the face of the earth, and it would not be wonderful to meet a Megalosaurus, 40 feet long or so, waddling like an elephantine lizard up Holborn Hill. Smoke lowering down from chimney-pots, making a soft black drizzle, with flakes of soot in it as big as full-grown snowflakes—gone into mourning, one might imagine, for the death of the sun. Dogs, undistinguishable in mire. Horses, scarcely better; splashed to their very blinkers. Foot passengers, jostling one another's umbrellas in a general infection of ill-temper, and losing their foot-hold at street-corners, where tens of thousands of other foot passengers have been slipping and sliding since the day broke (if the day ever broke), adding new deposits to the crust upon crust of mud, sticking at those points tenaciously to the pavement, and accumulating at compound interest.

Fog everywhere. Fog up the river, where it flows among green aits and meadows; fog down the river, where it rolls defiled among the tiers of shipping and the waterside pollutions of a great (and dirty) city. Fog on the Essex marshes, fog on the Kentish heights. Fog creeping into the cabooses of collier-brigs; fog lying out on the yards, and hovering in the rigging of great ships; fog drooping on the gunwales of barges and small boats. Fog in the eyes and throats of ancient Greenwich pensioners, wheezing by the firesides of their wards; fog in the stem and bowl of the afternoon pipe of the wrathful skipper, down in his close cabin; fog cruelly pinching the toes and fingers of his shivering little 'prentice boy on deck. Chance people on the bridges peeping over the parapets into a nether sky of fog, with fog all round them, as if they were up in a balloon, and hanging in the misty clouds.

Gas looming through the fog in divers places in the streets, much as the sun may, from the spongy fields, be seen to loom by husbandman and ploughboy. Most of the shops lighted two hours before their time—as the gas seems to know, for it has a haggard and unwilling look.

The raw afternoon is rawest, and the dense fog is densest, and the muddy streets are muddiest near that leaden-headed old obstruction, appropriate ornament for the threshold of a leaden-headed old corporation, Temple Bar. And hard by Temple Bar, in Lincoln's Inn Hall, at the very heart of the fog, sits the Lord High Chancellor in his High Court of Chancery.

Never can there come fog too thick, never can there come mud and mire too deep, to assort with the groping and floundering condition which this High Court of Chancery, most pestilent of hoary sinners, holds this day in the sight of heaven and earth.

On such an afternoon, if ever, the Lord High Chancellor ought to be sitting here—as here he is—with a foggy glory round his head, softly fenced in with crimson cloth and curtains, addressed by a large advocate with great whiskers, a little voice, and an interminable brief, and outwardly directing his contemplation to the lantern in the roof, where he can see nothing but fog. On such an afternoon some score of members of the High Court of Chancery bar ought to be—as here they are—mistily engaged in one of the ten

---

[1]**Michaelmas term:** the fall term in English schools and law courts

thousand stages of an endless cause, tripping one another up on slippery precedents, groping knee-deep in technicalities, running their goat-hair and horse-hair warded heads against walls of words and making a pretense of equity with serious faces, as players might. On such an afternoon the various solicitors in the cause, some two or three of whom have inherited it from their fathers, who made a fortune by it, ought to be—as are they not?—ranged in a line, in a long matted well (but you might look in vain for truth at the bottom of it) between the registrar's red table and the silk gowns, with bills, cross-bills, answers, rejoinders, injunctions, affidavits, issues, references to masters, masters' reports, mountains of costly nonsense, piled before them. Well may the court be dim, with wasting candles here and there; well may the fog hang heavy in it, as if it would never get out; well may the stained-glass windows lose their color and admit no light of day into the place; well may the uninitiated from the streets, who peep in through the glass panes in the door, be deterred from entrance by its owlish aspect and by the drawl, languidly echoing to the roof from the padded dais where the Lord High Chancellor looks into the lantern that has no light in it and where the attendant wigs are all stuck in a fog-bank!...

1 What is the author's purpose in writing the first three paragraphs of this passage?

   A to establish the setting as London

   B to create a tone of shadow and mystery

   C to complain humorously about the weather

   D to provide a vivid description of the setting

Did you notice how similar Dickens's description of the London fog and its effects are to Thomas Hood's? (They lived about the same time, though Hood was 13 years older than Dickens.) Yet the two authors had entirely different purposes in writing. Hood's poem is a self-contained observation, with a "punch line." Dickens's is the introduction to a very long novel. Instead of starting his book by introducing the characters or the plot, he begins by describing the setting. There is plenty of shadow, but the only mystery is how people can see where they're going. The correct answer is choice D.

Which of the following **best** characterizes the attitude of Dickens's narrator toward the Chancery court?

A mirth

B contempt

C detachment

D astonishment

Paragraphs 4–6 compare the literal fog outside to the figurative "fog" of the English court of Chancery. Chancery court, which plays a central role in *Bleak House*, was empowered to decide cases on the basis of "fairness" rather than the strict letter of the law, and so was subject to abuses. Dickens makes the judge and lawyers seem like cartoons, "engaged in one of the ten thousand stages of an endless cause, tripping one another up on slippery precedents, groping knee-deep in technicalities" and "inherit[ing] cases from their fathers, who made a fortune by it…" This blistering satire clearly shows the attitude of Dickens's narrator—and the author's purpose. Choice B is the correct answer.

What information, if added, could **best** support the author's purpose?

A an account of the legal case being argued

B an explanation of the Lord Chancellor's job

C a description of what the courtroom looks like

D a comparison of the English and American legal systems

The author's purpose in this passage is to bring his readers into the story. It focuses at first on the general setting and then on the legal system on which Dickens's story will turn. He is not interested in describing the Lord Chancellor's job, what a courtroom looks like, or how justice is done anywhere but in England. However, the case that is being argued has a great deal to do with the story Dickens is telling, and he will get to that soon enough. The correct answer is choice A.

Read a traditional ballad and answer the questions.

The Golden Vanity

Anonymous (English, early 17th century)

There was a lofty ship, and a gallant ship was she,

And the name of the ship was "The Golden Vanity"

And we feared she would be taken by the Turkish enemy

As she sailed upon the Lowland, Lowland, Lowland,

5   Sailed upon the Lowland Sea.

Then up came our little cabin boy, and boldly out spoke he,

And he said to our captain, "What would you give to me

If I would swim alongside of the Turkish enemy

And sink her in the Lowland, Lowland, Lowland,

10   Sink her in the Lowland Sea?"

"Oh, I will give you silver, and I will give you gold,

And my own fair young daughter your lovely bride shall be,

If you will swim alongside of the Turkish enemy

And sink her in the Lowland, Lowland, Lowland,

15   Sink her in the Lowland Sea."

The boy he made him ready, and overboard sprang he,

And he swam alongside of the Turkish enemy,

And with his brace and augur[1] in her side he bored holes three

And he sunk her in the Lowland, Lowland, Lowland,

20   Sunk her in the Lowland Sea.

The boy, he swam back to the cheering of the crew,

But the captain would not heed him, for his promise he did rue.[2]

And he scorned his poor entreatings when loudly did he sue.

And he left him in the Lowland, Lowland, Lowland,

25   He left him in the Lowland Sea.

Then quickly came 'round and swam to the port[3] side,

And up to his shipmates full bitterly he cried:

"Oh shipmates, draw me up! For I'm drifting with the tide,

And I'm sinking in the Lowland, Lowland, Lowland,

30   Sinking in the Lowland Sea."

Then his shipmates hauled him up, but on the deck he died,

And they sewed him in his hammock that was so fair and wide,

And they lowered him overboard, and he drifted with the tide

And sank beneath the Lowland, Lowland Lowland,

35   Sank beneath the Lowland Sea.

1   Explain what the author's purpose was for writing this passage.
    Use information from the passage to support your explanation.

_____

_____

_____

_____

_____

_____

_____

[1]**brace and augur:** drill
[2]**rue:** regret
[3]**port:** left (side of a ship)

2 What addition to the passage could **best** support the author's purpose?

    A   a battle in which "The Golden Vanity" is sunk

    B   a final stanza showing a conversation among the crew

    C   an explanation of why the English are at war with the Turks

    D   a stanza inserted between stanzas 3 and 4 that reveals the captain's thoughts

3 Read these lines from the ballad.

    "The boy he made him ready, and overboard sprang he,

    And he swam alongside of the Turkish enemy."

How does the use of the verb *sprang* help to communicate an idea in the ballad?

    A   It shows that the cabin boy is really quite young.

    B   It suggests the cabin boy's earnestness and courage.

    C   It contrasts the cabin boy's character with the captain's.

    D   It indicates what the speaker thinks about the cabin boy.

4 What is a purpose of the author in writing stanza 5?

    A   to highlight the captain's dishonor

    B   to emphasize the hazards of naval warfare

    C   to show how the crew responds to the cabin boy's deed

    D   to point out the class differences between officers and sailors

Module 1
Fiction

Unit 2
Analyzing and Interpreting Literature

This unit will focus on your ability to analyze and interpret literature. To *interpret* and *analyze* means to think deeply about what you are reading and to ask yourself questions:

What are the elements of the story?

What techniques is the author using to help me experience the reading?

Is the author using language in a special way?

How can I use what I already know to better understand what I am reading?

In this unit, you will review the elements of literature, such as character, setting, and plot. You will also pay attention to how authors use style, tone, and mood to tell their story, and how the author uses literary techniques such as irony, foreshadowing, and symbolism to convey a message. Literature can take different forms and this unit will look at why an author might choose a particular form to convey a particular message.

Making Inferences and Drawing Conclusions

L.F.2.1.1, L.F.2.1.2

Often as you read it's not enough just to understand the ideas and details the author states. You need to "read between the lines," to understand what the author means but doesn't state directly. You do that by **making inferences**—figuring out details by combining what you know with what the author tells you—and by **drawing conclusions**—putting facts together to determine other facts. From there it's only a small step to **making generalizations** about the ideas the author is trying to convey.

For example, an author may not introduce a character by describing her as "cold and calculating." She will lead you to that generalization based on the things the character does. From the opening paragraphs of *Bleak House*, you could infer that Charles Dickens is making fun of the processes of the law. This inference may lead you to the generalization that Dickens despises the workings of the law and that he will have nothing good to say about the courts, lawyers, or judges. In reading "The Golden Vanity," you could infer that the author was on the side of the cabin boy, and you could draw conclusions about his attitudes and social position. By making inferences and drawing conclusions, you enrich your reading by combining your prior knowledge and understanding with the writer's art.

GUIDED PRACTICE

Read the beginning of a novel by an African American author, and answer the questions.

from **The House Behind the Cedars**

by Charles Chesnutt

I. A Stranger from South Carolina

Time touches all things with destroying hand; and if he seem now and then to bestow the bloom of youth, the sap of spring, it is but a brief mockery, to be surely and swiftly followed by the wrinkles of old age, the dry leaves and bare branches of winter. And yet there are places where Time seems to linger lovingly long after youth has departed, and to which he seems loath to bring the evil day. Who has not known some even-tempered old man or woman who seemed to have drunk of the fountain of youth? Who has not seen somewhere an old town that, having long since ceased to grow, yet held its own without perceptible decline?

Some such trite reflection—as apposite to the subject as most random reflections are—passed through the mind of a young man who came out of the front door of the

Unit 2 Analyzing and Interpreting Literature

Patesville Hotel about nine o'clock one fine morning in spring, a few years after the Civil War, and started down Front Street toward the market-house. Arriving at the town late the previous evening, he had been driven up from the steamboat in a carriage, from which he had been able to distinguish only the shadowy outlines of the houses along the street; so that this morning walk was his first opportunity to see the town by daylight. He was dressed in a suit of linen duck—the day was warm—a panama straw hat, and patent leather shoes. In appearance he was tall, dark, with straight, black, lustrous hair, and very clean-cut, high-bred features. When he paused by the clerk's desk on his way out, to light his cigar, the day clerk, who had just come on duty, glanced at the register and read the last entry:—

> 'JOHN WARWICK, CLARENCE,
> SOUTH CAROLINA.'

"One of the South Ca'lina bigbugs, I reckon—probably in cotton, or turpentine." The gentleman from South Carolina, walking down the street, glanced about him with an eager look, in which curiosity and affection were mingled with a touch of bitterness. He saw little that was not familiar, or that he had not seen in his dreams a hundred times during the past ten years. There had been some changes, it is true, some melancholy changes, but scarcely anything by way of addition or improvement to counterbalance them. Here and there blackened and dismantled walls marked the place where handsome buildings once had stood, for Sherman's march to the sea had left its mark upon the town. The stores were mostly of brick, two stories high, joining one another after the manner of cities. Some of the names on the signs were familiar; others, including a number of Jewish names, were quite unknown to him.

A two minutes' walk brought Warwick— the name he had registered under, and as we shall call him—to the market-house, the central feature of Patesville, from both the commercial and the picturesque points of view. Standing foursquare in the heart of the town, at the intersection of the two main streets, a "jog" at each street corner left around the market-house a little public square, which at this hour was well occupied by carts and wagons from the country and empty drays awaiting hire. Warwick was unable to perceive much change in the market-house. Perhaps the surface of the red brick, long unpainted, had scaled off a little more here and there. There might have been a slight accretion of the moss and lichen on the shingled roof. But the tall tower, with its four-faced clock, rose as majestically and uncompromisingly as though the land had never been subjugated. Was it so irreconcilable, Warwick wondered, as still to peal out the curfew bell, which at nine o'clock at night had clamorously warned all negroes, slave or free, that it was unlawful for them to be abroad after that hour, under penalty of imprisonment or whipping? Was the old constable, whose chief business it had been to ring the bell, still alive and exercising the functions of his office, and had age lessened or increased the number of times that obliging citizens performed this duty for him during his temporary absences in the company of convivial spirits? A few moments later, Warwick saw a colored policeman in the old constable's place—a stronger reminder than even the burned buildings that war had left its mark upon the old town, with which Time had dealt so tenderly.

The lower story of the market-house was open on all four of its sides to the public square. Warwick passed through one of the wide brick arches and traversed the building with a leisurely step. He looked in vain into the stalls for the butcher who had sold fresh meat twice a week, on market days, and he felt a genuine thrill of pleasure when he recognized the red bandana turban of old Aunt Lyddy, the ancient negro woman who had sold him gingerbread and fried fish, and told him weird tales of witchcraft and conjuration, in the old days when, as an idle boy, he had loafed about the market-house. He did not speak to her, however, or give her any sign of recognition. He threw a glance toward a certain corner where steps led to the town hall above. On this stairway he had once seen a manacled free negro shot while being taken upstairs for examination under a criminal charge. Warwick recalled vividly how the shot had rung out. He could see again the livid look of terror on the victim's face, the gathering crowd, the resulting confusion. The murderer, he recalled, had been tried and sentenced to imprisonment for life, but was pardoned by a merciful governor after serving a year of his sentence. As Warwick was neither a prophet nor the son of a prophet, he could not foresee that, 30 years later, even this would seem an excessive punishment for so slight a misdemeanor.

Based on information from the passage, which conclusion can be made about the setting of the novel?

A   The novel is set in a small Southern town, around 1850.

B   The novel is set in a small Southern town, around 1875.

C   The novel is set in a large Southern city, around 1900.

D   The novel is set in a large Southern city, around 1925.

Chesnutt does not tell you when the story takes place because he knows his readers will figure it out. The setting is "a few years after the Civil War," and the man he calls Warwick has been away from Patesville for 10 years. You know that the Civil War was fought between 1861 and 1865, and the environment Chesnutt describes is not that of a large city. You can infer that choice B is the correct answer.

What does Warwick most likely do at the end of the passage after he leaves the market house?

A   He goes back to the hotel for supper.

B   He proceeds on to his purpose for being in town.

C   He goes to the railroad station, having seen enough.

D   He returns to ask Aunt Lyddy whether she remembers him.

Predicting what will happen next is a form of inference that helps move a narrative forward in your mind. Chesnutt has not told you so far why this man called Warwick is in Patesville, but he has told you that it's morning, so Warwick isn't going anywhere for supper, and he came by steamboat and carriage, so he isn't taking a train anywhere. Since he just walked past Aunt Lyddy without letting on that he recognizes her, why should we think he's going back to talk to her? Choice B is the answer you want.

Unit 2 Analyzing and Interpreting Literature

Which sentence from the passage **best** supports the generalization that the Civil War caused great changes in Patesville?

A "He saw little that was not familiar, or that he had not seen in his dreams a hundred times during the past ten years."

B "There had been some changes, it is true, some melancholy changes, but scarcely anything by way of addition or improvement to counterbalance them."

C "The stores were mostly of brick, two stories high, joining one another after the manner of cities."

D "Standing foursquare in the heart of the town, at the intersection of the two main streets, a 'jog' at each street corner left around the market-house a little public square, which at this hour was well occupied by carts and wagons from the country and empty drays awaiting hire."

Chesnutt tells several things explicitly that speak to the changes wrought by the war, but there are more subtle indications, too. Among the features of the town that look the same as Warwick remembers (choices A, C, and D), there are "melancholy changes" that are only for the worse. The correct answer is choice B.

Read the statement from the passage.

"Was it so irreconcilable, Warwick wondered, as still to peal out the curfew bell, which at nine o'clock at night had clamorously warned all negroes, slave or free, that it was unlawful for them to be abroad after that hour, under penalty of imprisonment or whipping?"

Explain the significance of this statement to the passage. Use information from the passage to support your explanation.

_____

_____

_____

_____

_____

_____

_____

_____

Chesnutt, an African American, is, through his narrator, making observations about the changes that have taken place in the South since the end of slavery. He is using **personification,** the literary technique of giving human characteristics to animals or inanimate things (like bells), to comment on these changes. Here is one way you could answer the question:

"Warwick is thinking about the bell in the clock tower that used to be rung every night at nine o'clock to order all African Americans off the street. He wonders whether the bell still rings, as though not accepting of the changes that have taken place. In that way, Chesnutt is comparing the bell to people who can't accept the changes. He emphasizes this point in describing Warwick's surprise at seeing a black policeman, and in his reflecting on having once seen a white man shoot an unarmed, shackled free African American and get away with only a year's sentence. The book was probably written some years after the events it describes, as Chesnutt remarks that "30 years later" (during the time of "Jim Crow" and lynchings), even this punishment would seem "excessive for so slight a misdemeanor."

Read a poem and answer the questions.

Mending Wall

by Robert Frost

Something there is that doesn't love a wall,

That sends the frozen-ground-swell under it,

And spills the upper boulders in the sun;

And makes gaps even two can pass abreast.

5 The work of hunters is another thing:

I have come after them and made repair

Where they have left not one stone on a stone,

But they would have the rabbit out of hiding,

To please the yelping dogs. The gaps I mean,

10 No one has seen them made or heard them made,

But at spring mending-time we find them there.

I let my neighbor know beyond the hill;

And on a day we meet to walk the line

And set the wall between us once again.

15 We keep the wall between us as we go.

To each the boulders that have fallen to each.

And some are loaves and some so nearly balls

We have to use a spell to make them balance:

"Stay where you are until our backs are turned!"

20 We wear our fingers rough with handling them.

Oh, just another kind of outdoor game,

One on a side. It comes to little more:

There where it is we do not need the wall:

He is all pine and I am apple orchard.

25 My apple trees will never get across

And eat the cones under his pines, I tell him.

He only says, "Good fences make good neighbors."

Spring is the mischief in me, and I wonder

If I could put a notion in his head:

30　　"Why do they make good neighbors? Isn't it

　　　Where there are cows? But here there are no cows."

　　　Before I built a wall I'd ask to know

　　　What I was walling in or walling out,

　　　And to whom I was like to give offence.

35　　Something there is that doesn't love a wall,

　　　That wants it down. I could say "Elves" to him,

　　　But it's not elves exactly, and I'd rather

　　　He said it for himself. I see him there

　　　Bringing a stone grasped firmly by the top

40　　In each hand, like an old-stone savage armed.

　　　He moves in darkness as it seems to me,

　　　Not of woods only and the shade of trees.

　　　He will not go behind his father's saying,

　　　And he likes having thought of it so well

45　　He says again, "Good fences make good neighbors."

1 Based on information in the poem, why does the speaker feel that "Something there is that does not love a wall"?

　A　His wall needs mending every spring.

　B　Hunters tear apart his wall to flush out game.

　C　The freeze each winter breaks and scatters the stones.

　D　He never sees the damage to the wall as it is happening.

2 Based on information in the poem, what does the speaker mean when he tells his neighbor,

　　　"My apple trees will never get across

　　　And eat the cones under his pines"?

　A　He is teasing the neighbor about his superstitions.

　B　He is ironically asking why they need a wall between them.

　C　He is complaining that his neighbor isn't doing his share of the work.

　D　He is wondering why his neighbor grows pine trees instead of edible fruit.

Unit 2 Analyzing and Interpreting Literature

3 Which of the following is the **best** generalization of what the speaker thinks of his neighbor's idea that "Good fences make good neighbors"?

  A My neighbor isn't acting very neighborly.

  B My neighbor thinks that I covet some of his land.

  C My neighbor must be planning to get some cows.

  D My neighbor is repeating an old saying without any thought.

4 Which lines from the poem **best** support the speaker's generalization that good fences do *not* make good neighbors?

  A "No one has seen them made or heard them made,
  But at spring mending-time we find them there."

  B "I let my neighbor know beyond the hill;
  And on a day we meet to walk the line
  And set the wall between us once again. "

  C "Before I built a wall I'd ask to know
  What I was walling in or walling out,
  And to whom I was like to give offence."

  D "I could say "Elves" to him,
  But it's not elves exactly, and I'd rather
  He said it for himself."

5 Read the lines from the poem.

  "… He moves in darkness as it seems to me,

  Not of woods only and the shade of trees."

  Explain the significance of this statement to the poem. Use information from the poem to support your explanation.

  _____

  _____

  _____

  _____

  _____

  _____

  _____

  _____

Literary Form

L.F.2.2.1, L.F.2.2.3, L.F.2.2.4, L.F.2.5.2, L.F.2.5.3

Any literary work tells a story. But there are many types of stories, and many ways of telling them. An author decides whether to tell her story as **narrative, poetry,** or **drama.** Her choice depends on the story she wants to tell and how she wants the reader to interact with it.

Narrative

A narrative may take the form of a short story, a novel, or a series made up of several volumes. A book-length novel unfolds more slowly than a short story, and a series might involve the same characters in a variety of plots and settings, but most narratives are told in substantially the same way:

- They are written in **prose,** which reads like ordinary speech.

- They are organized into **paragraphs,** which represent thought units.

- Larger story elements are organized as **chapters,** which may be of varying lengths.

- **Dialogue,** the conversations between characters, is usually enclosed within quotation marks (" "). A change in speakers between characters is usually indicated by a new paragraph.

You already know the narrative form very well. For example, the excerpt below describes a whale hunt from *Moby Dick.*

GUIDED PRACTICE

Read the passage and answer the questions.

To a landsman, no whale, nor any sign of a herring, would have been visible at that moment; nothing but a troubled bit of greenish white water, and thin scattered puffs of vapor hovering over it, and suffusingly blowing off to leeward, like the confused scud from white rolling billows. The air around suddenly vibrated and tingled, as it were, like the air over intensely heated plates of iron. Beneath this atmospheric waving and curling, and partially beneath a thin layer of water, also, the whales were swimming….

All four boats were now in keen pursuit of that one spot of troubled water and air. But it bade far outstrip them; it flew on and on, a mass of interblending bubbles borne down a rapid stream from the hills.

"Pull, pull, my good boys," said Starbuck, in the lowest possible but intensest concentrated whisper to his men; while the sharp fixed glance from his eyes darted straight ahead of the bow, almost seemed as two visible needles in two unerring binnacle compasses. He did not say much to his crew, though, nor did his crew say anything to him. Only the silence of the boat was at intervals startlingly pierced by one of his peculiar whispers, now harsh with command, now soft with entreaty....

It was a sight full of quick wonder and awe! The vast swells of the omnipotent sea; the surging, hollow roar they made, as they rolled along the eight gunwales, like gigantic bowls in a boundless bowling-green; the brief suspended agony of the boat, as it would tip for an instant on the knife-like edge of the sharper waves, that almost seemed threatening to cut it in two; the sudden profound dip into the watery glens and hollows; the keen spurrings and goadings to gain the top of the opposite hill; the headlong, sled-like slide down its other side;—all these, with the cries of the headsmen and harpooneers, and the shuddering gasps of the oarsmen, with the wondrous sight of the ivory *Pequod* bearing down upon her boats with outstretched sails, like a wild hen after her screaming brood;—all this was thrilling. Not the raw recruit, marching from the bosom of his wife into the fever heat of his first battle; not the dead man's host encountering the first unknown phantom in the other world;—neither of these can feel stranger and stronger emotions than that man does, who for the first time finds himself pulling into the charmed, churned circle of the hunted sperm whale.

The dancing white water made by the chase was now becoming more and more visible, owing to the increasing darkness of the dun cloud-shadows flung upon the sea. The jets of vapor no longer blended, but tilted everywhere to right and left; the whales seemed separating their wakes. The boats were pulled more apart; Starbuck giving chase to three whales running dead to leeward. Our sail was now set, and, with the still rising wind, we rushed along; the boat going with such madness through the water, that the lee oars could scarcely be worked rapidly enough to escape being torn from the row-locks.

Soon we were running through a suffusing wide veil of mist; neither ship nor boat to be seen.

"Give way, men," whispered Starbuck, drawing still further aft the sheet of his sail; "there is time to kill a fish yet before the squall comes. There's white water again!—close to! Spring!"

Soon after, two cries in quick succession on each side of us denoted that the other boats had got fast; but hardly were they overheard, when with a lightning-like hurtling whisper Starbuck said: "Stand up!" and Queequeg, harpoon in hand, sprang to his feet.

Though not one of the oarsmen was then facing the life and death peril so close to them ahead, yet with their eyes on the intense countenance of the mate in the stern of the boat, they knew that the imminent instant had come; they heard, too, an enormous wallowing sound as of 50 elephants stirring in their litter. Meanwhile the boat was still booming through the mist, the waves curling and hissing around us like the erected crests of enraged serpents.

"That's his hump. There, there, give it to him!" whispered Starbuck.

A short rushing sound leaped out of the boat; it was the darted iron of Queequeg. Then all in one welded commotion came an invisible push from astern, while forward the boat seemed striking on a ledge; the sail collapsed and exploded; a gush of scalding vapor shot up near by; something rolled and tumbled like an earthquake beneath us. The whole crew were half suffocated as they were tossed helter-skelter into the white curdling cream of the squall. Squall, whale, and harpoon had all blended together; and the whale, merely grazed by the iron, escaped.

Though completely swamped, the boat was nearly unharmed. Swimming round it we picked up the floating oars, and lashing them across the gunwale, tumbled back to our places. There we sat up to our knees in the sea, the water covering every rib and plank, so that to our downward gazing eyes the suspended craft seemed a coral boat grown up to us from the bottom of the ocean.

What characteristic of the passage **best** indicates to readers that it is narrative fiction rather than informational nonfiction?

   A   the inclusion of dialogue

   B   the tone of rising excitement

   C   the organization into paragraphs

   D   the narrator's expression of what he senses

Fiction and narrative nonfiction both are organized into paragraphs. Certain types of nonfiction may include dialogue in quotation marks, either to record actual conversations or to imagine what people might have said to one another. A reporter's account of an actual 19th-century whale hunt would most likely describe the tension and sense of danger. However, this passage is rich with imagery in the narrator's (Ishmael's) observations of what he sees, hears, and feels, and this is what the fictional form is especially good at conveying. Choice D is the correct answer.

How does the author's use of fiction as a literary form influence the meaning of the passage?

   A   It allows the reader to feel present in the whaleboat.

   B   It allows the author to present facts about whale hunting.

   C   It allows the author to advance the story through dialogue.

   D   It allows the reader to evaluate his opinions about hunting.

Moby Dick is full of facts about 19th-century whaling, and this passage is a fine example. However, nonfiction presents facts, too. Fiction certainly uses dialogue to advance the narrative, but the dialogue in this passage is sparse. You may have had an emotional reaction to the hunt, but the author's purpose is not to sway anybody for or against whale hunting. The fictional form allows you vividly to see what the narrator sees, hear what he hears, and feel what he feels. The correct answer is choice A.

Unit 2 Analyzing and Interpreting Literature

Read these sentences from the passage.

"It was a sight full of quick wonder and awe! The vast swells of the omnipotent sea; the surging, hollow roar they made, as they rolled along the eight gunwales, like gigantic bowls in a boundless bowling-green; the brief suspended agony of the boat, as it would tip for an instant on the knife-like edge of the sharper waves, that almost seemed threatening to cut it in two...."

What is the effect of the imagery in this sentence?

A   It creates a feeling of rollicking fun.

B   It indicates what the weather is like.

C   It emphasizes the danger of the hunt.

D   It shows Ishmael's love for the ocean.

"Vast swells." "Surging, hollow roar." "Suspended agony." "The knife edge... threatening to cut it in two." These are not images of fun, weather, or love. Melville here is emphasizing the constant danger of the crew in the open boat. The correct answer is choice C.

Poetry

Poetry has been called the purest form of literature, and is probably the oldest. There are as many types of poems as there are of narratives. Any poem presents an idea and aims to produce an emotional response in the reader. However, a **narrative poem,** like the ballad "The Golden Vanity" (page 42) tells a story, while a **lyric poem,** such as "No!" (page 36) expresses the author's feelings while telling a more subtle story. Then there are poems such as "Mending Wall" (page 51) that contain elements of both narrative and lyric poetry.

Poems express meaning through **form, sound devices,** and **imagery.**

Form gives structure to a poem. A poem is written of lines of regular or varying length, called **verse.** It may be divided into **stanzas,** such as this example by John Masefield:

Sea-Fever

by John Masefield

I must down to the seas again, to the lonely sea and the sky,

And all I ask is a tall ship and a star to steer her by,

And the wheel's kick and the wind's song and the white
    sail's shaking,

And a grey mist on the sea's face, and a grey dawn breaking.

5 I must down to the seas again, for the call of the running
    tide

Is a wild call and a clear call that may not be denied;

And all I ask is a windy day with the white clouds flying,

And the flung spray and the blown spume, and the sea-gulls
    crying.

I must down to the seas again, to the vagrant gypsy life,

10 To the gull's way and the whale's way where the wind's like
    a whetted knife;

And all I ask is a merry yarn from a laughing fellow-rover

And quiet sleep and a sweet dream when the long trick's
    over.

Here is a poem that has a formal structure but is not divided into stanzas. It is a **sonnet,** a 14-line structure that writers have used from the 1300s through today:

Sonnet XLIII

by Elizabeth Barrett Browning

How do I love thee? Let me count the ways.

I love thee to the depth and breadth and height

My soul can reach, when feeling out of sight

For the ends of Being and ideal Grace.

5 I love thee to the level of everyday's

Most quiet need, by sun and candle-light.

I love thee freely, as men strive for Right;

I love thee purely, as they turn from Praise.

I love thee with a passion put to use

10 In my old griefs, and with my childhood's faith.

I love thee with a love I seemed to lose

With my lost saints,—I love thee with the breath,

Smiles, tears, of all my life!—and, if God choose,

I shall but love thee better after death.

A **haiku** also has a formal structure of 17 syllables divided into three lines of 5, 7 and 5 syllables:

Mushroom

by Matsuo Bassho

See there a mushroom—

Fallen from an unknown tree,

A leaf sticks to it

Sound devices give poems a musical quality, set a mood for the poem, or emphasize the meanings of words. Many poems have **rhyme,** repeated sounds at the ends of words. The pattern of rhymed lines in a poem is called a **rhyme scheme.** In "Sea-Fever," for example, the first two lines of each stanza rhyme, and the third and fourth lines rhyme. This is called an **A A B B** rhyme scheme.

I must down to the seas again, to the lonely sea and the **sky, [A]**

And all I ask is a tall ship and a star to steer her **by, [A]**

And the wheel's kick and the wind's song and the white sail's **shaking, [B]**

And a grey mist on the sea's face, and a grey dawn **breaking. [B]**

In Browning's "Sonnet," the rhyme scheme is more complex:

How do I love thee? Let me count the ways. **[A]**

I love thee to the depth and breadth and height **[B]**

My soul can reach, when feeling out of sight **[B]**

For the ends of Being and ideal Grace. **[A]**

I love thee to the level of everyday's **[C]**

Most quiet need, by sun and candle-light. **[D]**

I love thee freely, as men strive for Right; **[D]**

I love thee purely, as they turn from Praise. **[C]**

In a haiku, or in poems like "Mending Wall," there is no rhyme.

"Mending Wall," like most poetry, has **rhythm**—a pattern of stressed and unstressed beats in a line of verse:

*Some*thing there *is* that *does*n't *love* a *wall,*

That *sends* the *frozen-ground*-swell *under it,*

And *spills* the *upper boul*ders *in* the *sun…*

But many poems, especially modern ones, have no formal structure, rhyme, or rhythm and are considered **free verse,** as is this example by Stephen Crane:

> A man said to the universe:
>
> "Sir, I exist!"
>
> "However," replied the universe,
>
> "The fact has not created in me
>
> "A sense of obligation."

Onomatopoeia is a sound device that you have probably known since you first began to talk. It is the use of words that imitate the sound of something, such as *ding, honk,* or *moo.*

Alliteration is the repetition of the same, or very similar, beginning consonant sounds in a line of poetry, as in this line of verse:

> Cake, cookies and candles at the close of day

Assonance is the repetition of vowel sounds in nearby words, as in this line of verse by Edgar Allen Poe:

> Hear the mellow wedding bells…

Imagery is the use of vivid and descriptive language that appeals to one or more of the senses. In "Sea-Fever," for example, Masefield's description allows you to feel, hear, and see what a sailor would when standing on the deck of a ship in the early morning.

> …the wheel's kick and the wind's song and the white sail's shaking,
>
> And a grey mist on the sea's face, and a grey dawn breaking.

Read the examples and answer the questions.

Read the first stanza of the poem "She Walks in Beauty" by George Gordon, Lord Byron.

> She walks in beauty, like the night
>
> Of cloudless climes and starry skies;
>
> And all that's best of dark and bright
>
> Meet in her aspect and her eyes:
>
> Thus mellowed to that tender light
>
> Which heaven to gaudy day denies.

What is the rhyme scheme of this stanza?

A A B A B A B

B A A B B C C

C A B C A B C

D A B A B C D

In this stanza, the three odd-numbered lines all rhyme with one another while the three even-numbered lines also rhyme with one another. If you call the lines with the first set of rhymes "A" and those with the second set "B," you'll readily see that choice A is the answer you want.

The second line of the stanza contains examples of

A free verse.

B assonance.

C alliteration.

D onomatopoeia.

Byron emphasizes the rhythm of his stanza in this line with two stressed *cl-* syllables and two stressed *s-* syllables. These are examples of alliteration, choice C.

How are the accounts of the sea in the poem "Sea-Fever" and the excerpt from *Moby Dick* **most** similar?

A in their use of vivid imagery

B in their economy of language

C in their feelings about the sea

D in their use of several characters

Here you're analyzing one of the differences between narrative fiction and lyric poetry. Both examples contain vivid imagery in describing the sea from a human point of view, on a ship and in an open rowboat respectively. But the poem is much more compressed in its imagery and in the language used to express it. Masefield's ocean is a place of romance and adventure, while Melville's is full of menace. And in a lyric poem such as "Sea-Fever," the only characters are the speaker and the reader. The correct answer is choice A.

Drama

Like other forms of narrative, dramatic writing tells a story. However, unlike other forms of narrative, it is meant to be performed—on a stage, a movie or TV screen, or the radio. This type of narrative also uses special features that give instructions to directors and performers for making the story come alive.

A **play** is a story that is performed by actors on a stage. A play is divided into **acts,** as a book is divided into chapters. Acts may be divided into **scenes.** A scene is part of the action that takes place in one place. Whether you watch a play or read one, it has acts and scenes. A **screenplay** is a story that is performed by actors before a camera to be shown as a movie, video, or TV program. It uses special techniques to guide the director and performers in expressing what the audience is meant to see.

Although dramatic literature has all the same elements as fiction, they are presented differently than in a novel or short story. Sometimes a **narrator** describes events and through whose point of view the narrative unfolds. Usually, however, character, plot, and conflict are advanced almost entirely through **dialogue**—the words the characters speak. In a **script,** or printed version of a play, dialogue comes directly after the speaker's name and is usually printed in a different form of type.

Setting and character may be conveyed in part through **stage directions** that describe what the audience sees and how the actors should move and speak. Some stage directions may be detailed while others may be sparse, leaving a great deal of the presentation to the discretion of the director and actors, and to the imagination of

Unit 2 Analyzing and Interpreting Literature

readers. In a script, stage directions are usually printed in a different style of type and set off from the characters' names and the dialogue.

Dramatic literature has its own special elements and terms. Here are a few that are useful for you to know as you read a play or screenplay:

- **Aside**—a statement made by a character that is directed to the audience, not another character. This device gives the audience more knowledge about the speaker's state of mind than the other characters have.

- **Lighting**—the types of lights used on stage. Lighting can suggest mood and tone, highlight specific characters, and suggest their relationships to one another.

- **Monologue**—a long speech spoken by one character.

- **Props**—the objects, such as a frying pan or hammer and nails, that the characters use on a stage.

- **Scenery**—backgrounds and larger objects that create the physical setting of the play such as a kitchen or a woodlands. When described in stage directions, scenery helps the reader to picture the setting.

- **Soliloquy**—a monologue spoken by a character who is alone on the stage. In a soliloquy, the character reveals her thoughts and feelings to the audience.

GUIDED PRACTICE

Read the beginning of a comedy and answer the questions.

from **Pygmalion**

by George Bernard Shaw

ACT I

[London.] Covent Garden at 11:15 p.m. Torrents of heavy summer rain. Cab whistles blowing frantically in all directions. Pedestrians running for shelter into the market and under the portico of St. Paul's Church, where there are already several people, among them a lady and her daughter in evening dress. They are all peering out gloomily at the rain, except one man with his back turned to the rest, who seems wholly preoccupied with a notebook in which he is writing busily.

The church clock strikes the first quarter.

THE DAUGHTER *[in the space between the central pillars, close to the one on her left]*. I'm getting chilled to the bone. What can Freddy be doing all this time? He's been gone 20 minutes.

THE MOTHER [*on her daughter's right*]. Not so long. But he ought to have got us a cab by this.

A BYSTANDER [*on the lady's right*]. He won't get no cab not until half-past 11, missus, when they come back after dropping their theatre fares.

THE MOTHER. But we must have a cab. We can't stand here until half-past 11. It's too bad.

THE BYSTANDER. Well, it ain't my fault, missus.

THE DAUGHTER. If Freddy had a bit of gumption, he would have got one at the theatre door.

THE MOTHER. What could he have done, poor boy?

THE DAUGHTER. Other people got cabs. Why couldn't he?

Freddy rushes in out of the rain from the Southampton Street side, and comes between them closing a dripping umbrella. He is a young man of 20, in evening dress, very wet around the ankles.

THE DAUGHTER. Well, haven't you got a cab?

FREDDY. There's not one to be had for love or money.

THE MOTHER. Oh, Freddy, there must be one. You can't have tried.

THE DAUGHTER. It's too tiresome. Do you expect us to go and get one ourselves?

FREDDY. I tell you they're all engaged. The rain was so sudden: nobody was prepared; and everybody had to take a cab. I've been to Charing Cross one way and nearly to Ludgate Circus the other; and they were all engaged.

THE MOTHER. Did you try Trafalgar Square?

FREDDY. There wasn't one at Trafalgar Square.

THE DAUGHTER. Did you try?

FREDDY. I tried as far as Charing Cross Station. Did you expect me to walk to Hammersmith?

THE DAUGHTER. You haven't tried at all.

THE MOTHER. You really are very helpless, Freddy. Go again; and don't come back until you have found a cab.

FREDDY. I shall simply get soaked for nothing.

THE DAUGHTER. And what about us? Are we to stay here all night in this draft, with next to nothing on. You selfish pig—

FREDDY. Oh, very well: I'll go, I'll go. [*He opens his umbrella and dashes off Strandwards, but comes into collision with a flower girl, who is hurrying in for shelter, knocking her basket out of her hands. A blinding flash of lightning, followed instantly by a rattling peal of thunder, orchestrates the incident.*]

Unit 2 Analyzing and Interpreting Literature

THE FLOWER GIRL. Nah then, Freddy: look wh' y' gowin, deah.

FREDDY. Sorry. [*he rushes off.*]

THE FLOWER GIRL [*picking up her scattered flowers and replacing them in the basket*]. There's menners f' yer! Te-oo banches o voylets trod into the mad. [*She sits down on the plinth of the column, sorting her flowers, on the lady's right. She is not at all an attractive person. She is perhaps eighteen, perhaps twenty, hardly older. She wears a little sailor hat of black straw that has long been exposed to the dust and soot of London and has seldom if ever been brushed. Her hair needs washing rather badly: its mousy color can hardly be natural. She wears a shoddy black coat that reaches nearly to her knees and is shaped to her waist. She has a brown skirt with a coarse apron. Her boots are much the worse for wear. She is no doubt as clean as she can afford to be; but compared to the ladies she is very dirty. Her features are no worse than theirs; but their condition leaves something to be desired; and she needs the services of a dentist.*]

How does the reader know that the passage is drama rather than narrative prose?

   A   The author uses dialogue.

   B   The author uses very little imagery.

   C   The author describes the characters.

   D   The author uses detailed stage directions.

> Dialogue may appear in narrative prose and even in poetry. There is no reason imagery may or may not be used in a play, and any author of fiction might include descriptions of the characters. Stage directions, however, are particular to dramatic writing, and Shaw's are richly detailed. The correct answer is choice D.

The playwright lets the reader discover the character of the daughter **mainly** through

   A   her dialogue.

   B   the stage directions.

   C   contrasting her with the flower girl.

   D   what Freddy and the mother say about her.

> You already know a lot about these characters. The daughter complains a great deal and speaks disrespectfully of and to her brother when he's the one getting soaked in the rain. This is all something you pick up from her dialogue, choice A.

What is the **main** effect of the use of dialect in the Flower Girl's speech?

   A   It makes her a comic figure.

   B   It reveals her lower-class origins.

   C   It suggests that she will be a main character.

   D   It sets up a conflict between her and the daughter.

> The way people speak is a key element of the theme of *Pygmalion*. You can tell at once the contrast between the flower girl and the other characters you have met so far. She is obviously poor, and the way she speaks emphasizes her poverty to the other characters and to the audience. The correct answer is choice B.

Which is an example of a prop used in this scene?

   A   a cab

   B   an umbrella

   C   a church portico

   D   a flash of lightning

> A prop is an object that can be carried by an actor on the stage. The church portico is part of the scenery; the flash of lightning is an effect of stage lighting; and did you notice in all the talk of cabs that the audience never actually sees one? Choice B is the answer you want.

IT'S YOUR TURN

Read a poem and an excerpt from a play and answer the questions.

Because I Could Not Stop for Death

by Emily Dickinson

Because I could not stop for Death,
He kindly stopped for me;
The carriage held but just ourselves
And Immortality.

5 We slowly drove, he knew no haste,
And I had put away
My labor, and my leisure too,

Unit 2 Analyzing and Interpreting Literature

For his civility.

We passed the school, where children strove

10 At recess, in the ring;

We passed the fields of gazing grain,

We passed the setting sun.

We paused before a house that seemed

A swelling of the ground;

15 The roof was scarcely visible,

The cornice but a mound.

Since then 'tis centuries, and yet each

Feels shorter than the day

I first surmised the horses' heads

20 Were toward eternity.

from Hamlet, Prince of Denmark

by William Shakespeare

Act III, Scene 1

Prince Hamlet believes that King Claudius, his father's brother, murdered his father to seize his throne and marry Hamlet's mother. On stage as this excerpt begins are the king, his advisor Polonius, and Polonius's daughter Ophelia, Hamlet's sweetheart, whom he has dismayed by his seeming indifference to her. They have arranged for Ophelia to meet Hamlet here, as though by accident, to see if they can find out what is troubling him.

POLONIUS: Ophelia, walk you here. Gracious, so please you,
We will bestow[1] ourselves.   *[to OPHELIA:]* Read on this book;
That show of such an exercise may color
Your loneliness. We are oft to blame in this,
'Tis too much proved—that with devotion's visage[2]
And pious action we do sugar o'er
The devil himself.

KING CLAUDIUS: *[Aside]* O, 'tis too true!
How smart a lash that speech doth give my conscience!
The harlot's cheek, beautied with plastering art,
Is not more ugly to the thing that helps it
Than is my deed to my most painted word.
O heavy burden!

---

[1]**bestow:** hide
[2]**visage:** face

POLONIUS: I hear him coming. Let's withdraw, my lord.

Exeunt KING CLAUDIUS and POLONIUS

Enter HAMLET

HAMLET: To be, or not to be: that is the question:
Whether 'tis nobler in the mind to suffer
The slings and arrows of outrageous fortune,
Or to take arms against a sea of troubles,
And by opposing end them? To die: to sleep
No more; and by a sleep to say we end
The heart-ache and the thousand natural shocks
That flesh is heir to. 'Tis a consummation
Devoutly to be wish'd. To die, to sleep,
To sleep—perchance to dream—ay, there's the rub;
For in that sleep of death what dreams may come
When we have shuffled off this mortal coil
Must give us pause. There's the respect
That makes calamity of so long life.
For who would bear the whips and scorns of time,
The oppressor's wrong, the proud man's contumely,[3]
The pangs of despised love, the law's delay,
The insolence of office and the spurns
That patient merit of the unworthy takes,
When he himself might his quietus[4] make
With a bare bodkin[5]? Who would these fardels[6] bear,
To grunt and sweat under a weary life,
But that the dread of something after death,
The undiscover'd country from whose bourn
No traveller returns, puzzles the will
And makes us rather bear those ills we have
Than fly to others that we know not of?
Thus conscience does make cowards of us all;
And thus the native hue of resolution
Is sicklied o'er with the pale cast of thought,
And enterprises of great pith and moment
With this regard their currents turn away,
And lose the name of action.—Soft[7] you now!
The fair Ophelia! Nymph, in thy orisons[8]
Be all my sins remember'd.

---

[3]**contumely:** rudeness
[4]**quietus:** release
[5]**bodkin:** a short dagger
[6]**fardels:** burdens
[7]**soft you now:** be quiet; stop talking
[8]**orisons:** prayers

Unit 2 Analyzing and Interpreting Literature

1 In what way are the poem and the play excerpt similar?

   A Both consider "Death" as if it were a person.

   B Both contain meditations on the taking of one's own life.

   C Both contemplate ideas on what may happen after life is over.

   D Both express a calm acceptance of death as the natural end of life.

2 What is the rhyme scheme of the first stanza of the poem?

   A A B A B

   B A A B B

   C A B C B

   D A B C C

3 Which pair of lines would **best** fit the rhythm of Dickinson's poem?

   A I fear not Death,
      Who has no power over me.

   B And if perchance Death could not wait,
      I'd gladly wait for him.

   C And when has come the time for me to die,
      I'll think of it as just a carriage ride.

   D And if in life I'd never lied,
      Just as I lived, so I'll have died.

4 Hamlet's famous speech in Act III, Scene 1 is known as "Hamlet's soliloquy." This indicates that Hamlet

   A is speaking to Ophelia.

   B believes himself to be alone.

   C is speaking directly to the audience.

   D stands on a bare stage with no scenery.

5 How does the reader know that the excerpt from *Hamlet* is drama rather than lyric poetry?

    A It is written in verse.

    B It is not written in paragraphs.

    C It contains directions for lighting.

    D It indicates which characters are speaking.

6 How do the authors' use of poetry and drama influence the meaning of the respective passages?

    A It allows them both to take solace in traditional religion.

    B It allows them both to critically examine their respective cultures' ideas about life after death.

    C It allows them both to use abstract imagery to express their feelings on a universal yet deeply personal theme.

    D It allows them both to imagine the way their respective speaker and character think about death without revealing their own feelings.

LESSON 6

Character, Setting, and Plot

L.F.2.3.1, L.F.2.3.2, L.F.2.3.3

Anything ever written, even an advertisement, tells a story, and as you know, there are many ways to tell one. What may not be so apparent is that every story, whether narrative, poetry, drama, or nonfiction, contains the same six elements:

- **Characters**—the people in a narrative. They may include a **narrator** or **speaker.** In some literary works, such as many poems, there may appear to be one character, the speaker. In fact, there are always at least two, including you, the reader or listener.

- **Setting**—the place and time that the story takes place.

- **Plot**—the events or action of the story.

- **Theme**—the main idea that the author is trying to advance.

- **Tone, style, mood**—the attitude of the author toward the subject, characters, and you, the reader or listener, as expressed in language, voice, and emotional content of the work.

- **Point of view**—the perspective from which the story is told, whether of one or more characters or of a narrator.

The ways these elements are presented differ depending on what literary form the author chooses, but they are always present, and they always interact in relation to one another. In this lesson, you'll examine the first three elements.

Characters

To understand any narrative you must be able to describe, analyze, and understand who the characters are. What characters say, how they act, how they change during the course of the narrative, and how they relate to and communicate with each other is important to understanding the overall meaning of a work of literature. Ask yourself these questions to better understand the characters and their contributions to the plot:

- Who is the most important character (the **protagonist**)?

- What does this character want?

- Is there a character that wants to prevent the main character from getting what he wants (the **antagonist**)?

- If so, what does this character want?

- Who are the supporting characters?

Unit 2 Analyzing and Interpreting Literature

71

- How do the characters relate to each other?

- What does each character want?

- How do the characters' words and actions reflect the conflict and action of the story?

- What can you tell about a character from what she says, what she does, what the narrative reveals about her, and how other characters respond to her?

- How do characters grow and change in *response* to the events of the story, and how does their growth and change *affect* the events of the story?

Setting

When reading any narrative, you need to be able to identify where and when the story takes place. Another important element to consider is how the setting will affect the overall meaning of the work.

Sometimes the author reveals the setting immediately. There may be a line that describes where or when the story takes place, as in the opening of Charles Dickens's *Bleak House* you read in Lesson 3:

LONDON. Michaelmas Term lately over, and the Lord Chancellor sitting in Lincoln's Inn Hall. Implacable November weather....

Dickens's readers know from this opening sentence where the story takes place (London), and at what time of year (November). If you know when *Bleak House* was written (1852–1853), you have an idea of what to expect in terms of the culture, technology, and social conditions that will be portrayed in the book.

In narratives that do not reveal their setting so directly, you can use what you know to pick up clues, as in the opening sentence of the story "One of the Missing," by Ambrose Bierce:

Jerome Searing, a private soldier of General Sherman's army, then confronting the enemy at and about Kennesaw Mountain, Georgia, turned his back upon a small group of officers with whom he had been talking in low tones, stepped across a light line of earthworks, and disappeared in a forest.

This sentence tells you where the story takes place—Georgia—but not when. However, the characters are soldiers, and you may know that William T. Sherman was a Northern general during the Civil War who led a devastating march through Georgia in 1864. So there is your setting in one sentence.

Unit 2 Analyzing and Interpreting Literature

In *To Kill a Mockingbird,* author Harper Lee tells you in the third paragraph that the narrative is set in Maycomb County, Alabama, but she holds off awhile before remarking that "Maycomb County had recently been told that it had nothing to fear but fear itself." That places the story in the year 1933, when President Franklin D. Roosevelt used that line in a famous speech.

Even if the setting is not explicitly stated, you can usually figure it out using clues in the reading passage, such as:

- the language characters use. Does it sound modern or historic? Do the characters speak in standard English or in dialect?

- the manner of transportation and other forms of technology. Are the characters traveling in cars or on horseback? Do they use telephones, watch television, use the Internet?

- the occupations and leisure activities of the characters

- the clothing styles of the characters

Plot and Conflict

The **plot,** or action, is made up of the events that happen in a story. The author tells the events of the story in a certain order or sequence. Understanding the time and sequence of events in a story helps you understand how one event contributes to another. Usually the events of the plot follow one another in **chronological order.** Sometimes, however, part of the narrative will be told in **flashback,** revealing events that happened at an earlier time. Less often, and nearly always in modern literature, an author will **flash forward** and relate events that happen *after* the main time sequence of the narrative.

If the time sequence of a story is complicated, sometimes it is helpful to take notes about which events occur at which point in the story. You could use a graphic organizer like this one:

What happens in the story		
Beginning	**Middle**	**End**

The main events of the plot are the **exposition, conflict, rising action, climax, falling action,** and/or **resolution.**

The exposition reveals who the main character will be and what you need to know about the characters and setting before the story properly begins.

The **conflict** is the disclosure of the problem the main character must solve. Sometimes it is a problem or obstacle that the protagonist faces alone. Sometimes it is a struggle between characters.

The **rising action** is the longest part of any narrative. The main character confronts the conflict, usually undergoing some sort of transformation in the process.

The **climax** is the point in the narrative when the main character (and the readers) learn how the conflict will turn out—in simple terms, whether or not the story will have a "happy ending."

The **falling action,** or **resolution,** describes the results of the conflict for the principal characters.

For example, in *The Lord of the Rings,* by J. R. R. Tolkien, the exposition describes the lives of hobbits, Bilbo's finding of the Ring of Power and his passing it along to Frodo, and the wizard Gandalf's relationship with the hobbits. The conflict is set in motion by Frodo's acceptance of Gandalf's mission to destroy the ring. The rising action consists of all the adventures that befall him and his companions. At the climax, the ring is destroyed and Middle-earth is saved. The falling action describes what happens to the various characters afterward, with the resolution coming as Frodo sails into the West with the Elves.

Sometimes it isn't as easy to identify the conflict as it is in *The Lord of the Rings.* To identify the conflict, think about these questions:

- Who is the main character?
- What problem does that character face?
- How is the problem solved?
- What lessons do the characters learn?

It can be helpful to look back at the reading passage to figure out how you know the answers to these questions. Do you get this information from the characters themselves, from other characters, or from the narrator?

Read a story and answer the questions.

The Last Lesson

by Alphonse Daudet

I started for school very late that morning and was in great dread of a scolding, especially because M. Hamel had said that he would question us on participles, and I did not know the first word about them. For a moment I thought of running away and spending the day out of doors. It was so warm, so bright! The birds were chirping at the edge of the woods; and in the open field back of the sawmill the Prussian soldiers were drilling. It was all much more tempting than the rule for participles, but I had the strength to resist, and hurried off to school.

When I passed the town hall there was a crowd in front of the bulletin-board. For the last two years all our bad news had come from there—the lost battles, the draft, the orders of the commanding officer—and I thought to myself, without stopping:

"What can be the matter now?"

Then, as I hurried by as fast as I could go, the blacksmith, Wachter, who was there, with his apprentice, reading the bulletin, called after me:

"Don't go so fast, bub; you'll get to your school in plenty of time!"

I thought he was making fun of me, and reached M. Hamel's little garden all out of breath.

Usually, when school began, there was a great bustle, which could be heard out in the street, the opening and closing of desks, lessons repeated in unison, very loud, with our hands over our ears to understand better, and the teacher's great ruler rapping on the table. But now it was all so still! I had counted on the commotion to get to my desk

without being seen; but, of course, that day everything had to be as quiet as Sunday morning. Through the window I saw my classmates, already in their places, and M. Hamel walking up and down with his terrible iron ruler under his arm. I had to open the door and go in before everybody. You can imagine how I blushed and how frightened I was.

But nothing happened. M. Hamel saw me and said very kindly:

"Go to your place quickly, little Franz. We were beginning without you."

I jumped over the bench and sat down at my desk. Not till then, when I had got a little over my fright, did I see that our teacher had on his beautiful green coat, his frilled shirt, and the little black silk cap, all embroidered, that he never wore except on inspection and prize days. Besides, the whole school seemed so strange and solemn. But the thing that surprised me most was to see, on the back benches that were always empty, the village people sitting quietly like ourselves; old Hauser, with his three-cornered hat, the former mayor, the former postmaster, and several others besides. Everybody looked sad; and Hauser had brought an old primer, thumbed at the edges, and he held it open on his knees with his great spectacles lying across the pages.

While I was wondering about it all, M. Hamel mounted his chair, and, in the same grave and gentle tone which he had used to me, said:

"My children, this is the last lesson I shall give you. The order has come from Berlin to teach only German in the schools of

Alsace and Lorraine. The new master comes tomorrow. This is your last French lesson. I want you to be very attentive."

What a thunderclap these words were to me!

Oh, the wretches; that was what they had put up at the town-hall!

My last French lesson! Why, I hardly knew how to write! I should never learn any more! I must stop there, then! Oh, how sorry I was for not learning my lessons, for seeking birds' eggs, or going sliding on the Saar! My books, that had seemed such a nuisance a while ago, so heavy to carry, my grammar, and my history of the saints, were old friends now that I couldn't give up. And M. Hamel, too; the idea that he was going away, that I should never see him again, made me forget all about his ruler and how cranky he was.

Poor man! It was in honor of this last lesson that he had put on his fine Sunday clothes, and now I understood why the old men of the village were sitting there in the back of the room. It was because they were sorry, too, that they had not gone to school more. It was their way of thanking our master for his 40 years of faithful service and of showing their respect for the country that was theirs no more.

While I was thinking of all this, I heard my name called. It was my turn to recite. What would I not have given to be able to say that dreadful rule for the participle all through, very loud and clear, and without one mistake? But I got mixed up on the first words and stood there, holding on to my desk, my heart beating, and not daring to look up. I heard M. Hamel say to me:

"I won't scold you, little Franz; you must feel bad enough. See how it is! Every day we have said to ourselves: 'Bah! I've plenty of time. I'll learn it tomorrow.' And now you see where we've come out. Ah, that's the great trouble with Alsace; she puts off learning till tomorrow. Now those fellows out there will have the right to say to you: 'How is it; you pretend to be Frenchmen, and yet you can neither speak nor write your own language?' But you are not the worst, poor little Franz. We've all a great deal to reproach ourselves with.

"Your parents were not anxious enough to have you learn. They preferred to put you to work on a farm or at the mills, so as to have a little more money. And I? I've been to blame also. Have I not often sent you to water my flowers instead of learning your lessons? And when I wanted to go fishing, did I not just give you a holiday?"

Then, from one thing to another, M. Hamel went on to talk of the French language, saying that it was the most beautiful language in the world—the clearest, the most logical; that we must guard it among us and never forget it, because when a people are enslaved, as long as they hold fast to their language it is as if they had the key to their prison. Then he opened a grammar and read us our lesson. I was amazed to see how well I understood it. All he said seemed so easy, so easy! I think, too, that I had never listened so carefully, and that he had never explained everything with so much patience. It seemed almost as if the poor man wanted to give us all he knew before going away, and to put it all into our heads at one stroke.

After the grammar, we had a lesson in writing. That day M. Hamel had new copies for us, written in a beautiful round hand: France, Alsace, France, Alsace. They looked like little flags floating everywhere in the schoolroom, hung from the rod at the top of our desks. You ought to have seen how every one set to work, and how quiet it was! The only sound was the scratching of the pens over the paper. Once some beetles flew in; but nobody paid any attention to them, not even the littlest ones, who worked right on tracing their fish-hooks, as if that was French, too. On the roof the pigeons cooed very low, and I thought to myself:

"Will they make them sing in German, even the pigeons?"

Whenever I looked up from my writing I saw M. Hamel sitting motionless in his chair and gazing first at one thing, then at another, as if he wanted to fix in his mind just how everything looked in that little school-room. Fancy! For 40 years he had been there in the same place, with his garden outside the window and his class in front of him, just like that. Only the desks and benches had been worn smooth; the walnut-trees in the garden were taller, and the hopvine that he had planted himself twined about the windows to the roof. How it must have broken his heart to leave it all, poor man; to hear his sister moving about in the room above, packing their trunks! For they must leave the country next day.

But he had the courage to hear every lesson to the very last. After the writing, we had a lesson in history, and then the babies chanted their *ba, be, bi, bo, bu.* Down there at the back of the room old Hauser had put on his spectacles and, holding his primer in both hands, spelled the letters with them. You could see that he, too, was crying; his voice trembled with emotion, and it was so funny to hear him that we all wanted to laugh and cry. Ah, how well I remember it, that last lesson!

All at once the church-clock struck 12. Then the Angelus. At the same moment the trumpets of the Prussians, returning from drill, sounded under our windows. M. Hamel stood up, very pale, in his chair. I never saw him look so tall.

"My friends," said he, "I—I—" But something choked him. He could not go on.

Then he turned to the blackboard, took a piece of chalk, and, bearing on with all his might, he wrote as large as he could:

"Vive La France!"

Then he stopped and leaned his head against the wall, and, without a word, he made a gesture to us with his hand:

"School is dismissed—you may go."

Which word best describes M. Hamel in the story?

A courageous

B proud

C sorrowful

D angry

M. Hamel is proud of being French and of his work teaching French to his pupils. He regrets that he cannot stay and that there is not enough time for Franz and his classmates to learn any more French, but he is unable to fight back against the government despite his sorrow and anger. Still, nothing can take away his pride in his French heritage. The correct answer is choice B.

Which sentence from the story **best** describes the narrator's feelings about the new rule about not speaking French?

- A "'Will they make them sing in German, even the pigeons?'"
- B "'Vive La France!'"
- C "What a thunderclap these words were to me!"
- D "Ah, how well I remember it, that last lesson!"

The narrator is stunned at the decision and has trouble understanding it at first. He wonders how the Germans can make such a rule and if it will change everything around him, even the way the pigeons sing. The correct answer is choice A.

Which sentence **best** describes the relationship of the setting to the plot of the passage?

- A The setting influences the rising action.
- B The setting is unimportant.
- C The setting provides the main source of the conflict.
- D The setting is essential to the resolution of the conflict.

The setting is a schoolroom in a small French town that is now ruled by Germany. It is the place where students learn not just the French language but also their country's history. Without learning their language and history, the students will not grow up with any knowledge or pride in their own country. The setting is essential to the development of the story and the consequences of the new German rule. The correct answer is choice A.

Why does M. Hamel write "Vive La France" on the blackboard?

- A He is sorry to be leaving France.
- B He wants to teach his students one more French phrase.
- C He wants his students to be proud of France no matter what.
- D He wants to defy the German rule.

"Vive La France" means "Long live France." M. Hamel writes this phrase on the board to tell his students that they will always be French and that no one can take their heritage away from them. This action shows pride in being French. The correct answer is choice C.

The resolution of the story signifies that

    A   things never stay the same.

    B   you must be strong no matter what happens to you.

    C   the Germans will be cruel to the people of the village.

    D   people are helpless to stop bad things from happening.

> M. Hamel writes "Vive La France" on the board to inspire his students before he dismisses them from school forever. Even though life may become difficult and the villagers cannot change what is happening, M. Hamel wants them to always be strong and proud and remember who they are. The correct answer is choice B.

IT'S YOUR TURN

Now read another story and answer the questions.

from **The Call of the Wild**

by Jack London

Buck did not read the newspapers, or he would have known that trouble was brewing, not alone for himself, but for every tide-water dog, strong of muscle and with warm, long hair, from Puget Sound to San Diego. Because men, groping in the Arctic darkness, had found a yellow metal, and because steamship and transportation companies were booming the find, thousands of men were rushing into the Northland. These men wanted dogs, and the dogs they wanted were heavy dogs, with strong muscles by which to toil, and furry coats to protect them from the frost.

Buck lived at a big house in the sun-kissed Santa Clara Valley. Judge Miller's place, it was called. It stood back from the road, half hidden among the trees, through which glimpses could be caught of the wide cool veranda that ran around its four sides. The house was approached by gravelled driveways which wound about through wide-spreading lawns and under the interlacing boughs of tall poplars. At the rear things were on even a more spacious scale than at the front. There were great stables, where a dozen grooms and boys held forth, rows of vine-clad servants' cottages, an endless and orderly array of outhouses, long grape arbors, green pastures, orchards, and berry patches. Then there was the pumping plant for the artesian well, and the big cement tank where Judge Miller's boys took their morning plunge and kept cool in the hot afternoon.

And over this great demesne Buck ruled. Here he was born, and here he had lived the four years of his life. It was true, there were other dogs, There could not but be other dogs on so vast a place, but they did not count. They came and went, resided in the populous kennels, or lived obscurely in the recesses of the house after the fashion of Toots, the Japanese pug, or Ysabel, the Mexican hairless,—strange creatures that rarely put nose out of doors or set foot to ground. On the other hand, there were the fox terriers, a score of them at least, who yelped fearful promises at Toots and Ysabel looking out of the windows at them and protected by a legion of housemaids armed with brooms and mops.

But Buck was neither house-dog nor kennel-dog. The whole realm was his. He plunged into the swimming tank or went hunting with the Judge's sons; he escorted Mollie and Alice, the Judge's daughters, on long twilight or early morning rambles; on wintry nights he lay at the Judge's feet before the roaring library fire; he carried the Judge's grandsons on his back, or rolled them in the grass, and guarded their footsteps through wild adventures down to the fountain in the stable yard, and even beyond, where the paddocks were, and the berry patches. Among the terriers he stalked imperiously, and Toots and Ysabel he utterly ignored, for he was king,—king over all creeping, crawling, flying things of Judge Miller's place, humans included.

His father, Elmo, a huge St. Bernard, had been the Judge's inseparable companion, and Buck bid fair to follow in the way of his father. He was not so large,—he weighed only 140 pounds,—for his mother, Shep, had been a Scotch shepherd dog. Nevertheless, 140 pounds, to which was added the dignity that comes of good living and universal respect, enabled him to carry himself in right royal fashion. During the four years since his puppyhood he had lived the life of a sated aristocrat; he had a fine pride in himself, was even a trifle egotistical, as country gentlemen sometimes become because of their insular situation. But he had saved himself by not becoming a mere pampered house-dog. Hunting and kindred outdoor delights had kept down the fat and hardened his muscles; and to him, as to the cold-tubbing races, the love of water had been a tonic and a health preserver.

And this was the manner of dog Buck was in the fall of 1897, when the Klondike strike dragged men from all the world into the frozen North. But Buck did not read the newspapers, and he did not know that Manuel, one of the gardener's helpers, was an undesirable acquaintance. Manuel had one besetting sin. He loved to play Chinese lottery. Also, in his gambling, he had one

besetting weakness—faith in a system; and this made his damnation certain. For to play a system requires money, while the wages of a gardener's helper do not lap over the needs of a wife and numerous progeny.

The Judge was at a meeting of the Raisin Growers' Association, and the boys were busy organizing an athletic club, on the memorable night of Manuel's treachery. No one saw him and Buck go off through the orchard on what Buck imagined was merely a stroll. And with the exception of a solitary man, no one saw them arrive at the little flag station known as College Park. This man talked with Manuel, and money chinked between them.

"You might wrap up the goods before you deliver 'm," the stranger said gruffly, and Manuel doubled a piece of stout rope around Buck's neck under the collar.

"Twist it, an' you'll choke 'm plentee," said Manuel, and the stranger grunted a ready affirmative.

Buck had accepted the rope with quiet dignit. To be sure, it was an unwonted performance: but he had learned to trust in men he knew, and to give them credit for a wisdom that outreached his own. But when the ends of the rope were placed in the stranger's hands, he growled menacingly. He had merely intimated his displeasure, in his pride believing that to intimate was to command. But to his surprise the rope tightened around his neck, shutting off his breath. In quick rage he sprang at the man, who met him halfway, grappled him close by the throat, and with a deft twist threw him over on his back. Then the rope tightened mercilessly, while Buck struggled in a fury, his tongue lolling out of his mouth and his great chest panting futilely. Never in all his life had he been so vilely treated, and never in all his life had he been so angry. But his strength ebbed, his eyes glazed, and he knew nothing when the train was flagged and the two men threw him into the baggage car.

Unit 2 Analyzing and Interpreting Literature

1 What event of plot is lacking in this story?

A exposition

B rising action

C falling action

D climax

2 Which word **best** describes the character of Buck?

A ferocious

B proud

C handsome

D spoiled

3 Which sentence **best** describes the relationship of the setting to the plot of the story?

A The setting enables the conflict in the story.

B The setting contributes little to the climax of the story.

C The setting provides the main source of the conflict in the story.

D The setting prevents the resolution of the conflict in the story.

4 Which sentence from the story **best** represents the conflict?

A "Buck did not read the newspapers or he would have known that trouble was brewing."

B "These men wanted dogs, and the dogs they wanted were heavy dogs, with strong muscles by which to toil, and furry coats to protect them from the frost."

C "During the four years since his puppyhood he had lived the life of a sated aristocrat."

D "He had learned to trust in men he knew, and give them credit for a wisdom that outstretched his own."

5 Which sentence **best** describes the function of the exposition of the story?

A It clarifies the setting of the story.

B It reveals the author's feelings toward Buck.

C It explains the historical conditions present at the time of the story.

D It sets up a contrast between the way Buck is treated at home and the way he will be treated in the future.

Elements of a Narrative

L.F.2.3.4, L.F.2.3.5, L.F.2.3.6

Character, setting, and plot are elements that are usually easy to recognize in any narrative. In this lesson, you'll analyze other aspects of a narrative that may not be so easy to identify but that deeply affect the meaning of a text:

- **Theme**—the main idea that the author is trying to advance.

- **Tone, style, mood**—the attitude of the author toward the subject, characters, and you, the reader or listener, as expressed in language, voice, and emotional content of the work.

- **Point of view**—the perspective from which the story is told, whether of one or more characters or of a narrator.

Theme

Every literary passage has a **theme** that is the main idea of the narrative. It is not the same as the plot but an underlying central concept. For example, the *plot* of "The Tell-Tale Heart" may be described in one sentence as "A man's madness leads him both to commit murder and to betray his crime to the police." The theme might be expressed in a religious way, such as "the sin that carries its own retribution," or as something closer to home such as "crime and punishment."

There are some universal themes that you encounter in literature from the earliest myths and poetic epics through contemporary popular novels. "Good versus evil," "struggle against nature," "a hero's quest," "family love" and "the pursuit of justice." In every era, these themes reflect the world of the author's own time, yet the characters and the challenges they face remain similar. Think of the books that you have enjoyed, including realistic fiction, fantasy, and other genres, and you'll see how many of them fit one or another of these timeless themes.

In some narratives, however, and especially in poetry, the theme might not be that easy to discern. For example, in "Mending Wall," is the theme "People need boundaries," or is it "People create artificial boundaries"? Or is it something else? The theme of a poem celebrating a sunrise may be to seize the day and enjoy the moment while it lasts. A poem about autumn weather may really be about growing old, the "autumn" of a person's life.

Tone, Style, and Mood

The **tone** of a work of literature is the way an author conveys emotion through her words. It is an attitude the author takes toward her theme, her characters, and her readers. Tone is conveyed through the voice of the narrator or speaker, which reveals the author's attitudes and feelings and reflects the author's purpose. For example, "Because I Could Not Stop for Death" has a deceptively cheery tone with a trace of a shiver, as Dickinson reflects that while death is universally inevitable, there is something universally scary and unknown about it, too.

The **style** of a literary work is the author's overall presentation. Word choice **(diction),** word arrangement **(syntax),** sentence variety, the use of figurative language and literary devices are some of the tools an author uses to construct his style. It influences how you think and feel about the writing. For example, 20th-century American author Ernest Hemingway is famous for his style. He loathed adverbs, thought little better of adjectives, used figurative language minimally, and recommended that writers rip the colon-and-semicolon key out of their typewriters. His style is characterized by simple declarative sentences and a realistic tone, as in this brief excerpt from *The Sun Also Rises:*

> The crowd was the boys, the dancers, and the drunks. Romero turned and tried to get through the crowd. They were all around him trying to lift him and put him on their shoulders. He fought and twisted away, and started running, in the midst of them, toward the exit. He did not want to be carried on people's shoulders. But they held him and lifted him.

Compare this to the breezy style and exaggerated imagery of Hemingway's contemporary, detective-story writer Raymond Chandler, in summarizing a description of a character's flashy clothes in *Farewell, My Lovely:*

> Even on Central Avenue, not the quietest dressed street in the world, he looked about as inconspicuous as a tarantula on a slice of angel food.

or to the complex sentences favored by 19th-century novelist Jane Austen:

> Mr. Darcy danced only once with Mrs. Hurst and once with Miss Bingley, declined being introduced to any other lady, and spent the rest of the evening in walking about the room, speaking occasionally to one of his own party. His character was decided. He was the proudest, most disagreeable man in the world, and everybody hoped that he would never come there again. Amongst the most violent against him was Mrs. Bennet, whose dislike of his general behavior was sharpened into particular resentment by his having slighted one of her daughters.

or to the compressed style of Emily Dickinson:

> Good Morning—Midnight—
>
> I'm coming Home—
>
> Day—got tired of Me—
>
> How could I—of Him?

Some techniques authors use to construct style are:

- the choice of speaker or narrator
- the way the work is organized
- word choice, rhythm, and imagery
- the use of sentences of different patterns and lengths
- the use of figurative language and literary devices

The **mood** of a literary work is its overall atmosphere and the emotional response it produces in a reader. The mood of a work may be closely connected to and may support the setting and the theme. A mood may be cheerful and full of light, as befits the theme of courtship and marriage Jane Austen presents in *Pride and Prejudice,* or it may be somber and shadowy to suit Mary Shelley's graveyard-haunted setting and theme of man-unwisely-tinkering-with-nature in *Frankenstein.*

When you think about the style, tone, and mood of a literary work, ask yourself the following questions:

- How does the author want me to feel when I read this?
- What techniques does the author use to make me feel this way?
- Do I feel what the author intends? Why, or why not?

Point of View

Every story is told from a particular point of view. In one sense, of course, the point of view is always the author's. But in a literary sense, "point of view" means the author's choice of a particular narrator or speaker and how this choice affects the tone, the events recounted, and even the believability of the story or poem. When reading any literary work, it is important to identify the point of view and to understand how it affects the story that is told.

Who is telling the story? If one of the characters tells the story in her own words, it is called **first-person** point of view. The narrator uses first-person pronouns such as *I* or *we.* An author may use the first-person point of view to let the reader feel close to the narrator and to the action of the story. This point of view limits what the narrator may discuss. It leaves it to the reader to determine the unspoken thoughts and motives of other characters.

Unit 2 Analyzing and Interpreting Literature

Other stories are told from a **third-person** point of view. Then the narrator exclusively uses third-person pronouns, such as *he, she,* and *they.* A **third-person limited** narrative tells the story from the point of view of one character. A **third-person objective** narrative expresses the point of view of someone outside the story. If the author chooses to tell a story from the **third-person omniscient** (all-knowing) point of view, his objective is to give the reader as much information as possible about all the characters and their thoughts and actions.

Here are some questions about point of view to consider when you are reading:

- Who is telling the story?

- What can you tell about the narrator from reading the story?

- Is the narrator reliable? Can you believe what the narrator says, or are there contradictions between what the narrator says and what other characters say?

- How does the author's choice of point of view and narrative style affect the story?

GUIDED PRACTICE

Read the beginning of the novel *Silas Marner* and answer the questions.

Silas Marner

by George Eliot (Mary Ann Evans)

CHAPTER I

In the days when the spinning-wheels hummed busily in the farmhouses—and even great ladies, clothed in silk and thread-lace, had their toy spinning-wheels of polished oak—there might be seen in districts far away among the lanes, or deep in the bosom of the hills, certain pallid undersized men, who, by the side of the brawny country-folk, looked like the remnants of a disinherited race. The shepherd's dog barked fiercely when one of these alien-looking men appeared on the upland, dark against the early winter sunset; for what dog likes a figure bent under a heavy bag?—and these pale men rarely stirred abroad without that mysterious burden. The shepherd himself, though he had good reason to believe that the bag held nothing but flaxen thread, or else the long rolls of strong linen spun from that thread, was not quite sure that this trade of weaving, indispensable though it was, could be carried on entirely without the help of the Evil One. In that far-off time superstition clung easily round every person or thing that was at all unwonted[1], or even intermittent and occasional merely, like the visits of the pedlar or the knife-grinder. No one knew where wandering men had their homes or their origin; and how was a man to be explained unless you at least knew somebody who knew his father and mother? To the peasants of old times, the world outside their own direct experience was a region of vagueness and mystery: to their

[1]**unwonted:** unaccustomed

untravelled thought a state of wandering was a conception as dim as the winter life of the swallows that came back with the spring; and even a settler, if he came from distant parts, hardly ever ceased to be viewed with a remnant of distrust, which would have prevented any surprise if a long course of inoffensive conduct on his part had ended in the commission of a crime; especially if he had any reputation for knowledge, or showed any skill in handicraft. All cleverness, whether in the rapid use of that difficult instrument the tongue, or in some other art unfamiliar to villagers, was in itself suspicious: honest folk, born and bred in a visible manner, were mostly not overwise or clever—at least, not beyond such a matter as knowing the signs of the weather; and the process by which rapidity and dexterity of any kind were acquired was so wholly hidden, that they partook of the nature of conjuring. In this way it came to pass that those scattered linen-weavers—emigrants from the town into the country—were to the last regarded as aliens by their rustic neighbors, and usually contracted the eccentric habits which belong to a state of loneliness.

In the early years of this century, such a linen-weaver, named Silas Marner, worked at his vocation in a stone cottage that stood among the nutty hedgerows near the village of Raveloe, and not far from the edge of a deserted stone-pit. The questionable sound of Silas's loom, so unlike the natural cheerful trotting of the winnowing-machine, or the simpler rhythm of the flail, had a half-fearful fascination for the Raveloe boys, who would often leave off their nutting or birds'-nesting to peep in at the window of the stone cottage, counterbalancing a certain awe at the mysterious action of the loom, by a pleasant sense of scornful superiority, drawn from the mockery of its alternating noises, along with the bent, tread-mill attitude of the weaver. But sometimes it happened that Marner, pausing to adjust an irregularity in his thread, became aware of the small

scoundrels, and, though chary of his time, he liked their intrusion so ill that he would descend from his loom, and, opening the door, would fix on them a gaze that was always enough to make them take to their legs in terror. For how was it possible to believe that those large brown protuberant eyes in Silas Marner's pale face really saw nothing very distinctly that was not close to them, and not rather that their dreadful stare could dart cramp, or rickets, or a wry mouth at any boy who happened to be in the rear? They had, perhaps, heard their fathers and mothers hint that Silas Marner could cure folks' rheumatism if he had a mind, and add, still more darkly, that if you could only speak the devil fair enough, he might save you the cost of the doctor. Such strange lingering echoes of the old demon-worship might perhaps even now be caught by the diligent listener among the grey-haired peasantry; for the rude mind with difficulty associates the ideas of power and benignity. A shadowy conception of power that by much persuasion can be induced to refrain from inflicting harm, is the shape most easily taken by the sense of the Invisible in the minds of men who have always been pressed close by primitive wants, and to whom a life of hard toil has never been illuminated by any enthusiastic religious faith. To them pain and mishap present a far wider range of possibilities than gladness and enjoyment: their imagination is almost barren of the images that feed desire and hope, but is all overgrown by recollections that are a perpetual pasture to fear. "Is there anything you can fancy that you would like to eat?" I once said to an old laboring man, who was in his last illness, and who had refused all the food his wife had offered him. "No," he answered, "I've never been used to nothing but common victual, and I can't eat that." Experience had bred no fancies in him that could raise the phantasm of appetite.

And Raveloe was a village where many of the old echoes lingered, undrowned by new voices. Not that it was one of those

Unit 2 Analyzing and Interpreting Literature

barren parishes lying on the outskirts of civilization—inhabited by meager sheep and thinly-scattered shepherds: on the contrary, it lay in the rich central plain of what we are pleased to call Merry England, and held farms which, speaking from a spiritual point of view, paid highly-desirable tithes. But it was nestled in a snug well-wooded hollow, quite an hour's journey on horseback from any turnpike, where it was never reached by the vibrations of the coach-horn, or of public opinion. It was an important-looking village, with a fine old church and large churchyard in the heart of it, and two or three large brick-and-stone homesteads, with well-walled orchards and ornamental weathercocks, standing close upon the road, and lifting more imposing fronts than the rectory, which peeped from among the trees on the other side of the churchyard:—a village which showed at once the summits of its social life, and told the practiced eye that there was no great park and manor-house in the vicinity, but that there were several chiefs in Raveloe who could farm badly quite at their ease, drawing enough money from their bad farming, in those war times, to live in a rollicking fashion, and keep a jolly Christmas, Whitsun, and Easter tide.

It was 15 years since Silas Marner had first come to Raveloe; he was then simply a pallid young man, with prominent short-sighted brown eyes, whose appearance would have had nothing strange for people of average culture and experience, but for the villagers near whom he had come to settle it had mysterious peculiarities which corresponded with the exceptional nature of his occupation, and his advent from an unknown region called "North'ard." So had his way of life:—he invited no comer to step across his door sill, and he never strolled into the village to drink a pint at the Rainbow, or to gossip at the wheelwright's: he sought no man or woman, save for the purposes of his calling, or in order to supply himself with necessaries; and it was soon clear to the Raveloe lasses that he would never urge one of them to accept him against her will—quite as if he had heard them declare that they would never marry a dead man come to life again. This view of Marner's personality was not without another ground than his pale face and unexampled eyes; for Jem Rodney, the mole-catcher, averred that one evening as he was returning homeward, he saw Silas Marner leaning against a stile with a heavy bag on his back, instead of resting the bag on the stile as a man in his senses would have done; and that, on coming up to him, he saw that Marner's eyes were set like a dead man's, and he spoke to him, and shook him, and his limbs were stiff, and his hands clutched the bag as if they'd been made of iron; but just as he had made up his mind that the weaver was dead, he came all right again, like, as you might say, in the winking of an eye, and said "Good-night", and walked off. All this Jem swore he had seen, more by token that it was the very day he had been mole-catching on Squire Cass's land, down by the old saw-pit. Some said Marner must have been in a "fit," a word which seemed to explain things otherwise incredible; but the argumentative Mr. Macey, clerk of the parish, shook his head, and asked if anybody was ever known to go off in a fit and not fall down. A fit was a stroke, wasn't it? and it was in the nature of a stroke to partly take away the use of a man's limbs and throw him on the parish, if he'd got no children to look to. No, no; it was no stroke that would let a man stand on his legs, like a horse between the shafts, and then walk off as soon as you can say "Gee!" But there might be such a thing as a man's soul being loose from his body, and going out and in, like a bird out of its nest and back; and that was how folks got over-wise, for they went to school in this shell-less state to those who could teach them more than their neighbors could learn with their five senses and the parson. And where did Master Marner get his knowledge of herbs from—and charms too, if he liked to give them away? Jem Rodney's story was no more than what might have been expected by anybody who had seen how Marner had cured Sally Oates, and made her sleep like a baby, when her heart had been beating enough to burst her body, for two months and more, while she had been under the doctor's care. He might cure more folks if he would; but he was worth speaking fair, if it was only to keep him from doing you a mischief.

What universal theme is **most** reflected in this passage?

A the loneliness of the outsider

B the familial closeness of village life

C the superstitious belief of country folk

D the dislocation brought about by change

Silas Marner is a novel, and it is hard to extract a "universal theme" from a few paragraphs. Yet you already know something about *Silas Marner,* the book, and Silas Marner, the man. He is a peculiar sort from another region of the country, which to the people of Raveloe might as well mean he is from Mars. As a result, he is both shunned and harassed by the people, who see his work as something like witchcraft. The portrait Eliot draws of him seems to reinforce the village's impression. Village life does not seem especially familial in this excerpt; there is as yet no sense of changes that have taken place, and the people's superstitions reinforce the theme rather than establish it. The correct answer is choice A.

How does the author's style help create the mood of the passage?

A The ironic language creates a humorous mood.

B The simple language creates a transparent mood.

C The objective language creates a sympathetic mood.

D The descriptive language creates a judgmental mood.

George Eliot—or her narrator—wants you to share her opinion about the village of Raveloe and the ways of its people. There is nothing ironic about the way she describes them—ignorant, superstitious, mistrusting of outsiders— and yet her language is too complex to be called transparent; she wants you to think about what you are reading. If there is any sympathy for Silas or his neighbors, it does not come through (yet) in her descriptions of them. She wants her descriptions to influence what you think of them. Choice D is the answer you want.

Unit 2 Analyzing and Interpreting Literature

Which sentence **best** describes the relationship of the setting to the tone in the passage?

   A The tone condemns the stifling nature of the setting.

   B The tone indicates the author's contempt for the setting.

   C The tone celebrates the timeless environment of the setting.

   D The tone establishes sympathy for the isolation of the setting.

Under her real name, Mary Ann Evans was well known in her time for her nonfiction writing about religion, and her tone in these opening paragraphs has something of the feeling of a sermon. She is not contemptuous of the people of Raveloe, nor does she celebrate them. She sees their lives and attitude as resulting from the limits of their setting, but she wants you to care about them, or else you would not read much further in her book. The correct answer is choice D.

What point of view does the author use in this passage?

   A first person

   B third-person limited

   C third-person objective

   D third-person omniscient

Is the narrator a character in the story? Toward the end of the second paragraph, the narrator uses the pronoun *I* in her anecdote about the dying man who wouldn't eat unfamiliar food. But this is the author (or her narrator) revealing herself as a close observer of the events of the story. That is a third-person objective point of view, choice C.

Why is an objective narrator most likely used to describe events in the passage?

A   to describe conditions in Raveloe

B   to develop a negative attitude toward Silas

C   to explain why Silas kept himself apart from the villagers

D   to provide a sympathetic understanding of the villagers' ways

> The narrator so far has described Silas only as he appears to the villagers. They are the ones with the negative attitude, not the narrator. There is no explanation of his loneliness (as there might be, if he were telling the story), and while Eliot wants you to understand the villagers' ways, she doesn't waste much sympathy on them. But she does effectively present the village and its people as they are. Choice A is the correct answer.

IT'S YOUR TURN

Now read a narrative poem and answer the questions.

My Last Duchess

Ferrara[1]

by Robert Browning

That's my last Duchess painted on the wall,

Looking as if she were alive. I call

That piece a wonder, now: Frà Pandolf's[2] hands

Worked busily a day, and there she stands.

5   Will't please you sit and look at her? I said

"Frà Pandolf" by design, for never read

Strangers like you that pictured countenance,

The depth and passion of its earnest glance,

But to myself they turned (since none puts by

10   The curtain I have drawn for you, but I)

And seemed as they would ask me, if they durst,[3]

How such a glance came there; so, not the first

---

[1]**Ferrara:** a city in Italy. The setting of the poem is the 16th century.
[2]**Frà Pandolf:** a fictitious artist, as is Claus of Innsbruck (line 56)
[3]**durst:** dare

Unit 2 Analyzing and Interpreting Literature

Are you to turn and ask thus. Sir, 'twas not

Her husband's presence only, called that spot

15   Of joy into the Duchess' cheek: perhaps

Frà Pandolf chanced to say "Her mantle laps

Over my Lady's wrist too much," or "Paint

Must never hope to reproduce the faint

Half-flush that dies along her throat": such stuff

20   Was courtesy, she thought, and cause enough

For calling up that spot of joy. She had

A heart—how shall I say?—too soon made glad,

Too easily impressed; she liked whate'er

She looked on, and her looks went everywhere.

25   Sir, 'twas all one! My favor at her breast,

The dropping of the daylight in the West,

The bough of cherries some officious fool

Broke in the orchard for her, the white mule

She rode with round the terrace—all and each

30   Would draw from her alike the approving speech,

Or blush, at least. She thanked men,—good! but thanked

Somehow—I know not how—as if she ranked

My gift of a nine-hundred-years-old name

With anybody's gift. Who'd stoop to blame

35   This sort of trifling? Even had you skill

In speech—(which I have not)—to make your will

Quite clear to such an one, and say, "Just this

Or that in you disgusts me; here you miss,

Or there exceed the mark"—and if she let

40   Herself be lessoned so, nor plainly set

Her wits to yours, forsooth, and made excuse,

—E'en then would be some stooping, and I choose

Never to stoop. Oh sir, she smiled, no doubt,

Whene'er I passed her; but who passed without

45   Much the same smile? This grew; I gave commands;

Then all smiles stopped together. There she stands

As if alive. Will't please you rise? We'll meet

The company below, then. I repeat,

The Count your master's known munificence

50 Is ample warrant that no just pretence

Of mine for dowry will be disallowed;

Though his fair daughter's self, as I avowed

At starting, is my object. Nay, we'll go

Together down, sir. Notice Neptune, though,

55 Taming a sea-horse, thought a rarity,

Which Claus of Innsbruck cast in bronze for me!

1 Why is a first-person narrator most likely used as the speaker in this poem?

A to reveal the character of the Duke of Ferrara

B to provide a deeper understanding of the setting

C to develop an objective attitude toward the duchess

D to indicate how impressed the Duke's guest is by his wealth

2 What universal theme is **most** reflected in the passage?

A jealousy

B grief and loss

C truth in beauty

D the magnetism of power

3 Which sentence **best** describes the relationship of the tone to the character of the speaker in the poem?

A The haughty tone reflects the duke's family pride.

B The alarming tone hints that the duke is possibly mad.

C The anxious tone suggests that the duke wants to impress his guest.

D The glittering tone illustrates the superficiality of the duke and his possessions.

4 How does the poet's style help the reader understand how the duke's thoughts change when he talks about the duchess from when he talks about her portrait?

    A The point of view changes.

    B The diction becomes more formal.

    C The speaker frequently interrupts himself.

    D The sentences do not conclude at the ends of lines.

5 Write a sentence that contrasts the tone and mood of "My Last Duchess." Use it as the opening sentence of a paragraph that explains that contrast. Use evidence from the poem to compose your response.

_____

_____

_____

_____

_____

_____

_____

_____

Authors throughout time and around the globe have created works that deal with such universal themes as love, family, courage, or attachment to place. You know that such themes may be expressed as narrative, poetry, or drama, and that the author's choice of one form or another can influence the meaning of his work. For example, in *Silas Marner,* "George Eliot" tells the tale of a lonely, selfish man redeemed by love for an abandoned child—a theme closely related to the Protestant Christian religious ideas she expressed under her real name, Mary Ann Evans. However, her choice of the novel as her literary form also allows her to comment on the cruelty of the English class structure (a frequent theme of British writers) and the social disruption caused by the Industrial Revolution. These are ideas that would have been awkward or impossible to convey in a play or poem, and that would not have touched the human heart nearly as effectively in nonfiction.

Cultural and historical factors are often at play in the choices an author makes. It is important to be able to recognize these factors in order to interpret and analyze a literary work. For example, the legends of King Arthur and his knights, which took their classic form in the 1400s, reflect the values that the "noble" classes of Europe liked to attribute to themselves. The tales of Robin Hood, which arose around the same time, celebrate an outlaw who was the hero of the common people. In fact, most medieval knights were brutal, uncouth warriors who despised anyone not of their class, while if Robin Hood really existed he was probably just a robber. If their contemporaries had portrayed them accurately, we would not have the stories to enjoy as literature. Likewise, in the history plays of William Shakespeare, the kings that were the ancestors of his patron, Queen Elizabeth I, are always the "good guys" (like Henry V), while the kings that Elizabeth's ancestors fought against are always the "bad guys" (like Richard III).

In modern literature, an author's choice of **genre** also influences the way a theme is presented. The term *genre* is used to classify literary works by form or technique (such as novel, drama, lyric poetry, and so on), but it can also refer to the content of the work. For example, **mystery** is a popular genre. In its usual form, the detective story, it generally represents the themes of good battling against evil and of the lone individual seeking hidden knowledge. **Science fiction** and **fantasy** are genres in which authors may use such settings as alien planets or imaginary worlds to express themes that relate to the here and now. For example, in *Frankenstein,* written in 1817, Mary Shelley expresses the fear of many of her contemporaries about science unleashing forces it cannot control. In *The Time Machine,* written in 1895, H. G. Wells saw a future in which the English class system of his day had divided humans' descendants into two species, the lazy, passive Eloi and the brutal, cave-dwelling Morlocks. In our time, Suzanne Collins's *Hunger Games* trilogy explores a similar theme as reflected in the author's perception of early 21st-century America. Collins in turn credits as inspirations for her novels the ancient Greek myth of Theseus and the gladiatorial games of the ancient Romans.

The myths and history of Greece and Rome in fact set forth many of the themes that have been explored by authors in many genres ever since. Earlier in this book, you read an excerpt from George Bernard Shaw's comedy *Pygmalion.* The plot of the play is focused on a bet made by Professor Henry Higgins (the "note taker" described in the stage directions) that he can take a "common," lower-class woman (the "flower girl") and pass her off as a duchess by teaching her to speak proper English. Where, then, does that odd title come from? From the Greek myth of Pygmalion, a sculptor who creates his ideal woman in the form of a statue and then falls in love with her. Audiences for Shaw's play were familiar with the myth and would have appreciated his twist on the tale—that Higgins's "creation" is not made of marble, and that it is the way people treat one another, not speech or social position, that truly determines who has "class" and who doesn't.

Epic is another genre that is part of the literary traditions of many cultures, from India to Greece to Iceland. Epics are long narrative poems that relate in great detail the tales of human heroes assisted by supernatural forces. The tradition and themes of epic has found their way into many modern works of fantasy, including *The Lord of the Rings* and J. K. Rowling's *Harry Potter* cycle.

Let's look at Greek myth and an American novel to see how universal themes may appear in literary works across time, genres, and cultures.

Read an excerpt from a play and answer the questions.

from Antigone

by Sophocles

> *The tragedy of Antigone was written by the Athenian dramatist Sophocles in 442 B.C. Antigone has defied the order of her uncle King Creon, decreed under penalty of death, by giving funeral honors to her brother, Polyneices, who was killed leading an army against his own city. In this scene, the king confronts Antigone.*

CREON: You, whose head is bent low to the ground,
do you admit, or do you deny this deed?

ANTIGONE: I say I did it; I deny it not.

CREON: *(to the guard)* Get out of here. Go where you wish;
you are free of blame. *(to Antigone)* You—tell me yes or no—
You knew I ordered not to do this deed?

ANTIGONE: Of course I knew. Your word was plain.

CREON: And yet you dared to violate the law?

ANTIGONE: For me, it was not Zeus who gave that order,
Nor did Justice, who lives among the gods
write out such laws for mortals to obey.
Nor did I think your power was so great
that you, a human being, could abrogate
the gods' inviolable, unwritten laws.
They are not for today, or yesterday,
but for all time, and none knows their beginning.
So I would not, for fear of one man's pride,
be likely, then, to disrespect these laws,
bring on myself the gods' sure punishment.
I knew 't would mean my death; how could I not,
even without the warning of a king?
If I die young, I say I'd gain something.
For one who bears such sorrows as are mine,
how can she not be glad to yield to death?
And so I do not grieve to meet this fate.
But if I left my brother's corpse unburied,
Then surely I would have good cause to grieve.
And if you think I've done a foolish thing,
Perhaps you see it with a foolish eye.

Unit 2 Analyzing and Interpreting Literature

Based on the passage, what cultural ideal is emphasized in the play?

A   patriotism

B   the cruelty of war

C   individual conscience

D   the corruption of power

In Sophocles's Greece, obedience to one's city-state was among the highest cultural values. However, the playwright chose to portray as a tragic hero a teen girl who defies state power to obey what she sees as the gods' "higher law." What figures of recent times, both in literature and in history, have embodied that same cultural ideal? Choice C is the correct answer.

How does the reader know that the passage is drama rather than poetry or narrative fiction?

A   The author uses dialogue.

B   The text is written in verse.

C   The speaker's name precedes each line of dialogue.

D   The scene involves two characters confronting one another.

Well into the 1600s, drama was commonly written in verse, and there are even some 20th-century verse dramas. You have seen examples of dialogue in narrative fiction and even in poetry, and, of course, characters confronting one another can be the essence of conflict in any genres. But indicating the speaker by putting her name in front of the lines she speaks is characteristic only of drama, choice C.

How does the author's use of drama as a genre influence the meaning of the passage?

A It allows the author to advance a political agenda.

B It allows the author to give immediacy to the conflict.

C It allows the reader to learn about the culture of ancient Greece.

D It allows the reader to understand how the main character feels.

> Sophocles was writing for Athenians, not for people 2,500 years later to study their culture. Many genres would have allowed him to express a political point of view, and indeed that might be one aspect of his purpose. But the immediacy of drama, of having two characters confronting one another directly without the author's observations distracting the audience, heightens the conflict between Antigone and Creon that provides meaning to the play. Choice B is the answer you want.

Now read an excerpt from a novel and answer the questions.

from **The Adventures of Huckleberry Finn**

by Mark Twain

> Huckleberry Finn, *published in 1884 but set some 40 years earlier, has often been called the greatest novel written by an American. In this excerpt, Huck realizes that his friend, the escaped slave Jim, has been betrayed, and so has his own role in aiding Jim's escape.*

Once I said to myself it would be a thousand times better for Jim to be a slave at home where his family was, as long as he'd *got* to be a slave, and so I'd better write a letter to Tom Sawyer and tell him to tell Miss Watson where he was. But I soon give up that notion for two things: she'd be mad and disgusted at his rascality and ungratefulness for leaving her, and so she'd sell him straight down the river again; and if she didn't, everybody naturally despises an ungrateful [slave], and they'd make Jim feel it all the time, and so he'd feel ornery and disgraced. And then think of *me*! It would get all around that Huck Finn helped a [slave] to get his freedom; and if I was ever to see anybody from that town again I'd be ready to get down and lick his boots for shame. That's just the way: a person does a low-down thing, and then he don't want to take no consequences of it. Thinks as long as he can hide it, it ain't no disgrace. That was my fix exactly. The more I studied about this the more my conscience went to grinding me, and the more wicked and low-down and ornery I got to feeling. And at last, when it hit me all of a sudden that here was the plain hand of Providence slapping me in the face and letting me know my wickedness was being watched all the time from up there in heaven, whilst I

Unit 2 Analyzing and Interpreting Literature

was stealing a poor old woman's [slave] that hadn't ever done me no harm, and now was showing me there's One that's always on the lookout, and ain't a-going to allow no such miserable doings to go only just so fur and no further, I most dropped in my tracks I was so scared. Well, I tried the best I could to kinder soften it up somehow for myself by saying I was brung up wicked, and so I warn't so much to blame; but something inside of me kept saying, "There was the Sunday-school, you could a gone to it; and if you'd a done it they'd a learnt you there that people that acts as I'd been acting about that [slave] goes to everlasting fire."

It made me shiver. And I about made up my mind to pray, and see if I couldn't try to quit being the kind of a boy I was and be better. So I kneeled down. But the words wouldn't come. Why wouldn't they? It warn't no use to try and hide it from Him. Nor from *me*, neither. I knowed very well why they wouldn't come. It was because my heart warn't right; it was because I warn't square; it was because I was playing double. I was letting *on* to give up sin, but away inside of me I was holding on to the biggest one of all. I was trying to make my mouth *say* I would do the right thing and the clean thing, and go and write to that [slave]'s owner and tell where he was; but deep down in me I knowed it was a lie, and He knowed it. You can't pray a lie—I found that out.

So I was full of trouble, full as I could be; and didn't know what to do. At last I had an idea; and I says, I'll go and write the letter—and then see if I can pray. Why, it was astonishing, the way I felt as light as a feather right straight off, and my troubles all gone. So I got a piece of paper and a pencil, all glad and excited, and set down and wrote:

Miss Watson, your runaway [slave] Jim is down here two mile below Pikesville, and Mr. Phelps has got him and he will give him up for the reward if you send.

Huck Finn.

I felt good and all washed clean of sin for the first time I had ever felt so in my life, and I knowed I could pray now. But I didn't do it straight off, but laid the paper down and set there thinking—thinking how good it was all this happened so, and how near I come to being lost and going to hell. And went on thinking. And got to thinking over our trip down the river; and I see Jim before me all the time: in the day and in the night-time, sometimes moonlight, sometimes storms, and we a-floating along, talking and singing and laughing. But somehow I couldn't seem to strike no places to harden me against him, but only the other kind. I'd see him standing my watch on top of his'n, 'stead of calling me, so I could go on sleeping; and see him how glad he was when I come back out of the fog; and when I come to him again in the swamp, up there where the feud was; and such-like times; and would always call me honey, and pet me and do everything he could think of for me, and how good he always was; and at last I struck the time I saved him by telling the men we had small-pox aboard, and he was so grateful, and said I was the best friend old Jim ever had in the world, and the *only* one he's got now; and then I happened to look around and see that paper.

It was a close place. I took it up, and held it in my hand. I was a-trembling, because I'd got to decide, forever, betwixt two things, and I knowed it. I studied a minute, sort of holding my breath, and then says to myself:

"All right, then, I'll *go* to hell"—and tore it up.

It was awful thoughts and awful words, but they was said. And I let them stay said; and never thought no more about reforming. I shoved the whole thing out of my head, and said I would take up wickedness again, which was in my line, being brung up to it, and the other warn't. And for a starter I would go to work and steal Jim out of slavery again; and if I could think up anything worse, I would do that, too; because as long as I was in, and in for good, I might as well go the whole hog.

Based on the passage, what American historical theme is **most** emphasized?

A respect for rights

B the conflict over slavery

C governance versus liberty

D attachment to one's native place

Twain wrote *Huckleberry Finn* 20 years after the Civil War settled the conflict over slavery, but he sets the book in the South of his boyhood. You can see the ideas of respect for life, the tug between individual liberty and community pressure, and attachment to place in this brief excerpt (it's a big, complex novel!), but clearly at the forefront is Huck's internal conflict over whether to let Jim be recaptured. The correct answer is choice B.

How does the author's use of dialect help to communicate an idea in this novel?

A It shows Huck as representing "the people."

B It emphasizes the point that Huck is a Southerner.

C It conveys the author's memory of his own boyhood.

D It suggests that the reader need not respect Huck's opinions.

Twain wants to present the choices made by a young boy in the years when African American slavery was taken for granted by most white Americans. The use of dialect does not represent Twain's own experiences—unlike Huck he was a polished speaker who came from a stable family—and no author wants you to disrespect his main character, no matter what negative characteristics he may have. Huck is more poorly educated than most Americans of Twain's day or ours, but he is no fool. Choice A is the correct answer.

How does the author's use of realistic fiction as a literary form influence the meaning of the passage?

A   It allows the author to show the irony in Huck's choice.

B   It allows the author to present facts about life in the South.

C   It allows the reader to understand the moral issue of slavery.

D   It allows the reader to appreciate the realities of life in the 1840s.

Here is Huck making the moral decision to tear up the letter he had written betraying Jim's whereabouts—and deciding that doing so makes him a wicked person! Southern culture, the issues of slavery, and life in the 1840s might have been revealed through other genres, but Huck's internal monologue detailing his thought process and his feelings about Jim and what his culture demands of him is possible only in narrative fiction. Choice A is the answer you want.

Analyze and discuss the similarities and differences in the themes of *Antigone* and *The Adventures of Huckleberry Finn* as represented in these two passages. Use examples from the passages in your analysis.

_____

_____

_____

_____

_____

_____

_____

_____

Here are two literary works written 23 centuries apart, both dealing with human choices and conflicts in values. The following is one way you might answer the question:

Both Antigone and Huck Finn face moral choices between what their culture expects of them and what their conscience demands of them. Antigone chooses to give her traitor brother a proper funeral even though her king has forbidden it. She thinks she is obeying a "higher law"—the unchanging law of the gods. She tells

Creon she would fear the gods' punishment if she did otherwise, and that her grief over her brother would be even greater if she did not give him due respect. Huck, too, believes that his actions are being watched by a "higher power" and fears God's punishment if he makes the wrong choice. Ultimately he makes the right choice, but that's where the similarities end and the differences begin. Huck's culture teaches him that slavery is right and proper and that helping a slave to escape is a form of stealing. He can't get his mind around this idea and thinks he's bound to be condemned if he saves Jim. His affection for Jim and his understanding that Jim is a human being like himself—even though he can't express it that way—lead him to make the same choice Antigone does. But while she thinks she is obeying a higher law, Huck feels in his heart that he is disobeying God's law. His choice is harder than hers, but he ends up doing the right thing.

IT'S YOUR TURN

Now read two more passages and answer the questions.

from **The Iliad**, *Book IV*

by Homer

> *Homer's two epic poems,* The Iliad *and* The Odyssey, *were written about 800 B.C. and are considered along with the Bible as the foundation texts of Western literature. In this account of a war between the Greeks and Trojans, the gods and goddesses of Mount Olympus take sides in the struggle and help their favorites. This is a prose translation of the Greek verse.*

"Hush, my friend, pay heed to what I say," Diomedes intervened, with an angry glance at Sthenelus, "I'll not fault Agamemnon, king of men, for urging the bronze-greaved Greeks on to battle. Glory will be his if the Achaeans[1] win, and raze sacred Ilium[2], but his will be the pain if we Achaeans lose. Let us, rather, turn our thoughts to acts of conspicuous bravery."

---

[1]**Achaeans:** Greeks
[2]**Ilium:** Troy

Unit 2 Analyzing and Interpreting Literature

So saying, fully armored, he leapt down from his chariot, and the bronze at his breast rang so loud even the stoutest heart might well have trembled.

Now, as the sea-swell beats on the sounding shore, wave on wave driven before the westerly gale, each crest rising out of the depths to break thundering on the beach or rearing its head to lap the headland and spew out briny foam, so the Danaan ranks advanced, battalion on battalion, remorselessly into battle, while the captains' voices rose in command as the men marched on in silence, as if that moving mass lacked tongues to speak, mute as they were, fearful of their generals, while on every man the inlaid armor glittered. But the Trojan clamor rang out from their ranks, like the endless bleating of countless ewes in a rich man's yard, there to yield their white milk, when they hear the cries of their lambs, for the Trojan army, gathered from many lands, lacked a common language, speaking a myriad tongues.

Ares urged on the Trojans, bright-eyed Athene[3], the Greeks, and Terror, Panic, and Strife were there, Strife the sister and ally to man-killer Ares[4], she whose anger never ceases, who barely raises her head at first, but later lifts it to the high heavens though her feet still trample the earth. Now she brought the evil of war among them, as she sped through the ranks, filling the air with the groans of dying men.

So they met in fury with a mighty crash, with the clash of spears, shields-bosses, bronze-clad warriors, till the last moans of the fallen mingled with the victory cries of their killers, and the earth ran red with blood. Like the sound a shepherd deep in the mountains hears; the mighty clash of two wintry torrents that pour down from high sources to their valleys' meeting place in a deep ravine; such was the tumult raised by those armies toiling together in battle.

Of the Trojans, noble Echepolos, son of Thalysius, was first to die, fighting in the vanguard, downed in his armor by Antilochus. The spear struck the ridge of his horse-hair crested helmet, and the point drove through the skin of his forehead into the bone. Darkness filled his eyes, and he dropped like a fallen tower on the field. Once downed, Elephenor, son of Chalcodon, prince of the fierce Abantes, seizing him by the feet, tried to drag his body out of range, ready to strip it swiftly of armor; yet not for long, for brave Agenor saw him drag the corpse aside, and with a thrust of his bronze-tipped spear, striking him in the flank exposed by his shield as he stooped, loosened all his limbs. His spirit fled, and the Greeks and Trojans struggled grimly over the corpse. They leapt at one another like wolves, and staggered locked in each other's fierce embrace.

---

[3]**Athene:** goddess who inspires men with courage
[4]**Ares:** god of war

Anthem for Doomed Youth

by Wilfred Owen

> *Wilfred Owen fought in the British army during World War I (1914–1918).*
> *All of his famous poems came out of his experiences in the war. Owen*
> *was killed in action on November 4, 1918, a week before the war ended.*

What passing-bells[1] for these who die as cattle?

Only the monstrous anger of the guns.

Only the stuttering rifles' rapid rattle

Can patter out their hasty orisons.[2]

5   No mockeries now for them; no prayers nor bells;

Nor any voice of mourning save the choirs,—

The shrill, demented choirs of wailing shells;

And bugles calling for them from sad shires.

What candles may be held to speed them all?

10 Not in the hands of boys but in their eyes

Shall shine the holy glimmers of goodbyes.

The pallor of girls' brows shall be their pall[3];

Their flowers the tenderness of patient minds,

And each slow dusk a drawing-down of blinds.

---

1   Based on the passage from *The Iliad,* what ancient Greek
cultural idea is **most** emphasized in the poem?

   A   the gods as the governors of human affairs

   B   war as the natural condition of human beings

   C   courage as the virtue that makes all others possible

   D   arrogant pride as a fault that brings the gods' retribution

---

[1]**passing-bells:** bells rung in churches to announce the death of someone from the community
[2]**orisons:** prayers
[3]**pall:** cover for a coffin or tomb

Unit 2 Analyzing and Interpreting Literature

2 How does Homer's use of epic as a literary form influence the meaning of the passage from *The Iliad?*

A   It allows the author to use mythical gods as characters.

B   It allows the reader to appreciate ancient Greek culture.

C   It allows the reader to learn about the characters' feelings.

D   It allows the author to express loyalty to his side in the war.

3 Which sentence **best** describes the relationship of the theme of "Anthem for Doomed Youth" to that of *The Iliad?*

A   It expresses contempt for Homer's glorification of war.

B   It suggests that courage is unchanged throughout the ages.

C   It emphasizes that there is no place for individual heroism in a modern army.

D   It declares that God (unlike "the gods") is not concerned with human conflict.

4 Based on "Anthem for Doomed Youth," what 20th-century historical trend is **most** emphasized?

A   the suffering of noncombatants in war

B   the young being sent to fight by the old

C   the mass death caused by modern weaponry

D   the rush to war by politicians to benefit business interests

5 Read these lines from the poem.

"No mockeries now for them; no prayers nor bells;

Nor any voice of mourning save the choirs,—

The shrill, demented choirs of wailing shells"

How does the poet's reference to choirs help to communicate an idea in the poem?

A   It indicates the speaker's love of music.

B   It conveys the speaker's nostalgia for his lost religious faith.

C   It uses sensory language to reproduce the sounds of the battlefield.

D   It emphasizes the difference between death in war and death in peace.

Figurative Language and Literary Devices

L.F.2.5.1

> All the world's a stage,
>
> And all the men and women merely players:
>
> They have their exits and their entrances;
>
> And one man in his time plays many parts,
>
> His acts being seven ages: At first the infant…

You may have recognized these words as Shakespeare's, from his play *As You Like It.* A character named Jacques is comparing life to a play, with all of us as actors who enter the world's stage when we are born and exit it when we die. In these famous lines, Shakespeare is using **figurative language.** It's a form of imagery that writers use to create a special effect or feeling. Figurative language is not meant to be taken literally—our lives are not performances in a theater, after all—but it prods our mind into thinking about things in new and different ways.

Here is another literary sentence that you may have read before:

> It is a truth universally acknowledged that a single man in possession of a good fortune must be in want of a wife.

This famous first sentence of Jane Austen's *Pride and Prejudice* makes use of two **literary devices**—techniques used by an author to enliven a text and provide voice to it. The statement is certainly not "a truth universally acknowledged"! It is a statement of **irony** that hints at the novel's theme and the conflict involving its two main characters, Elizabeth Bennet and Mr. Darcy. It is also an example of **foreshadowing,** telling the readers that they are going to meet "a single man in possession of a good fortune" and a woman who *may* end up as his wife.

Authors use figurative language and literary devices to make readers sense and think in unusual ways about what they are reading. They are aspects of an author's style. Some writers, and certain forms of literature, make free use of these techniques, while others use them sparingly. Our reading experience, however, would be impoverished indeed if a writer refrained from using them at all.

Unit 2 Analyzing and Interpreting Literature

Figurative Language

Several types of imagery let readers perceive a writer's ideas in unusual ways:

Personification gives human qualities to an object, animal, or abstract idea. For example, in Emily Dickinson's poem "Because I Could Not Stop for Death," the idea of death is made to seem like a gallant gentleman. Here is another example from Shakespeare's *Romeo and Juliet,* in which the sun and moon are given human qualities:

Arise, fair sun, and kill the envious moon,

Who is already sick and pale with grief

That thou her maid art far more fair than she.

A **simile** compares two unlike things by using *like* or *as.* A simile can be gentle, like this familiar one by Robert Burns:

My love is like a red, red rose

or it can be a more arresting comparison that brings a character into focus, as in this simile from a story by James Joyce:

She dealt with moral problems as a cleaver deals with meat.

A metaphor compares two things without using *like* or *as.* Instead of saying that one thing is like another, it states that one thing is the same as another or substitutes for it in some way. Read the beginning of Alfred Noyes's poem "The Highwayman":

The wind was a torrent of darkness among the gusty trees,

The moon was a ghostly galleon tossed upon cloudy seas,

The road was a ribbon of moonlight over the purple moor…

Three lines, three metaphors. They let you *feel* the wind as "a torrent [flood] of darkness," *see* the moon as a "ghostly galleon" [sailing ship] on an ocean made of clouds, and *see* that the road looks like a ribbon in the moonlight.

Symbolism is a higher-level form of metaphor. It uses language in ways that reminds the reader of images or abstract ideas not directly expressed by the words. A police officer's badge, for example, is a symbol of authority.

In a work of literature, symbols may have more than one meaning. An island may be a symbol either of solitude or of self-sufficiency. In F. Scott Fitzgerald's 1925 novel *The Great Gatsby,* the color green is a symbol for the empty pursuit of wealth and pleasure—it's the color of money, after all. But as the green light at the end of the dock that represents the corrupt Jay Gatsby's hopes and dreams, it's also a symbol of the futility of trying to recapture a more innocent past.

Symbolism often has cultural significance. Only in the United States, for example, would green be a symbol of money. In Western writing, yellow may symbolize cowardice, while to the Chinese it is often a symbol for wisdom.

Hyperbole is the use of exaggeration to make a point. People use hyperbole in everyday speech, as when your mother says, "I've told you a million times to clean your room," or when you comment to a friend, "This homework is killing me!" Neither of these statements is literally true, but they make an effective point. Here Harper Lee uses hyperbole in describing the setting of *To Kill a Mockingbird:*

> People moved slowly then. There was no hurry, for there was nowhere to go, nothing to buy and no money to buy it with, nothing to see outside the boundaries of Maycomb County.

Literary Devices

Literary devices help authors create the mood, tone, and style of a work by emphasizing meaning in vivid ways.

Satire is a literary device that ridicules or examines human weaknesses and faults. It is often directed at politicians, celebrities, and popular fads. George Orwell's novel *Animal Farm* is a famous satire that uses a fable about talking animals to critique Communism. In the opening passage from *Bleak House* on pages 39–40, Dickens uses biting satire to portray the lawyers and judges in Chancery court. Here Mark Twain uses it in Huck Finn's observations about a slave-owning farmer-preacher and just what his preaching was worth:

> He was the innocentest, best old soul I ever see. But it warn't surprising; because he warn't only just a farmer, he was a preacher, too, and had a little one-horse log church down back of the plantation, which he built it himself at his own expense, for a church and schoolhouse, and never charged for his preaching, and it was worth it, too.

Flashback interrupts the time flow of a narrative to describe events that happened in the past. It is often used to reveal something that the author has until then kept secret about a character. In the excerpt from *The House Behind the Cedars* on pages 46–48, Charles Chesnutt uses flashback to show his character, Warwick, remembering his boyhood and a lynching he once witnessed.

Foreshadowing is the opposite of flashback. It is a device authors use to create expectation—to keep the reader turning the pages—or to set up an explanation of later developments. In *Romeo and Juliet,* Shakespeare foreshadows Romeo's death when he has Juliet say:

> Methinks I see thee, now thou art below
>
> As one dead in the bottom of a tomb:
>
> Either my eyesight fails, or thou lookst pale.

Allegory is a form of extended metaphor in which characters, actions, and themes throughout a narrative are compared with persons, events, or abstract qualities that lie outside the narrative. In an allegory, characters are often personifications of ideas or qualities such as greed, jealousy, or "the devil." Though J. R. R. Tolkien claimed to dislike allegory, many readers have seen in *The Lord of the Rings* an allegory of the alliance of nations against Nazi Germany in World War II. *Moby Dick* uses allegory on so many levels that readers have been offering new interpretations of it ever since it was published in 1851.

Allusion is a form of metaphor that is simpler to analyze than allegory. It's an implied or indirect reference to a famous person, place, or event. Mythology, the Bible, and Shakespeare are frequent sources of allusion. George Bernard Shaw's *Pygmalion* is an example of an allusion to Greek myth. Jane Smiley's novel *A Thousand Acres* resets Shakespeare's play *King Lear* on a present-day Iowa farm. Examples of allusion are part of our everyday speech as well as of literature. A sports team competing against a heavily favored opponent is called "David versus Goliath." A young man with an eye for the ladies is a "Romeo." Hidden invasive code in a software program is a "Trojan horse." Can you think of others?

Irony is the use of words or phrases to mean the opposite of their literal meaning **(verbal irony)**, a contrast between what a character believes and what the reader knows **(dramatic irony)**, or a result of events that is very different than expected **(situational irony)**. You use irony when you say "Yeah, right!" to mean "I don't believe it!" The opening paragraph of "The Tell-Tale Heart" contains a splendid example of irony. The narrator, protesting that he is not mad, claims to have "heard many things in hell," thus demonstrating himself to be (as the simile has it) "crazy as a jaybird."

Dialect is a variety of language that differs in pronunciation, grammar, or vocabulary from standard, "proper" speech. Authors use it as a literary device to convey authenticity in their characters. Dialect can be used in a demeaning way to make fun of characters' origins, but the absence of it in certain cases can make for dishonest writing. The uneducated Huckleberry Finn, for example, speaks in dialect, and we would not believe him as a character if he did not. Eliza, the flower girl of Shaw's *Pygmalion,* speaks in a dialect of London English known as "cockney," and her speech is a focus of the theme of the play.

Read a poem and answer the questions.

The Garden of Love
by William Blake

I went to the Garden of Love,

And saw what I never had seen;

A Chapel was built in the midst,

Where I used to play on the green.

5 And the gates of this Chapel were shut,

And 'Thou shalt not' writ over the door;

So I turned to the Garden of Love

That so many sweet flowers bore.

And I saw it was filled with graves,

10 And tombstones where flowers should be;

And priests in black gowns were walking their rounds,

And binding with briars my joys and desires.

In this poem, the garden can **best** be said to be a symbol of

A love.

B freedom.

C innocence.

D springtime.

Images are not symbolic by themselves. They acquire symbolism through their cultural context. In Western culture, and particularly in the religious world of Blake's England around 1800 when everyone was familiar with the Bible, the idea of the garden suggests an allusion to the Garden of Eden, a place of innocence before Adam and Eve were cast out. The image is reinforced by Blake's use of the verb *play,* which suggests childhood. Choice C is the correct answer.

The speaker uses irony when he refers to

A   priests in black gowns.

B   a garden filled with graves.

C   writing over the door of the chapel.

D   never having seen the chapel before.

Keep in mind that there is more than one kind of irony. The speaker does not use verbal irony, in which words connote the opposite of their literal meaning, or dramatic irony, in which the reader knows something that a character or speaker does not. There is situational irony in the idea of a garden "filled with graves, and tombstones where flowers should be." The correct answer is choice B.

What is the effect of the imagery of the last two lines?

A   It suggests that the speaker is mourning his lost childhood.

B   It makes an appeal for the freedom of the individual heart.

C   It expresses the speaker's loss of faith and disbelief in God.

D   It personifies the garden's thorny overgrowth as hooded men.

The figurative imagery in these lines uses metaphor that compares the repressive power of the Church of Blake's day with thorny cords that choke off the speaker's "joys and desires," his human spirit. Blake is not protesting against religion—the speaker can't even get into the chapel in the midst of the garden because its gates are shut. He is dismayed by the way religious *power* stifles the individual conscience. The answer is choice B.

Now read a passage from a story and answer the questions.

from **Girl**

by O. Henry (William S. Porter)

In gilt letters on the ground glass of the door of room No. 962 were the words: "Robbins & Hartley, Brokers." The clerks had gone. It was past five, and with the solid tramp of a drove of prize Percherons, scrub-women were invading the cloud-capped 20-story office building. A puff of red-hot air flavored with lemon peelings, soft-coal smoke and train oil came in through the half-open windows.

Robbins, 50, something of an overweight beau, and addicted to first nights and hotel palm-rooms, pretended to be envious of his partner's commuter's joys.

"Going to be something doing in the humidity line tonight," he said. "You out-of-town chaps will be the people, with your katydids and moonlight and long drinks and things out on the front porch."

Hartley, 29, serious, thin, good-looking, nervous, sighed and frowned a little.

"Yes," said he, "we always have cool nights in Floralhurst, especially in the winter."

A man with an air of mystery came in the door and went up to Hartley.

"I've found where she lives," he announced in the portentous half-whisper that makes the detective at work a marked being to his fellow men.

Hartley scowled him into a state of dramatic silence and quietude. But by that time Robbins had got his cane and set his tie pin to his liking, and with a debonair nod went out to his metropolitan amusements.

"Here is the address," said the detective in a natural tone, being deprived of an audience to foil.

Hartley took the leaf torn out of the sleuth's dingy memorandum book. On it were penciled the words "Vivienne Arlington, No. 341 East —th Street, care of Mrs. McComus."

"Moved there a week ago," said the detective. "Now, if you want any shadowing done, Mr. Hartley, I can do you as fine a job in that line as anybody in the city. It will be only $7 a day and expenses. Can send in a daily typewritten report, covering—"

"You needn't go on," interrupted the broker. "It isn't a case of that kind. I merely wanted the address. How much shall I pay you?"

"One day's work," said the sleuth. "A tenner will cover it."

Hartley paid the man and dismissed him. Then he left the office and boarded a Broadway car. At the first large crosstown artery of travel he took an eastbound car that deposited him in a decaying avenue, whose ancient structures once sheltered the pride and glory of the town.

Walking a few squares, he came to the building that he sought. It was a new flathouse, bearing carved upon its cheap stone portal its sonorous name, "The Vallambrosa." Fire-escapes zigzagged down its front—these laden with household goods, drying clothes, and squalling children evicted by the midsummer heat. Here and there a pale rubber plant peeped from the miscellaneous mass, as if wondering to what kingdom it belonged—vegetable, animal or artificial.

Hartley pressed the "McComus" button. The door latch clicked spasmodically— now hospitably, now doubtfully, as though in anxiety whether it might be admitting friends or duns. Hartley entered and began to climb the stairs after the manner of those who seek their friends in city flat-houses— which is the manner of a boy who climbs an apple-tree, stopping when he comes upon what he wants.

On the fourth floor he saw Vivienne standing in an open door. She invited him inside, with a nod and a bright, genuine smile. She placed a chair for him near a window, and poised herself gracefully upon the edge of one of those Jekyll-and-Hyde pieces of furniture that are masked and mysteriously hooded, unguessable bulks by day and inquisitorial racks of torture by night.

Read the sentences from the passage.

> *"The clerks had gone. It was past five, and with the solid tramp of a drove of prize Percherons, scrub-women were invading the cloud-capped 20-story office building."*

What is the effect of the imagery used to describe the scrub-women?

A It indicates that they have the bearing of soldiers.

B It suggests their pride despite their humble occupation.

C It implies that their footsteps are heavy and purposeful.

D It emphasizes the differences between them and the office workers.

At the time this story was written, about 1900, readers knew that Percherons were large horses used to pull heavy vehicles. Today we can understand O. Henry's metaphor through the phrase "solid tramp." Choice C is the correct answer, and did you note the use of hyperbole in describing the "cloud-capped" skyscraper?

Read the sentence from the passage.

> *"Here and there a pale rubber plant peeped from the miscellaneous mass, as if wondering to what kingdom it belonged—vegetable, animal or artificial."*

What figure of speech or literary device does the narrator use to help you picture the rubber plants?

A satire

B simile

C flashback

D personification

The author describes the plants as "peeping," suggesting that they have eyes, and as "wondering," suggesting that they have thoughts. They are being compared with people, which is an example of personification, choice D.

Read the sentence from the passage.

"She placed a chair for him near a window, and poised herself gracefully upon the edge of one of those Jekyll-and-Hyde pieces of furniture that are masked and mysteriously hooded, unguessable bulks by day and inquisitorial racks of torture by night."

What is the effect of the imagery used to describe the furniture?

A   It uses satire to suggest that the furniture is ugly.

B   It humorously evokes the idea that the furniture is menacing.

C   If foreshadows that the furniture will be significant in the story.

D   It ironically emphasizes the shabby appearance of the apartment.

The sentence alludes to Robert Louis Stevenson's horror story, "The Strange Case of Dr. Jekyll and Mr. Hyde," in which a respected doctor transforms his form and personality into that of a brutal murderer by drinking a chemical potion. Even today, anything that seems to have two opposed personalities, be it a person, a cat, or a basketball team, may be described as "Jekyll and Hyde." But even if you didn't catch the allusion, the description of a piece of furniture as "mysteriously hooded" and suggesting "racks of torture" tells you that the correct answer is choice B.

Read a poem and answer the questions.

To Mistress Margaret Hussey

by John Skelton

Merry Margaret
    As midsummer flower
    Gentle as falcon
    Or hawk of the tower[1]:
5 With solace and gladness,
Much mirth and no madness,
All good and no badness;
    So joyously,
    So maidenly,
10   So womanly
    Her demeaning
    In everything,
    Far, far passing
    That I can indite[2]
15   Or suffice to write
Of Merry Margaret
As midsummer flower,
Gentle as falcon
Or hawk of the tower.
20 As patient and still
And as full of good will
As fair Isaphill[3],
    Coliander[4],
    Sweet pomander[5],
25 Good Cassander[6];
Steadfast of thought,
Well made, well wrought,
Fair may be sought
Ere that ye can find
30 So courteous, so kind
As Merry Margaret,
This midsummer flower,
Gentle as falcon
Or hawk of the tower.

---

[1]**hawk of the tower:** high-flying hawk
[2]**indite:** to describe in literary writing
[3]**Ishapill:** Hypsipyle, queen in Greek mythology who helped her father escape from women who wanted him killed
[4]**coliander:** coriander, an aromatic seed
[5]**pomander:** a ball made of perfumes
[6]**Cassander:** a princess in Greek mythology who was given the gift of prophecy by the gods

1 The form of figurative language the speaker **most** uses in portraying Mistress Margaret is

    A   simile.

    B   metaphor.

    C   hyperbole.

    D   personification.

2 What is the effect of the imagery the poet uses in lines 2, 23, and 24?

    A   It shows that the speaker likes how Margaret smells.

    B   It indicates that Margaret has hurt the speaker's feelings.

    C   It implies that the speaker feels socially superior to Margaret.

    D   It suggests that the speaker feels bashful in Margaret's presence.

3 The speaker's mythical allusions in the poem suggest that Margaret

    A   is like a Greek goddess.

    B   is devoted to her family.

    C   has rescued him from physical danger.

    D   has the pride and graciousness of royalty.

4 In which grouping of lines does the poet **most** use an ironic description of Margaret?

    A   "Gentle as falcon
        Or hawk of the tower"

    B   "Much mirth and no madness,
        All good and no badness"

    C   "So joyously,
        So maidenly,
        So womanly"

    D   "Steadfast of thought,
        Well made, well wrought,"

5 Which of the following **best** describes the relationship between the form of the poem and its imagery?

 A The shortness of the lines are a metaphor for Margaret's youth.

 B The use of rhymes in threes parallel the imagery the speaker uses to describe Margaret.

 C The playfulness of the rhythm and rhyme reflect the speaker's feelings about Margaret.

 D The regularity of the rhythm contrasts with the contradictory images the speaker uses to depict Margaret.

Read the following passage. Then answer questions 1–11.

The Gift of the Magi

by O. Henry (William S. Porter)

> *O. Henry's most famous short story first appeared in a magazine in December 1905.*

One dollar and 87 cents. That was all. And 60 cents of it was in pennies. Pennies saved one and two at a time by bulldozing the grocer and the vegetable man and the butcher until one's cheeks burned with the silent imputation of parsimony that such close dealing implied. Three times Della counted it. One dollar and 87 cents. And the next day would be Christmas.

There was clearly nothing to do but flop down on the shabby little couch and howl. So Della did it. Which instigates the moral reflection that life is made up of sobs, sniffles, and smiles, with sniffles predominating.

While the mistress of the home is gradually subsiding from the first stage to the second, take a look at the home. A furnished flat at $8 per week. It did not exactly beggar description, but it certainly had that word on the lookout for the mendicancy squad.

In the vestibule below was a letter-box into which no letter would go, and an electric button from which no mortal finger could coax a ring. Also appertaining thereunto was a card bearing the name "Mr. James Dillingham Young."

The "Dillingham" had been flung to the breeze during a former period of prosperity when its possessor was being paid $30 per week. Now, when the income was shrunk to $20, the letters of "Dillingham" looked blurred, as though they were thinking seriously of contracting to a modest and unassuming D. But whenever Mr. James Dillingham Young came home and reached his flat above he was called "Jim" and greatly hugged by Mrs. James Dillingham Young, already introduced to you as Della. Which is all very good.

Della finished her cry and attended to her cheeks with the powder rag. She stood by the window and looked out dully at a gray cat walking a gray fence in a gray backyard. Tomorrow would be Christmas Day, and she had only $1.87 with which to buy Jim a present. She had been saving every penny she could for months, with this result. Twenty dollars a week doesn't go far. Expenses had been greater than she had calculated. They always are. Only $1.87 to buy a present for Jim. Her Jim. Many a happy hour she had spent planning for something nice for him. Something fine and rare and sterling— something just a little bit near to being worthy of the honor of being owned by Jim.

There was a pier-glass between the windows of the room. Perhaps you have seen a pier-glass in an $8 flat. A very thin and very agile person may, by observing his reflection in a rapid sequence of longitudinal strips, obtain a fairly accurate conception of his looks. Della, being slender, had mastered the art.

Suddenly she whirled from the window and stood before the glass. Her eyes were shining brilliantly, but her face had lost its color within 20 seconds. Rapidly she pulled down her hair and let it fall to its full length.

Now, there were two possessions of the James Dillingham Youngs in which they both took a mighty pride. One was Jim's gold watch that had been his father's and his grandfather's. The other was Della's hair. Had the Queen of Sheba lived in the flat across the airshaft, Della would have let her hair hang out the window some day to dry just to depreciate Her Majesty's jewels and gifts. Had King Solomon been the janitor, with all his treasures piled up in the basement, Jim would have pulled out his watch every time he passed, just to see him pluck at his beard from envy.

So now Della's beautiful hair fell about her rippling and shining like a cascade of brown waters. It reached below her knee and made itself almost a garment for her. And then she did it up again nervously and quickly. Once she faltered for a minute and stood still while a tear or two splashed on the worn red carpet.

On went her old brown jacket; on went her old brown hat. With a whirl of skirts and with the brilliant sparkle still in her eyes, she fluttered out the door and down the stairs to the street.

Where she stopped the sign read: "Mme. Sofronie. Hair Goods of All Kinds." One flight up Della ran, and collected herself, panting. Madame, large, too white, chilly, hardly looked the "Sofronie."

"Will you buy my hair?" asked Della.

"I buy hair," said Madame. "Take yer hat off and let's have a sight at the looks of it."

Down rippled the brown cascade.

"Twenty dollars," said Madame, lifting the mass with a practised hand.

"Give it to me quick," said Della.

Oh, and the next two hours tripped by on rosy wings. Forget the hashed metaphor. She was ransacking the stores for Jim's present.

She found it at last. It surely had been made for Jim and no one else. There was no other like it in any of the stores, and she had turned all of them inside out. It was a platinum fob chain simple and chaste in design, properly proclaiming its value by substance alone and not by meretricious ornamentation—as all good things should do. It was even worthy of The Watch. As soon as she saw it she knew that it must be Jim's. It was like him. Quietness and value—the description applied to both. Twenty-one dollars they took from her for it, and she hurried home with the 87 cents. With that chain on his watch Jim might be properly anxious about the time in any company. Grand as the watch was, he sometimes looked at it on the sly on account of the old leather strap that he used in place of a chain.

When Della reached home her intoxication gave way a little to prudence and reason. She got out her curling irons and lighted the gas and went to work repairing the ravages made by generosity added to love. Which is always a tremendous task, dear friends—a mammoth task.

Within 40 minutes her head was covered with tiny, close-lying curls that made her look wonderfully like a truant schoolboy. She looked at her reflection in the mirror long, carefully, and critically.

"If Jim doesn't kill me," she said to herself, "before he takes a second look at me, he'll say I look like a Coney Island chorus girl. But what could I do—oh! what could I do with a dollar and 87 cents?"

At 7 o'clock the coffee was made and the frying-pan was on the back of the stove hot and ready to cook the chops. Jim was never late. Della doubled the fob chain in her hand and sat on the corner of the table near the door that he always entered. Then she heard his step on the stair away down on the first flight, and she turned white for just a moment. She had a habit of saying little silent prayers about the simplest everyday things, and now she whispered:

"Please God, make him think I am still pretty." The door opened and Jim stepped in and closed it. He looked thin and very serious. Poor fellow, he was only 22—and to be burdened with a family! He needed a new overcoat and he was without gloves.

Jim stopped inside the door, as immovable as a setter at the scent of quail. His eyes were fixed upon Della, and there was an expression in them that she could not read, and it terrified her. It was not anger, nor surprise, nor disapproval, nor horror, nor any of the sentiments that she had been prepared for. He simply stared at her fixedly with that peculiar expression on his face.

Della wriggled off the table and went for him.

"Jim, darling," she cried, "don't look at me that way. I had my hair cut off and sold it because I couldn't have lived through Christmas without giving you a present. It'll grow out again—you won't mind, will you? I just had to do it. My hair grows awfully fast. Say 'Merry Christmas!' Jim, and let's be happy. You don't know what a nice—what a beautiful, nice gift I've got for you."

"You've cut off your hair?" asked Jim, laboriously, as if he had not arrived at that patent fact yet even after the hardest mental labor.

"Cut it off and sold it," said Della. "Don't you like me just as well, anyhow? I'm me without my hair, ain't I?"

Jim looked about the room curiously.

"You say your hair is gone?" he said, with an air almost of idiocy.

"You needn't look for it," said Della. "It's sold, I tell you—sold and gone, too. It's Christmas Eve, boy. Be good to me, for it went for you. Maybe the hairs of my head were numbered," she went on with a sudden serious sweetness, "but nobody could ever count my love for you. Shall I put the chops on, Jim?"

Out of his trance Jim seemed quickly to wake. He enfolded his Della. For ten seconds let us regard with discreet scrutiny some inconsequential object in the other direction. Eight dollars a week or a million a year— what is the difference? A mathematician or a wit would give you the wrong answer. The magi brought valuable gifts, but that was not among them. This dark assertion will be illuminated later on.

Jim drew a package from his overcoat pocket and threw it upon the table.

"Don't make any mistake, Dell," he said, "about me. I don't think there's anything in the way of a haircut or a shave or a shampoo that could make me like my girl any less. But if you'll unwrap that package you may see why you had me going a while at first."

White fingers and nimble tore at the string and paper. And then an ecstatic scream of joy; and then, alas! a quick feminine change to hysterical tears and wails, necessitating the immediate employment of all the comforting powers of the lord of the flat.

For there lay The Combs—the set of combs, side and back, that Della had worshipped for long in a Broadway window. Beautiful combs, pure tortoise shell, with jewelled rims—just the shade to wear in the beautiful vanished hair. They were expensive combs, she knew, and her heart had simply craved and yearned over them without the least hope of possession. And now, they were hers, but the tresses that should have adorned the coveted adornments were gone.

But she hugged them to her bosom, and at length she was able to look up with dim eyes and a smile and say: "My hair grows so fast, Jim!"

And then Della leaped up like a little singed cat and cried, "Oh, oh!"

Jim had not yet seen his beautiful present. She held it out to him eagerly upon her open palm. The dull precious metal seemed to flash with a reflection of her bright and ardent spirit.

"Isn't it a dandy, Jim? I hunted all over town to find it. You'll have to look at the time a hundred times a day now. Give me your watch. I want to see how it looks on it."

Instead of obeying, Jim tumbled down on the couch and put his hands under the back of his head and smiled.

"Dell," said he, "let's put our Christmas presents away and keep 'em a while. They're too nice to use just at present. I sold the watch to get the money to buy your combs. And now suppose you put the chops on."

The magi, as you know, were wise men—wonderfully wise men—who brought gifts to the Babe in the manger. They invented the art of giving Christmas presents. Being wise, their gifts were no doubt wise ones, possibly bearing the privilege of exchange in case of duplication. And here I have lamely related to you the uneventful chronicle of two foolish children in a flat who most unwisely sacrificed for each other the greatest treasures of their house. But in a last word to the wise of these days let it be said that of all who give gifts these two were the wisest. Of all who give and receive gifts, such as they are wisest. Everywhere they are wisest. They are the magi.

1 The word <u>parsimony</u> as used in the first paragraph has the connotation of

A   thrift.

B   economy.

C   stinginess.

D   dishonesty.

2 What word **best** describes Jim in the passage?

A   proud

B   foolish

C   hapless

D   supportive

3 What does Madame Sofronie most likely do with the hair she buys from Della?

A   She makes a wig.

B   She stuffs a pillow.

C   She sells it to a bald-headed man.

D   She makes Christmas ornaments.

4 Read this sentence from the passage.

> "'You've cut off your hair?' asked Jim, laboriously, as if he had not arrived at that patent fact yet even after the hardest mental labor."

The suffixes -*ous* and -*ly* help the reader know that <u>laboriously</u> means

A after laboring.

B the result of labor.

C the condition of labor.

D in the manner of laboring.

5 Which sentence **best** describes the relationship of the setting to the plot in the passage?

A The setting helps explain the conflict.

B The setting is not relevant to the climax.

C The setting brings the falling action into focus.

D The setting makes it easy for the problem to be resolved.

6 Why is the third-person limited point of view most likely used to narrate the passage?

A to allow the readers to empathize with Della

B to make possible the "surprise twist" at the climax

C to show why the couple are happy despite their poverty

D to explain the importance of Della's decision to sell her hair

7 Which sentence marks the climax of the story?

A "For there lay The Combs—the set of combs, side and back, that Della had worshipped for long in a Broadway window."

B "'Dell,' said he, 'let's put our Christmas presents away and keep 'em a while.'"

C "'I sold the watch to get the money to buy your combs.'"

D "But in a last word to the wise of these days let it be said that of all who give gifts these two were the wisest."

8 How does the author's use of fiction as a literary device influence the meaning of the passage?

   A It allows the reader to learn how Christmas was celebrated in 1905.

   B It allows the reader to empathize with the feelings of the two characters.

   C It allows the author to present facts about American urban life around 1900.

   D It allows the author to use persuasive techniques to show that people can be happy without money.

9 What characteristic of the passage **best** indicates to readers that it is fiction rather than informational nonfiction?

   A the use of imagery

   B the inclusion of dialogue

   C the development of style

   D the description of the setting

10 Based on the passage, what American cultural value is **most** emphasized in this story? Use evidence from the text to support your answer.

_____

_____

_____

_____

_____

_____

_____

11 Summarize the key events and details of the passage.

_____

_____

_____

_____

_____

_____

_____

Read the poem and answer questions 12–20.

Sonnet 116

by William Shakespeare

Let me not to the marriage of true minds

Admit impediments. Love is not love

Which alters when it alteration finds,

Or bends with the remover to remove:

5 O no! it is an ever-fixed mark

That looks on tempests and is never shaken;

It is the star to every wandering bark[1],

Whose worth's unknown, although his height be taken.

Love's not Time's fool, though rosy lips and cheeks

10 Within his bending sickle's compass come:

Love alters not with his brief hours and weeks,

But bears it out even to the edge of doom.

If this be error and upon me proved,

I never writ, nor no man ever loved.

---

[1]**bark:** a small ship

Unit 2 Analyzing and Interpreting Literature

12 What is the author's purpose in writing this poem?

   A   to express his views on marriage

   B   to describe a person that he loves

   C   to reflect on the ideal of romantic love

   D   to warn people against hasty marriage

13 Which word is a synonym for <u>impediments</u>?

   A   reasons

   B   obstacles

   C   emotions

   D   celebrations

14 Read the lines from the poem.

   "O no! it is an ever-fixed mark

   That looks on tempests and is never shaken;

   It is the star to every wandering bark,

   Whose worth's unknown, although his height be taken."

   What is the rhyme scheme of these lines?

   A   A A B B

   B   A B A B

   C   A B C B

   D   A B B A

15 How does Shakespeare's use of metaphor in the lines quoted
    above help to communicate an idea in the poem?

   A   It indicates the speaker's memory of a lost love.

   B   It establishes the speaker's age and experience with love.

   C   It conveys the speaker's feelings about the constancy of
       love.

   D   It shows the speaker's view of love as an adventurous
       voyage.

16 Which lines from the poem **best** support the generalization that love is unchanging?

    A "Let me not to the marriage of true minds
       Admit impediments."

    B "Love is not love
       Which alters when it alteration finds"

    C "It is the star to every wandering bark,
       Whose worth's unknown, although his height be taken."

    D "If this be error and upon me proved,
       I never writ, nor no man ever loved."

17 What is the effect of the poet's personification of time?

    A It implies that it is foolish to waste time thinking about love.

    B It contrasts the long duration of time with the brevity of life.

    C It suggests that one becomes wiser about love as time passes.

    D It declares that love does not change with the passage of time.

18 How does the poet's style help to create the mood of the passage?

    A The playful language creates an upbeat mood.

    B The ironic language creates a humorous mood.

    C The cautionary language creates a formal mood.

    D The descriptive language creates a thoughtful mood.

19 In what way is the poem similar to the story "The Gift of the Magi"?

    A Both express a romantic view of love.

    B Both depict a love relationship in a realistic setting.

    C Both use figurative language to convey the idea of love.

    D Both examine how hard yet how rewarding it is to nurture love.

20 Compare and contrast how the universal theme of love is treated in the story and in the poem.

_____

_____

_____

_____

_____

_____

_____

_____

Read the beginning of a play and answer questions 21–27.

The Wild Duck

by Henrik Ibsen

Ibsen, a Norwegian who lived 1828–1906, is said to be the second-most translated playwright in world literature, after Shakespeare.

At WERLE'S house. A richly and comfortably furnished study; bookcases and upholstered furniture; a writing table, with papers and documents, in the center of the room; lighted lamps with green shades, giving a subdued light. At the back, open folding doors with curtains drawn back. Within is seen a large and handsome room, brilliantly lighted with lamps and branching candlesticks. In front, on the right (in the study), a small baize door leads into WERLE'S Office. On the left, in front, a fireplace with a glowing coal fire, and farther back a double door leading into the dining room.

WERLE'S servant, PETTERSEN, in livery, and JENSEN, the hired waiter, in black, are putting the study in order. In the large room, two or three other hired waiters are moving about, arranging things and lighting more candles. From the dining room, the hum of conversation and laughter of many voices are heard; a glass is tapped with a knife; silence follows, and a toast is proposed; shouts of "Bravo!" and then again a buzz of conversation.

PETTERSEN: *(lights a lamp on the chimney-place and places a shade over it)* Hark to them, Jensen! Now the old man's on his legs holding a long palaver about Mrs. Sorby.

JENSEN: *(pushing forward an armchair)* Is it true, what folks say, that they're very good friends, eh?

PETTERSON: Lord knows.

JENSEN: I've heard tell as he's been a lively customer in his day.

PETTERSON: May be.

JENSEN: And he's giving this spread in honor of his son, they say.

PETTERSEN: Yes. His son came home yesterday.

JENSEN: This is the first time I ever heard as Mr. Werle had a son.

PETTERSEN: Oh yes, he has a son, right enough. But he's a fixture, as you might say, up at the Hoidal works. He's never once come to town all the years I've been in service here.

A WAITER: *(in the doorway of the other room)* Pettersen, here's an old fellow wanting—

PETTERSEN: *(mutters)* The devil—who's this now?

OLD EKDAL appears from the right, in the inner room. He is dressed in a threadbare overcoat with a high collar; he wears woollen mittens, and carries in his hand a stick and a fur cap. Under his arm, a brown paper parcel. Dirty red-brown wig and small grey moustache.

PETTERSEN: *(goes towards him)* Good Lord—what do you want here?

EKDAL: *(in the doorway)* Must get into the office, Pettersen.

PETTERSON: The office was closed an hour ago, and—

EKDAL: So they told me at the front door. But Graberg's in there still. Let me slip in this way, Pettersen; there's a good fellow. *(Points towards the baize door.)* It's not the first time I've come this way.

PETTERSEN: Well, you may pass. *(Opens the door.)* But mind you go out again the proper way, for we've got company.

EKDAL: I know, I know—h'm! Thanks, Pettersen, good old friend! Thanks! *(Mutters softly.)* Pain!

He goes into the Office; PETTERSEN shuts the door after him.

JENSEN: Is he one of the office people?

PETTERSEN: No he's only an outside hand that does odd jobs of copying. But he's been a tip-topper in his day, has old Ekdal.

JENSEN: You can see he's been through a lot.

PETTERSEN: Yes; he was an army officer, you know.

JENSEN: You don't say so?

PETTERSEN: No mistake about it. But then he went into the timber trade or something of the sort. They say he once played Mr. Werle a very nasty trick. They were partners in the Hoidal works at the time. Oh, I know old Ekdal well, I do. Many a nip of bitters and bottle of ale we two have drunk at Madam Eriksen's.

JENSEN: He don't look as if he'd much to stand treat with.

PETTERSEN: Why, bless you, Jensen, it's me that stands treat. I always think there's no harm in being a bit civil to folks that have seen better days.

JENSEN: Did he go bankrupt then?

Unit 2 Analyzing and Interpreting Literature

Pettersen: Worse than that. He went to prison.

Jensen: To prison!

Pettersen: Or perhaps it was the Penitentiary. *(Listens.)* Sh! They're leaving the table.

The dining-room door is thrown open from within, by a couple of waiters. MRS. SORBY comes out conversing with two gentlemen. Gradually the whole company follows, amongst them WERLE. Last come HIALMAR EKDAL and GREGERS WERLE.

Mrs. Sorby: *(in passing, to the servant)* Tell them to serve the coffee in the music-room, Pettersen.

Pettersen: Very well, Madam.

She goes with the two Gentlemen into the inner room, and thence out to the right. PETTERSEN and JENSEN go out the same way.

21 How does the reader know that the passage is drama rather than narrative prose?

    A   The author uses dialogue.

    B   The author uses stage directions.

    C   The author includes detailed description.

    D   The author introduces his characters at once.

22 Read this sentence from the passage.

    "A richly and comfortably furnished study; bookcases and upholstered furniture; a writing table, with papers and documents, in the center of the room; lighted lamps with green shades, giving a <u>subdued</u> *light."*

What does the word <u>subdued</u> mean as used in the sentence?

    A   conquered

    B   cultivated

    C   made submissive

    D   reduced in intensity

23 In this passage, Old Ekdal uses an aside to

    A   flaunt his superiority over the servants.

    B   show what he really thinks of Pettersen.

    C   indicate that life has treated him harshly.

    D   hint that he will be an important character.

24 Pettersen's attitude toward Old Ekdal in this passage could **best** be described as

    A flattering.

    B deferential.

    C indifferent.

    D condescending.

25 What addition to the text could **best** support the author's purpose in this selection?

    A an explanation of why Werle's son rarely comes to town

    B details of the relationship between Werle and Mrs. Sorby

    C an indication of how long Pettersen has worked for Werle

    D a soliloquy by Old Ekdal explaining why he went to prison

26 Which sentence **best** describes the relationship between the setting and the tone in this passage?

    A The formal setting contributes to a stuffy tone.

    B The dark setting contributes to a menacing tone.

    C The foreign setting contributes to an exotic tone.

    D The realistic setting contributes to a neutral tone.

27 Analyze how the author uses exposition in this selection. Use evidence from the passage to explain your answer.

_____

_____

_____

_____

_____

_____

_____

_____

Module 2
Nonfiction

Unit 3
Reading for Meaning

In this unit, you will sharpen the skills you need to read and understand nonfiction literature. You will review vocabulary words, including affixes, synonyms, and antonyms. Gaining meaning from context is another skill you will review. This is helpful in teasing out the meaning of words you encounter when studying a particular subject, but with which you may be unfamiliar. This is especially true in the sciences and social sciences. You will also assess your comprehension skills. You will read passages, and then answer questions about the main idea and important supporting details. Understanding why an author has chosen to write in a particular form or style is helpful when reading nonfiction.

Vocabulary Skills

L.N.1.2.1, LN.1.2.2, L.N.1.2.3, L.N.1.2.4

Identifying unfamiliar words in an informational text involves the same skills as it does in fiction. You read about them in Lesson 1:

- identifying and using **synonyms** and **antonyms**
- identifying how **affixes** change the meaning of a word
- using **context clues** to determine the meaning of unfamiliar words or words that have multiple meanings
- drawing conclusions about the **connotations** of words

In addition, some nonfiction texts use specialized vocabulary—words that are exclusive to a certain subject, or that have special meaning within that subject. For example, do you know the difference between a *boson* and a *bosun?* One is something you'd encounter in an article about science, the other in a book about ships. An *assembly* is something that happens at school on special occasions, but what does it connote in an article about the United States Bill of Rights, in the phrase "freedom of assembly"? And how about an advertisement for a product that says "no assembly required"? What about foreign words that have become part of English or that are not easily translated with a simple synonym, words like *subpoena* or *coup d'etat?* Or words that mean something different in British English than they do in American English, such as *bonnet* and *boot?* You may encounter words like these in some of the passages you'll read in the second half of this book, and in any nonfiction passage you may read in print or on the Internet.

Read this sentence.

> *About once an hour Mrs. Lincoln would <u>repair</u> to the bedside of her husband and with <u>lamentation</u> and tears remain until overcome by emotion.*

Which word is a synonym for <u>lamentation</u> as used in this sentence?

A wailing

B fainting

C apologizing

D understanding

> A context clue in this sentence is the word *tears*. <u>Lamentation</u> is something that goes with crying. And if you know what the word *lament* means, you can figure out from the suffix that the word means "the act of lamenting," crying out in sorrow. Choice A is the correct answer.

What does the word <u>repair</u> mean in the sentence above?

A go

B fix

C make up for

D condition for use

> This sentence comes from the diary of a government official who was present at Abraham Lincoln's bedside when he died. It uses the word *repair* in a way that doesn't come up so often in American English anymore. The context tells you that <u>repair</u> in this sentence means "to go (to a place)," choice A.

Read this sentence.

Using data from NASA's Chandra X-ray Observatory, astronomers have discovered an <u>unprecedented</u> <u>bonanza</u> of black holes in the Andromeda Galaxy, one of the nearest galaxies to the Milky Way.

What does <u>unprecedented</u> mean in this sentence?

A   very far away

B   teeming with life

C   of extraordinary size

D   never done or known before

Your prior knowledge combined with context clues might help you to eliminate choice A (it's too obvious) and choice B (this isn't science fiction). But that prefix *un-* means "not," which tells you that <u>unprecedented</u> means "not" something. If you recognize the root word *precede*, it's easy to conclude that choice D is the correct answer.

What does the word <u>bonanza</u> mean in the sentence above?

A   a rich mineral deposit

B   a thing or person worthy of fame

C   something very valuable or rewarding

D   an event that had someone had predicted earlier

Sometimes identifying a context clue requires reading more than one sentence. Here is the next sentence of the Smithsonian Institution's press release about the discovery:

Using more than 150 Chandra observations, spread over 13 years, researchers identified 26 black hole candidates, the largest number to date, in a galaxy outside our own.

If you were unsure about the meaning of <u>bonanza</u> from reading just the first sentence, this second sentence tells you something more about the discovery— it was the greatest number yet found in a galaxy outside our own. This context clue tells you that the correct answer is choice C, and did you notice that the sentence also confirms the answer to the previous question?

Read this sentence.

> Jerry Lee Lewis's <u>arresting</u> piano <u>glissando</u> was a trademark of his style and a factor in his <u>installation</u> in the Rock and Roll Hall of Fame

What does the word <u>glissando</u> mean in this sentence?

A   like glass

B   elaborately decorated

C   sliding from one note to another

D   singing high above the usual range

Legal terms are in Latin, martial-arts terms in Japanese, and musical terms in Italian—even in a sentence about an American rock and country star. The context tells you that it a noun, not an adjective, and that in Lewis's case it's a musical technique used in playing the piano, not singing. Choice C is the correct answer.

What is being suggested by the use of the word <u>arresting</u> in the sentence above?

A   celebrity

B   dishonesty

C   lack of polish

D   stunning surprise

<u>Arresting</u> in this sentence has nothing to do with the police. But it has the connotation of being stopped suddenly, to be grabbed and diverted from one's purpose, in this case by musical artistry. Choice D is the answer you want.

The suffix -*tion* helps the reader know that the word <u>installation</u> means

A   previously established in a place.

B   the result of establishing in a place

C   a person who is established in a place.

D   tending toward being established in a place.

If you need help in finding the answer, you can turn to the suffix chart on page 13. It will tell you that the -*tion* ending turns a verb to a noun and means "the act of." <u>Installation</u> in this sentence means the act or result of Lewis's being installed in the Rock and Roll Hall of Fame, so choice B is the answer you want.

Read this sentence.

The industrious ant has long been used by fabulists and entomologists alike as an example of purposeful endeavor.

The word industrious in this sentence is an antonym for

A   lazy.

B   busy.

C   rural.

D   cooperative.

Industrious suggests industry, which in turn may suggest machines and factories. When applied to an ant, however, that connection doesn't make sense. The phrase "purposeful endeavor" gives you the context to understand that the sentence is referring to the ant's constant busy-ness, so you're looking for a word that can be an antonym of *busy*. The correct answer is choice A.

What is the meaning of entomologists in the sentence above?

A   abstract thinkers

B   industrial engineers

C   scientists who study insects

D   doctors who treat digestive disorders

You may have recognized the suffix *-ologists* as relating to medicine or other scientists. Doctors who treat human beings generally would not have much to do with ants, so you can conclude here that choice C is the correct answer.

IT'S YOUR TURN

Read this excerpt from a speech and answer the questions.

Lincoln's Speech on the Supreme Court's Dred Scott Decision

Given at Springfield, Illinois, June 26, 1857

Chief Justice Taney, in his opinion in the Dred Scott case, admits that the language of the Declaration [of Independence] is broad enough to include the whole human family, but he and Judge Douglas argue that the authors of that instrument did not intend to include Negroes, by the fact that they did not at once, actually place them on an equality with the whites. Now this grave argument comes to just nothing at all, by the other fact, that they did not at once, or ever afterwards, actually place all white people on an equality with one or another. And this is the staple argument of both the Chief Justice and the Senator [Stephen Douglas], for doing this obvious violence to the plain unmistakable language of the Declaration. I think the authors of that notable instrument intended to include all men, but they did not intend to declare all men equal in all respects. They did not mean to say all were equal in color, size, intellect, moral developments, or social capacity. They defined with tolerable distinctness, in what respects they did consider all men created equal—equal in "certain inalienable rights, among which are life, liberty, and the pursuit of happiness." This they said, and this meant. They did not mean to assert the obvious untruth, that all were then actually enjoying that equality, nor yet, that they were about to confer it immediately upon them. In fact they had no power to confer such a boon. They meant simply to declare the right, so that the enforcement of it might follow as fast as circumstances should permit. They meant to set up a standard maxim for free society, which should be familiar to all, and revered by all; constantly looked to, constantly labored for, and even though never perfectly attained, constantly approximated, and thereby constantly spreading and deepening its influence, and augmenting the happiness and value of life to all people of all colors everywhere. The assertion that "all men are created equal" was of no practical use in effecting our separation from Great Britain; and it was placed in the Declaration, nor for that, but for future use. Its authors meant it to be, thank God, it is now proving itself, a stumbling block to those who in after times might seek to turn a free people back into the hateful paths of despotism. They knew the proneness of prosperity to breed tyrants, and they meant when such should re-appear in this fair land and commence their vocation they should find left for them at least one hard nut to crack.

1 As used in this passage, the word instrument means

   A   mechanical implement.

   B   measuring tool used in science.

   C   thing by which something is done.

   D   device for producing musical sounds.

2 Read the sentence from the passage.

   "And this is the staple argument of both the Chief Justice and the Senator, for doing this obvious violence to the plain unmistakable language of the Declaration."

   What does the word staple refer to in this sentence?

   A   a raw material

   B   a main element

   C   a principal crop

   D   a metal fastener

3 Which word or phrase defines the word <u>tolerable</u> as Lincoln uses it?

   A unfair

   B mediocre

   C fairly good

   D able to be endured

4 The prefix *in-* and the suffix *-able* help the reader to know that the word <u>inalienable</u> means

   A in the mind of a foreigner.

   B not subject to being removed.

   C against the act of transferring.

   D after being carefully considered.

5 As used in this passage, the word <u>confer</u> is a synonym for

   A give.

   B discuss.

   C compare.

   D separate.

6 Read this sentence from the passage.

> *"They meant to set up a standard maxim for free society, which should be familiar to all, and <u>revered</u> by all; constantly looked to, constantly labored for, and even though never perfectly attained, constantly approximated, and thereby constantly spreading and deepening its influence, and augmenting the happiness and value of life to all people of all colors everywhere."*

What is Lincoln suggesting by the use of the word <u>revered</u>?

   A patriotism

   B admiration

   C hard work

   D religious devotion

Unit 3 Reading for Meaning

Author's Purpose in Nonfiction

L.N.1.1.1, L.N.1.1.2, L.N.1.1.3, L.N.1.1.4

When you're reading fiction, finding the main idea is a step toward determining the author's purpose. With nonfiction, it's often the other way around. While authors of fiction have different motivations for writing, their main purpose is to entertain their readers. Authors of nonfiction may write for a number of different purposes, and it's important to be able to determine what they are.

Suppose that you're reading an article about the Battle of Gettysburg. Such a selection, full of facts and details about a historical event, is obviously intended to **explain, inform,** or **teach**. However, there are sections that quote from a soldier's diary and are plainly meant to **describe.** They include details about the soldier's daily life, the things he saw and heard and smelled every day, and his personal account of the battle. It's also possible that the book's author is blending facts with her own opinions about the Civil War in order to **persuade** readers to her point of view. Consider how your own purposes would differ if you were writing:

- a set of instructions for a task

- a journal entry

- a report for a science class

- a magazine feature

- an editorial about a news story

- a guide to your school for incoming students

- a politician's campaign biography

- an advertisement for a service

- a personal essay about a memorable experience

Read the passage and answer the questions.

Pennsylvania Dutch Chicken Corn Soup

In 1683, the Plain Sects began to arrive in William Penn's Colony seeking a land of peace and plenty. They were a mixed people; Moravians from Bohemia and Moravia, Mennonites from Switzerland and Holland, the Amish, the Dunkards, the Schwenkfelds, and the French Huguenots. After the lean years of clearing the land and developing their farms, they established the peace and plenty they sought. These German-speaking people were originally called the Pennsylvania Deutsch, but time and custom have caused them to be known to us as the Pennsylvania Dutch.

The Pennsylvania Dutch are a hard-working people and as they say, "Them that works hard, eats hearty." The blending of recipes from their many home lands and the ingredients available in their new land produced tasty dishes that have been handed down for generations. Their cooking was truly a folk art requiring much intuitive knowledge, for recipes contained measurements such as "flour to stiffen," "butter the size of a walnut," and "large as an apple." Many of the recipes have been made more exact…, providing us with a regional cookery we can all enjoy.

Soups are a traditional part of Pennsylvania Dutch cooking…. One of the favorite summer soups in the Pennsylvania Dutch country is Chicken Corn Soup. Few Sunday School picnic suppers would be considered complete without gallons of this hearty soup.

Chicken Corn Soup

1 stewing hen, about 4 lbs

4 qts water

1 onion, chopped

10 ears corn

½ cup celery, chopped with leaves

2 hard-boiled eggs

salt and pepper

rivels

    Put cut-up chicken and onion into the water and cook slowly until tender, add salt. Remove chicken, cut the meat into small (1-inch) pieces and return to broth, together with corn, which has been cut from the cob, celery, and seasoning. Continue to simmer.

    Make rivels by combining 1 cup flour, a pinch of salt, 1 egg, and a little milk. Mix well with fork or fingers to form small crumbs. Drop these into the soup, also the chopped, hard-boiled eggs. Boil for 15 minutes longer.

What is the main purpose in writing the passage?

A   to explain what rivels are

B   to describe the taste of a favorite soup

C   to instruct readers in making a type of soup

D   to explain the origins of Pennsylvania Dutch cooking

This recipe comes from an old cookbook, author anonymous. *Rivels* is a term you don't hear so often, but explaining what they are is only a minor detail in this account. To know how the soup tastes you'd have to make it yourself, and while the author does discuss Pennsylvania Dutch cooking, her main purpose is to give readers directions for doing just that. Choice C is the correct answer.

What additional information would **best** support the author's purpose?

A   a note on how many people the recipe serves

B   the name of the person who provided the recipe

C   a list of farmers' markets in the Pennsylvania Dutch country

D   a statement of the author's credentials for writing a cookbook

Consider that the author's purpose is to explain to the reader how to make the soup. You wouldn't need the name of the person who provided the recipe or any indication that the author is an expert. Farmers' markets are nice, but these ingredients can be found in any grocery or supermarket. Four quarts of water and a whole chicken make a lot of soup, however, and it would be useful to know just how many people it will feed. Choice A is the answer you want.

What is the author's purpose in writing the first two paragraphs of this passage?

A   to provide nutritional information about the recipe

B   to compare traditional and modern cookbook recipes

C   to provide background information on the Pennsylvania Dutch

D   to persuade the reader that the recipe is authentically American

Often a section of a passage can have a different purpose than the main one. The first two paragraphs aren't about the recipe, though they do generalize about Pennsylvania Dutch cooking. They mainly furnish information about the tradition that the recipe comes from. The correct answer is choice C.

GUIDED PRACTICE

Read the passage and answer the questions.

The scene changed again as they descended. On either hand ran ranges of woody hills, following the course of the river; and when they mounted to their tops, they saw beyond them a rolling sea of dull green prairie, a boundless pasture of the buffalo and the deer, in our own day strangely transformed—yellow in harvest time with ripened wheat, and dotted with the roofs of a hardy and valiant yeomanry.

They passed the site of the future town of Ottawa, and saw on their right the high plateau of Buffalo Rock, long a favorite dwelling place of Indians. A league below, the river glided among islands bordered with stately woods. Close on their left towered a lofty cliff, crested with trees that overhung the rippling current; while below them spread the valley of the Illinois, in broad low meadows, bordered on the right by graceful hills at whose foot now lies the village of Utica.

What is the author's main purpose in writing these paragraphs?

A   to serve as a guide for tourists

B   to describe the setting he is writing about

C   to persuade readers to visit the region for the scenery

D   to compare the site in prehistoric and contemporary times

This passage almost reads like an adventure story, doesn't it? Such was the expansive style of 19th-century historian Francis Parkman, here describing the early French exploration of the North American Midwest. Parkman's main purpose was writing history, but he colored his accounts with detailed descriptions of the locations of events for readers of his day. Choice B is the correct answer.

How does the author's use of imagery in this selection help communicate an idea?

A   It uses words that vividly appeal to the sense of sight.

B   It gives information that indicates the presence of danger.

C   It suggests that American settlement has spoiled the land.

D   It gives a bountiful description to attract settlers to the valley.

Key words or phrases in a text can provide information to a reader and influence him to perceive it from the author's point of view. Here Parkman's purpose is description, and he uses words like "woody hills," "rolling sea of… prairie," "boundless pasture of the buffalo and the deer," and "rippling current" to achieve it. The correct answer is choice A.

Read the passage and answer the questions.

Your laptop's been stolen!

…or maybe you just left it in the bathroom at the airport. The trouble is, you're home in Wichita but the airport is in Singapore! Your personal files, your business records, your family photos— gone! Maybe your computer will be recovered, but maybe it won't.

That's why you need Kryptonite. It backs up your files online, automatically and securely. So no matter where your laptop is, your files and documents are recoverable in seconds. Get full Kryptonite protection starting at $69 per year.

ORDER NOW at www.kryptonitesecurity.com

What is the author's purpose in writing this passage?

A   to warn the reader against computer theft

B   to advise the reader about Internet security

C   to describe a company's products and services

D   to persuade the reader to buy a product or service

You recognized this passage as an advertisement, and you know the purpose of an advertisement is to persuade you to buy something. Be aware, however, that some advertisements are not so straightforward in their approach: You may be persuaded to watch an entertaining video on a website or to read something disturbing that may or may not be true, and only then be presented with an appeal to separate you from your money. Choice D is the correct answer.

Unit 3 Reading for Meaning

Which statement **best** describes how the author's use of the sentence "Your laptop's been stolen!" influences the reader?

   A   The sentence indicates that crime in airports is a growing problem.

   B   The sentence suggests that the company's product can deter thieves.

   C   The sentence reminds you of the consequences if your laptop really was stolen.

   D   The sentence implies that you should never leave a computer unattended in public.

In Lesson 18, you will learn about techniques of persuasion and how to spot them. Here, however, the purpose of the sentence is to get you to actually *read* the text of the advertisement and hopefully to order the product from the company's website. It got your attention, didn't it? Made you think of what a hassle it would be if all your school papers (not to mention your private information) were to be lost or to fall into a stranger's hands? The correct answer is choice C.

Read the passage and answer the questions.

Chief Joseph

from a speech given at Washington, D.C., in 1879

Chief Joseph (1840–1904) of the Nez Percé is best known for his resistance to the U.S. government's attempts to force his people onto a reservation.

…I have seen the Great Father Chief [President Hayes]… and many other law chiefs and they all say they are my friends, and that I shall have justice, but while all their mouths talk right I do not understand why nothing is done for my people. I have heard talk and talk, but nothing is done. Good words do not last long unless they amount to something. Words do not pay for my dead people. They do not pay for my country now overrun by white men. They do not protect my father's grave. They do not pay for my horses and cattle. Good words will not give me back my children. Good words will not make good the promise of your war chief, General Miles. Good words will not give my people good health and stop them from dying. Good words will not get my people a home where they can live in peace and take care of themselves.

I am tired of talk that comes to nothing. It makes my heart sick when I remember all the good words and all the broken promises. There has been too much talking by men who had no right to talk. Too many misrepresentations have been made, too many misunderstandings have come up between the white men about the Indians. If the white man wants to live in peace with the Indian, he can live in peace. There need be no trouble. Treat all men alike. Give them the same law. Give them an even chance to live and grow. All men were made by the same Great Spirit Chief. They are all brothers. The earth is the mother of all people, and all people should have equal rights upon it. You might as well expect all rivers to run backward as that any man who was born a free man should be contented penned up and denied liberty to go where he pleases. If you tie a horse to a stake, do you expect he will grow fat? If you pen an Indian up on a small spot of earth and compel him to stay there, he will not be contented, nor will he grow and prosper. I have asked some of the Great White Chiefs where they get their authority to say to the Indian that he shall stay in one place, while he sees white men going where they please. They cannot tell me.

I only ask of the government to be treated as all other men are treated. If I cannot go to my own home, let me have a home in a country where my people will not die so fast….

Let me be a free man, free to travel, free to stop, free to work, free to trade where I choose, free to choose my own teachers, free to follow the religion of my fathers, free to talk, think, and act for myself—and I will obey every law or submit to the penalty….

1   What is Chief Joseph's purpose in writing this passage?

   A   to describe in detail the sorry situation of his people

   B   to persuade the government to give his people justice

   C   to express his indignation about settlers on the reservation

   D   to inform the public about how his people have been treated

2   Which additional information would **best** support Chief Joseph's purpose?

   A   an explanation of how he came to Washington

   B   a record of his conversation with President Hayes

   C   the names of the government officials he has met with

   D   details of the promises the government has made and broken

3 Read the sentence from the passage.

> *"You might as well expect all rivers to run backward as that any man who was born a free man should be contented penned up and denied liberty to go where he pleases."*

How does Chief Joseph's use of imagery in this sentence help to communicate an idea?

  A   It gives details about the reality his people face.

  B   It emphasizes the impossibility of life on a reservation.

  C   It suggests that his people will go to war to keep their land.

  D   It offers a vivid description of the country his people call home.

4 Which statement best describes how Chief Joseph's repetition of the phrase "good words" influences the reader?

  A   It builds intensity toward a climax.

  B   It offers conciliation to the government.

  C   It uses figurative language to make his point.

  D   It contrasts the government's words with its actions.

5 Read the sentence from the passage.

> *"The earth is the mother of all people, and all people should have equal rights upon it."*

Explain how Chief Joseph's use of the phrase "equal rights" influences the reader. Use information from the passage to support your explanation.

_____

_____

_____

_____

_____

_____

_____

Unit 3 Reading for Meaning

Main Idea in Informational Text

L.N.1.3.1, L.N.1.3.2, L.N.1.3.3

Identifying the main idea and supporting details in a nonfiction text and summarizing the most important ideas is almost exactly the same skill it is in fiction—almost, because the author's purpose is a clue toward determining "What's it about?" and what the most important details are.

If the author's purpose is to inform or instruct, look for the ideas that indicate *what* he's trying to teach you. If her purpose is plainly to persuade, then the main idea is *what* she's trying to sell you (whether it's a product, a service, an idea, or a candidate for mayor) and what techniques she's using to persuade you. If the author's purpose is to describe, somewhere in his account of sensory images is a concept that unifies and makes sense of them all.

GUIDED PRACTICE

Read an article and answer the questions.

Digging a Vegetarian Diet

Plant-Based Eating Can Reap Rewards

Vegetarians miss out on lots of foods. No grilled burgers or franks at picnics. No holiday turkey or fries cooked in animal fat. Strict vegetarians may even forego honey made by bees. But vegetarians also tend to miss out on major health problems that plague many Americans. They generally live longer than the rest of us, and they're more likely to bypass heart-related and other ailments.

The fact is, eating a more plant-based diet can boost your health, whether you're a vegetarian or not.

What is it about the vegetarian lifestyle that can protect your health? And are there risks to being vegetarian? NIH-funded researchers are looking for answers. They're exploring the many ways that diet and other factors affect our health.

Vegetarian meals focus on fruits and vegetables, dried beans, whole grains, seeds and nuts. By some estimates, about 2% of the U.S. adult population follows this type of diet.

People have many reasons for becoming vegetarians. Some want to eat more healthy foods. Others have religious or economic reasons or are concerned about animal welfare. "Vegetarian diets are also more sustainable and environmentally sound than diets that rely heavily on meat, poultry, and fish," says NIH nutritionist Dr. Susan Krebs-Smith, who monitors trends in cancer risk factors.

Most people think of vegetarian diets as simply eating plant foods and not eating meat, poultry and fish. "But in fact, there are many different types of vegetarian diets,"

Krebs-Smith explains. "Some are more restrictive than others."

Strict vegetarians, or vegans, eat plant foods and reject all animal products—meat, poultry, fish, eggs, dairy, and sometimes honey. Those who also eat dairy products are called lacto vegetarians. Vegetarians who eat both dairy and eggs are called lacto-ovo vegetarians.

Some vegetarians eat fish but not meat or poultry. They're called pescatarians (*pesce* is Italian for fish).

"Then there are the so-called flexitarians, or semi-vegetarians. These are people who eat a mostly vegetarian diet, but they occasionally eat meat," says Jody Engel, a nutritionist and registered dietitian at NIH. "They might say 'I'm a vegetarian, but I need to eat my burgers every Sunday.' People tend to follow their own rules, which is one reason why it's hard for researchers to study vegetarians. There's so much variance."

Despite the different definitions, "there's tremendous agreement among nutrition experts and health organizations that a more plant-based diet is beneficial, whether you're a true vegetarian or not," says Krebs-Smith. "Most Americans don't eat enough fruit, vegetables, legumes, or whole grains. There's a huge consensus that eating more of these foods would be a good idea for everyone."

Vegetarian diets tend to have fewer calories, lower levels of saturated fat and cholesterol, and more fiber, potassium, and vitamin C than other eating patterns. Vegetarians tend to weigh less than meat-eaters, and to have lower cancer rates. "Evidence also suggests that a vegetarian diet is associated with a lower risk of death from certain heart diseases, and that those who follow a vegetarian diet tend to have lower LDL ["bad"] cholesterol levels," says Engel.

In some cases, though, it's unclear if certain health benefits come from plant-based eating or from the healthy lifestyle of most vegetarians. "Vegetarians are generally more physically active and have healthier habits than nonvegetarians. They also typically have a higher socioeconomic status, at least in the United States," says Krebs-Smith.

To tease out the effects of diet, scientists have to conduct large, carefully controlled studies that account for other factors. One of the world's largest studies of plant-based diets is now underway at Loma Linda University in California. Cardiologist Dr. Gary Fraser is leading an NIH-funded team of scientists to analyze data on 96,000 Seventh-day Adventists in all 50 states and in Canada. Members of this religious group have unique dietary habits and a generally healthy lifestyle.

Adventists are encouraged to follow a vegetarian diet, but about half the population sometimes eats meat. These variable eating patterns allow scientists to compare a wide range of dietary habits and look for links between diet and disease.

To date, the researchers have found that the closer people are to being vegetarian, the lower their risk of diabetes, high blood pressure, and metabolic syndrome (a condition that raises your risk for heart disease and stroke). "The trend is almost like a stepladder, with the lowest risks for the strict vegetarians, then moving up for the lacto vegetarians and then the pescatarians and then the nonvegetarians," Fraser explains. Earlier studies found that vegetarian Adventists also tend to live longer than both meat-eating Adventists and non-Adventists. The vegetarians also have less coronary heart disease and lower rates of some cancers.

Because vegetarians by definition don't eat meat, some people jump to the conclusion that simply cutting meat from your diet will lead to health benefits. "But it's actually more complicated than that," says Fraser. "Differences in life expectancy and other health matters might be related to the extra fruits, vegetables, nuts, and legumes—

including soy—that vegetarians tend to eat. You can't necessarily conclude it's based on the absence of meat," he says.

Experts generally agree that vegetarians who eat a wide variety of foods can readily meet all their body's needs for nutrients. "At any stage of life, you should be able to eat a healthy diet by consuming vegetarian foods. But it does take a little planning," says Rachel Fisher, a registered dietitian involved in nutrition research at NIH.

Vegetarians need to be sure they take in enough iron, calcium, zinc, and vitamin B12. Studies show that most vegetarians do get enough, in part because so many cereals, breads, and other foods are fortified with these nutrients. "Vegans in particular need to be certain to get enough vitamin B12 and omega-3 fatty acids," says Fisher. Omega-3—found in fish, flax seed, walnuts, and canola oil—is important for heart health and vision.

Some vegetarians take dietary supplements to make sure they're getting everything they need. It's a good idea to talk to a registered dietitian or other health professional if you're a vegetarian or thinking of becoming one.

Whether you're a vegetarian or not, Fisher says, you can benefit from the high fiber, low fat, and rich nutrients of a vegetarian diet. "Vegetarian foods can be so delicious, and they're so good for you," she says.

Try using a variety of spices and herbs to make things interesting. And make sure not to overcook your vegetables, or they might lose some of their valuable nutrients.

Which of these sentences from the passage **best** states the main idea of the passage?

A "But vegetarians also tend to miss out on major health problems that plague many Americans."

B "The fact is, eating a more plant-based diet can boost your health, whether you're a vegetarian or not."

C "Vegetarian diets tend to have fewer calories, lower levels of saturated fat and cholesterol, and more fiber, potassium, and vitamin C than other eating patterns."

D "In some cases, though, it's unclear if certain health benefits come from plant-based eating or from the healthy lifestyle of most vegetarians."

The author's purpose here is not to persuade people to become vegetarians. It's to provide facts about the benefits *and* the drawbacks of a diet based more on plants and less on meat, and to explain the science behind the facts. Choices A, C, and D are details that support that purpose, but the message is that there are health benefits to eating more plant-based foods, even if one enjoys an occasional steak or burger. Choice B is the correct answer.

According to the passage, how do scientists determine the health benefits of a vegetarian diet?

   A   by interviewing people who have variable eating patterns

   B   by analyzing the nutrient content of animal and plant foods

   C   by conducting controlled studies with large population groups

   D   by studying groups whose religion prescribes a vegetarian diet

> This question asks you to identify a key detail that supports the main idea. Since there is such a wide variety in the types of diets people eat, scientists must select large population groups to account for as much variation in diet as possible. Carefully controlled experiments are an essential characteristic of the scientific method. The correct answer is choice C.

Read this paragraph from the passage.

> *"People have many reasons for becoming vegetarians. Some want to eat more healthy foods. Others have religious or economic reasons or are concerned about animal welfare. 'Vegetarian diets are also more sustainable and environmentally sound than diets that rely heavily on meat, poultry, and fish,' says NIH nutritionist Dr. Susan Krebs-Smith, who monitors trends in cancer risk factors."*

Which sentence expresses the main idea of this paragraph?

   A   "People have many reasons for becoming vegetarians."

   B   "Some want to eat more healthy foods."

   C   "Others have religious or economic reasons or are concerned about animal welfare."

   D   "'Vegetarian diets are also more sustainable and environmentally sound than diets that rely heavily on meat, poultry, and fish,' says NIH nutritionist Dr. Susan Krebs-Smith, who monitors trends in cancer risk factors."

> One of the four sentences in the paragraph is the **topic sentence.** It effectively summarizes what the paragraph is about. The other three sentences are details that support or explain the topic sentence. They state some of the reasons that people become vegetarians—health, religious or economic concerns, animal welfare, and environmental consciousness. All these are among the "many reasons" stated in the first sentence. Choice A is the answer you want.

Unit 3 Reading for Meaning

Based on information in the passage, what factor made it difficult for scientists to determine the health benefits of a vegetarian diet?

A   Vegetarians tend to have healthier habits in general.

B   Most Americans don't eat enough fruit, vegetables, legumes, or whole grains.

C   Vegetarians have lower incidences of coronary heart disease and some forms of cancer.

D   Many cereals, breads, and other foods are fortified with nutrients that are also found in meat.

All four of the answer choices are facts, according to the passage. You are being asked to choose which detail best relates to the idea that scientists had to design their studies carefully to determine the health effects of a vegetarian diet. Only one answer choice directly interacts with and affects this problem: Vegetarians tend to exercise more and make other healthier choices, which makes it hard to control for the effects of diet. Choice A is the correct answer.

Read the incomplete summary of the passage.

- *Eating a more plant-based diet is beneficial to your health.*

- *There are many degrees of vegetarianism, but the closer one is to a meat-free diet, the lower the risk of many life-shortening diseases.*

- *Science has demonstrated the value of a vegetarian diet through controlled experiments.*

- _____

Which sentence **best** completes the summary?

A   Cutting meat from your diet will lead to health benefits.

B   Overcooking vegetables can cause them to lose some of their nutrients.

C   Vegetarians must plan carefully to meet all their bodies' nutritional needs.

D   Vegetarians can take dietary supplements to get the nutrients that are found in meat.

A summary should include only the most important ideas. Most of this passage focuses on the benefits of a vegetarian diet, but the author also points out that it can be harder to get all the body's necessary nutrients if you don't eat meat. Choices B and D support this idea, while choice A is an oversimplification that ignores the fact. The correct answer is choice C.

Read the passage. Then answer the questions.

from Life on the Mississippi

by Mark Twain

Now when I had mastered the language of this water and had come to know every trifling feature that bordered the great river as familiarly as I knew the letters of the alphabet, I had made a valuable acquisition. But I had lost something, too. I had lost something which could never be restored to me while I lived. All the grace, the beauty, the poetry had gone out of the majestic river! I still keep in mind a certain wonderful sunset which I witnessed when steamboating was new to me. A broad expanse of the river was turned to blood; in the middle distance the red hue brightened into gold, through which a solitary log came floating, black and conspicuous; in one place a long, slanting mark lay sparkling upon the water; in another the surface was broken by boiling, tumbling rings, that were as many-tinted as an opal; where the ruddy flush was faintest, was a smooth spot that was covered with graceful circles and radiating lines, ever so delicately traced; the shore on our left was densely wooded, and the somber shadow that fell from this forest was broken in one place by a long, ruffled trail that shone like silver; and high above the forest wall a clean-stemmed dead tree waved a single leafy bough that glowed like a flame in the unobstructed splendor that was flowing from the sun. There were graceful curves, reflected images, woody heights, soft distances; and over the whole scene, far and near, the dissolving lights drifted steadily, enriching it, every passing moment, with new marvels of coloring.

I stood like one bewitched. I drank it in, in a speechless rapture. The world was new to me, and I had never seen anything like this at home. But as I have said, a day came when I began to cease noting the glories and the charms which the moon and the sun and the twilight wrought upon the river's face; another day came when I ceased altogether to note them. Then, if that sunset scene had been repeated, I would have looked upon it without rapture, and would have commented upon it, inwardly, after this fashion: This sun means that we are going to have wind tomorrow: that floating log means that the river is rising, small thanks to it; that slanting mark on the water refers to a bluff reef which is going to kill somebody's steamboat one of these nights, if it keeps on stretching out like that; those tumbling "boils" show a dissolving bar and a changing channel there; the lines and circles in the slick water over yonder are a warning that that execrable place is shoaling up dangerously; that silver streak in the shadow of the forest is the "break" from a new snag, and he has located himself in the very best place he could have found to fish for steamboats; that tall, dead tree, with a single living branch, is not going to last long, and then how is a body ever going to get through this blind place at night without the friendly old landmark?

1 What is the **main** point Mark Twain makes in this excerpt?

A Sunsets on the river were the most beautiful he ever saw.

B Becoming a Mississippi River pilot spoiled the river's beauty for him.

C The river is always changing and looks different to a pilot on each trip.

D As a Mississippi River pilot, he had to memorize every small detail of its course.

2 Based on information in the passage, what did a slanting mark on the water mean to Twain as a river pilot?

A an underwater obstruction that could sink a boat

B a landmark that guided him in navigating the river

C the memory of a beautiful sunset he once witnessed

D the wreck of another boat that had passed that point

3 According to the passage, why could Twain no longer appreciate the effect of the sun and moon on the water?

A It was no longer new to him.

B Every detail signified danger to him.

C The river had changed too much since his youth.

D Construction and other human activity had spoiled the scenery.

4 Read the incomplete summary of the passage.

• *Twain reflects on what he gained and what he lost by "learning the river."*

• *Twain describes a sunset he saw when steamboating was new to him.*

• *Twain expresses regret that he could no longer appreciate such a sight.*

• _____

Which sentence **best** completes the summary?

A   Twain explains why he gave up steamboat piloting.

B   Twain describes a dangerous voyage down the river.

C   Twain explains why the river has lost its charm for him.

D   Twain describes some techniques a pilot uses to "read" the river.

Module 2
Nonfiction

Unit 4
Analyzing and Interpreting Nonfiction

This unit will focus on your ability to analyze and interpret nonfiction. You will learn to use your critical thinking skills to think deeply about what you are reading and to ask yourself questions:

What is the author's purpose?

What techniques is the author using?

How is the author using language to support his purpose?

How can I use what I already know to better understand what I am reading?

In this unit, you will pay attention to how the author develops and supports his argument. You will analyze the language and supporting evidence the author uses. Making connections is an important part of reading, and helps deepen your understanding of the author's subject or theme. To judge the validity and accuracy of what you are reading, you will differentiate between the facts and opinions in a selection. Authors convey and emphasize meaning through the way they organize their text.

Inferences, Conclusions, and Generalizations

L.N.2.1.1, L.N.2.1.2

If you absorb only the information an author explicitly tells you as you read, you may be missing something important. An author assumes that you will also understand the *implicit* information she is trying to convey. In Lesson 4, you learned how to combine what an author tells you with your prior knowledge to **make inferences** about a text, to put pieces of information together to **draw conclusions,** and to use these inferences and conclusions to **make generalizations** about what an author means.

These are skills you apply when reading for information, too. In an article about space science, for example, the author may assume you know what stars are and what a galaxy is, and so will understand some of his points without his having to explain them. He may describe a series of causes and effects without ever actually stating that A was the result of B. Or, he may explain a natural process and assume that his readers can put together the facts and details to determine other facts. Similarly, in a historical document, you're reading something that an author wrote for people in his own time. In order to understand the events and social issues, you need to know something about the culture of that time and combine that knowledge with what you read.

GUIDED PRACTICE

Read the passage and answer the questions.

from **Walden**

by Henry David Thoreau

> In 1845, teacher and writer Henry David Thoreau left his home in Concord, Massachusetts, to live in a cabin he built himself on a 17-acre tract at nearby Walden Pond. As he wrote, "I went to the woods because I wished to live deliberately, to front only the essential facts of life, and see if I could not learn what it had to teach, and not, when I came to die, discover that I had not lived." It has been said of the book he wrote about his two years in the woods that it "surpasses everything we have had in America."

But while we are confined to books, though the most select and classic, and read only particular written languages, which are themselves but dialects and provincial, we are in danger of forgetting the language which all things and events speak without metaphor, which alone is copious and standard. Much is published, but little

Unit 4 Analyzing and Interpreting Nonfiction

printed.... No method nor discipline can supersede the necessity of being forever on the alert. What is a course of history or philosophy, or poetry, no matter how well selected, or the best society, or the most admirable routine of life, compared with the discipline of looking always at what is to be seen? Will you be a reader, a student merely, or a seer? Read your fate, see what is before you, and walk on into futurity.

I did not read books the first summer; I hoed beans. Nay, I often did better than this. There were times when I could not afford to sacrifice the bloom of the present moment to any work, whether of the head or hands. I love a broad margin to my life. Sometimes, in a summer morning, having taken my accustomed bath, I sat in my sunny doorway from sunrise till noon, rapt in a reverie, amidst the pines and hickories and sumacs, in undisturbed solitude and stillness, while the birds sing around or flitted noiseless through the house, until by the sun falling in at my west window, or the noise of some traveller's wagon on the distant highway, I was reminded of the lapse of time. I grew in those seasons like corn in the night, and they were far better than any work of the hands would have been. They were not time subtracted from my life, but so much over and above my usual allowance. I realized what the Orientals mean by contemplation and the forsaking of works. For the most part, I minded not how the hours went. The day advanced as if to light some work of mine; it was morning, and lo, now it is evening, and nothing memorable is accomplished. Instead of singing like the birds, I silently smiled at my incessant good fortune. As the sparrow had its trill, sitting on the hickory before my door, so had I my chuckle or suppressed warble which he might hear out of my nest. My days were not days of the week, bearing the stamp of any heathen deity, nor were they minced into

hours and fretted by the ticking of a clock; for I lived like the Puri Indians[1], of whom it is said that "for yesterday, today, and tomorrow they have only one word, and they express the variety of meaning by pointing backward for yesterday forward for tomorrow, and overhead for the passing day." This was sheer idleness to my fellow-townsmen, no doubt; but if the birds and flowers had tried me by their standard, I should not have been found wanting. A man must find his occasions in himself, it is true. The natural day is very calm, and will hardly reprove his indolence.

I had this advantage, at least, in my mode of life, over those who were obliged to look abroad for amusement, to society and the theatre, that my life itself was become my amusement and never ceased to be novel. It was a drama of many scenes and without an end. If we were always, indeed, getting our living, and regulating our lives according to the last and best mode we had learned, we should never be troubled with ennui[2]. Follow your genius[3] closely enough, and it will not fail to show you a fresh prospect every hour. Housework was a pleasant pastime. When my floor was dirty, I rose early, and, setting all my furniture out of doors on the grass, bed and bedstead making but one budget, dashed water on the floor, and sprinkled white sand from the pond on it, and then with a broom scrubbed it clean and white; and by the time the villagers had broken their fast the morning sun had dried my house sufficiently to allow me to move in again, and my meditations were almost uninterrupted. It was pleasant to see my whole household effects out on the grass, making a little pile like a gypsy's pack, and my three-legged table, from which I did not remove the books and pen and ink, standing amid the pines and hickories. They seemed glad to get out themselves, and as if unwilling to be brought in. I was sometimes tempted to stretch an

---

[1]**Puri Indians:** a native people of Brazil
[2]**ennui:** boredom
[3]**genius:** here meaning a person's distinctive character

awning over them and take my seat there. It was worth the while to see the sun shine on these things, and hear the free wind blow on them; so much more interesting most familiar objects look out of doors than in the house. A bird sits on the next bough, life-everlasting grows under the table, and blackberry vines run round its legs; pine cones, chestnut burs, and strawberry leaves are strewn about. It looked as if this was the way these forms came to be transferred to our furniture, to tables, chairs, and bedsteads—because they once stood in their midst.

My house was on the side of a hill, immediately on the edge of the larger wood, in the midst of a young forest of pitch pines and hickories, and half a dozen rods from the pond, to which a narrow footpath led down the hill. In my front yard grew the strawberry, blackberry, and life-everlasting, johnswort and goldenrod, shrub oaks and sand cherry, blueberry and groundnut. Near the end of May, the sand cherry…adorned the sides of the path with its delicate flowers arranged in umbels cylindrically about its short stems,

which last, in the fall, weighed down with goodsized and handsome cherries, fell over in wreaths like rays on every side. I tasted them out of compliment to Nature, though they were scarcely palatable. The sumac… grew luxuriantly about the house, pushing up through the embankment which I had made, and growing five or six feet the first season. Its broad pinnate tropical leaf was pleasant though strange to look on. The large buds, suddenly pushing out late in the spring from dry sticks which had seemed to be dead, developed themselves as by magic into graceful green and tender boughs, an inch in diameter; and sometimes, as I sat at my window, so heedlessly did they grow and tax their weak joints, I heard a fresh and tender bough suddenly fall like a fan to the ground, when there was not a breath of air stirring, broken off by its own weight. In August, the large masses of berries, which, when in flower, had attracted many wild bees, gradually assumed their bright velvety crimson hue, and by their weight again bent down and broke the tender limbs.

What is the language Thoreau refers to in the first sentence?

A Latin

B English

C his own thoughts

D the language of nature

> To answer this question, you need to draw a conclusion based on the context of the passage. Thoreau is comparing the study of human knowledge through books with the appreciation of nature gained from observation. Nature is "the language which all things and events speak without metaphor"; the language in which "Much is published, but little printed." The correct answer is choice D.

Unit 4 Analyzing and Interpreting Nonfiction

Based on information from the passage, what inference can be drawn about Thoreau's life at Walden Pond?

A He spent a lot of time reading.

B He had little physical labor to do.

C He was not prepared for a solitary life.

D He valued his hours of quiet contemplation.

What comes through in this passage is Thoreau's love for the sights and sounds of nature. There was plenty of work to do at Walden Pond—he speaks of hoeing beans, housecleaning, and building an embankment—and he seems more than content to be alone most of the time. What most seems to please him is time spent observing the sights and sounds of nature. Choice D is the correct answer.

What statement from the passage **best** supports the generalization that Thoreau found satisfaction in his solitude?

A "What is a course of history or philosophy, or poetry, no matter how well selected, or the best society, or the most admirable routine of life, compared with the discipline of looking always at what is to be seen?"

B "I grew in those seasons like corn in the night, and they were far better than any work of the hands would have been."

C "I had this advantage, at least, in my mode of life, over those who were obliged to look abroad for amusement, to society and the theatre, that my life itself was become my amusement and never ceased to be novel."

D "My house was on the side of a hill, immediately on the edge of the larger wood, in the midst of a young forest of pitch pines and hickories, and half a dozen rods from the pond, to which a narrow footpath led down the hill."

Thoreau spends a great deal of his time in ways he knows his neighbors would find strange. As he expresses it, however, simply being himself and following "his genius" makes for a life in which he never has to look elsewhere for amusement and in which he is never bored. Choice C is the answer you want.

Read this sentence from the passage.

"My days were not days of the week, bearing the stamp of any heathen deity, nor were they minced into hours and fretted by the ticking of a clock; for I lived like the Puri Indians, of whom it is said that 'for yesterday, today, and tomorrow they have only one word, and they express the variety of meaning by pointing backward for yesterday forward for tomorrow, and overhead for the passing day.'"

What does Thoreau imply by this statement?

A   He has no clocks or calendars at his cabin.

B   He is so busy that time seems to pass quickly.

C   He does not worry about how he spends his time.

D   He thinks that living by the clock is an obsolete custom.

You can't conclude from this sentence that Thoreau doesn't know what time it is or day of the week. He's not criticizing how other people think about time, and his very point in this passage is that he values most the time spent in activities that one would not call "busy." His life at Walden simply makes such distinctions as "days" and "hours" irrelevant. The correct answer is choice C.

Read a document from a web page and then answer the questions.

www.waldenpond.com

Walden Pond State Reservation
Concord, MA

About Walden Pond State Reservation

Walden Pond was once home to the renowned author, Henry David Thoreau. Now part of the Massachusetts Forests and Parks system, Walden Pond State Reservation includes 460 acres of protected open space so that visitors may come to experience the pond that inspired Thoreau, as well as to hike, swim, fish, canoe and kayak and cross-country ski.

In 1845, Henry David Thoreau came to Walden Pond to live. He stayed for just over two years. He didn't come to inspire a myth or a legend, or to found movements, or to make a name for himself. He came instead for the simplest of reasons: to live simply in nature, and find out what it could teach him.

A replica of Thoreau's house and the location of his modest accommodations are available for viewing by the public. Year-round interpretive programs and guided walks are offered as well as a gift shop/bookstore.

In March of 1845, Thoreau began planning and building his one-room house. On July 4th of that year, he took up residence. He studied natural history, gardened, wrote in his journal, read, and drafted his first book, *A Week on the Concord and Merrimack Rivers,* a story of a trip taken with his brother in 1839. He also made the first accurate survey of the pond. By no means a hermit, he frequently walked to the village, entertained visitors at his house and hired himself out as a surveyor. In September of 1847, Thoreau completed his experiment in simplicity and became a sojourner in civilized life again.

Thoreau's sojourn at Walden started a long tradition of people coming to the pond and its surrounding woods for recreation and inspiration. The emergence of Walden as a public park was in keeping with a belief that nature is meant to be enjoyed by people. "I think that each town should have a park… a common possession forever, for instruction and recreation," he wrote in an 1859 journal entry lamenting the deforestation that had taken place around Walden. "All Walden wood might have been preserved for our park forever, with Walden in its midst."

In 1922, the Emerson, Forbes, and Heywood families granted approximately 80 acres surrounding the pond to the Commonwealth of Massachusetts with the stipulation of "preserving the Walden of Emerson and Thoreau, its shores and nearby woodlands for the public who wish to enjoy the pond, that woods and nature, including bathing, boating, fishing, and picnicking." Middlesex County was given the responsibility for management of the reservation. In the summer of 1936, some 485,000 people visited Walden Pond, with Sunday crowds numbering as high as 25,000 visitors.

Today, it is estimated that approximately 600,000 people visit the reservation each year. In 1985, a number of additions were made, including the constructing of a replica of Thoreau's house. In an effort to balance public recreation with protection of these resources, the DCR established a "people capacity" at the park to ensure a positive visitor experience and to maintain the integrity of the resources.

By the time the Commonwealth acquired the property in 1922, much of Walden's forest had been cut down. The woods have since grown back so that the vegetation resembles the hard and soft wood mix of Thoreau's day and includes mostly berry bushes, sumac, pitch pine, hickory and oak. Above Thoreau's house site are stumps of some of the 400 white pines planted by Thoreau and leveled by the great hurricane of 1938.

Fun Times: The Amusement Park at Walden Pond

Wednesday July 31st, 5:30–6:30

Meet a Park Interpreter at the Thoreau house replica for a walk to the back of Walden Pond where once the voices of merry making from the Amusement Park echoed by the shore. Learn about the boat rentals, dancing, and picnicking of "day trippers" coming from the city on the railroad who came in large numbers starting in 1865. Be prepared for a moderate 1.5-mile walk.

Unit 4 Analyzing and Interpreting Nonfiction

Much of the wildlife of Thoreau's time can still be found here. Gray squirrels, chipmunks, and rabbits are common. Skunks, raccoons, and red foxes are active at night, but can occasionally be seen shortly before sunset or after sunrise. Kingfishers, blackbirds, chickadees, and red-tailed hawks can often be seen flying among the trees or over the water. In the spring and fall, migratory ducks and geese pass overhead and land in nearby marshes for food and rest. As noted by Thoreau, the pond "is not very fertile in fish. Its pickerel, though not very abundant, are its chief boast." The pickerel disappeared around the turn of the century and the pond is now stocked annually. In addition, sunfish, perch, and small-mouth bass compete for crayfish.

Walden Pond is a kettle hole, a deep (103 foot) pond formed over 12,000 years ago when the last glacier to cover New England slowly melted away. As it did, large chunks of ice broke off and became surrounded and covered by vast amounts of sand and gravel carried by streams flowing from the glacier. As they melted, they left behind depressions that eventually filled with water. Because of this geological history, most kettle holes like Walden Pond have no streams flowing into or out of them.

An updated Walden Pond Trail Map and a Walden Pond Historical Pamphlet are available here.

The interpretive staff at the reservation offers a wide array of programs for visitors. Children's seasonal programs include nature crafts, story time, and the Junior Ranger series. Adult and family activities include poetry readings, tracking programs, and Thoreau walks. Accessible hiking and boating programs are scheduled in the spring and summer. School and group tours are available when scheduled in advance. Tour themes focus on the natural history of Walden Pond and Thoreau's life and his impact on society. Reservations may be made by calling 978-369-3254.

915 Walden St. Concord, MA 01742 (978) 369-3254

Summer Season Park Hours: **7 a.m.–7:30 p.m.**
(Out Gate in Parking Lot closes @ **8 p.m.**)

Walden Pond State Reservation is located near Lincoln and Concord in the Greater Boston Area.

1 Based on information in the web page, what conclusion can be drawn about Thoreau's life after his experience at Walden Pond?

    A He never lost his appreciation of nature.

    B He became wealthy from the sale of his books.

    C He returned frequently to Walden for vacations.

    D He established the property at Walden as a park.

2 Based on information in the web page, what inference can you make about a visit to the Walden Pond State Reservation?

    A Visitors can tour the house that Thoreau lived in.

    B Entry is limited so that the park does not get too crowded.

    C Much of the land around Walden Pond is covered with buildings.

    D The grounds look much the same as they did when Thoreau lived there.

3 Which statement from the web page **best** supports the generalization that Thoreau would approve of the use to which Walden Pond is put to today?

    A "Thoreau's sojourn at Walden started a long tradition of people coming to the pond and its surrounding woods for recreation and inspiration."

    B "In the summer of 1936, some 485,000 people visited Walden Pond, with Sunday crowds numbering as high as 25,000 visitors."

    C "The woods have since grown back so that the vegetation resembles the hard and soft wood mix of Thoreau's day and includes mostly berry bushes, sumac, pitch pine, hickory, and oak."

    D "Adult and family activities include poetry readings, tracking programs, and Thoreau walks."

Unit 4 Analyzing and Interpreting Nonfiction

4 Read the sentence from the web page.

"Accessible hiking and boating programs are scheduled in the spring and summer."

What does the web page imply with this statement?

A   The park is closed during the winter months.

B   People in wheelchairs can enjoy some of the park activities.

C   Visitors must make reservations for hiking or boating activities.

D   Users should click on this statement for a map of the hiking trails.

Varieties of Nonfiction

L.F.2.2.2, L.N.2.2.1., L.N.2.2.2, L.N.2.2.3

Nonfiction writing deals with facts and opinions. It is not intended to entertain the reader, as literary fiction is. However, there is such a thing as **literary nonfiction**—factual writing that for many readers can be as entertaining as a novel, poem, or dramatic script.

Some literary nonfiction is almost indistinguishable from fiction. For example, on pages 142–143, you read a brief excerpt from *LaSalle and the Discovery of the Great West,* by 19th-century historian Francis Parkman. It reads like a passage from a novel. Parkman's histories include detailed descriptions and dialogue that could be easily mistaken for fiction, were it not for his citations of sources—letters, journals, and government records that inform his work. Likewise, many historical novels could be confused with actual historical writing. Author Gore Vidal's novel *Burr* relates events of the American Revolution and the first few decades of our country's history. Persons such as George Washington, Aaron Burr, and Dolley Madison are shown to be in the places where they actually were at specific times, doing what they actually did. But the author of a historical novel can mingle made-up characters with the real ones, put their own words in their historical characters' mouths and motivations in their heads, and weave events that didn't happen among those that did—as Vidal did in writing *Burr* and other novels based on American history. It's important to be able to distinguish between fiction and literary nonfiction, and to discern the author's purpose in such varying types of nonfiction as these:

- **informational nonfiction**—narrative prose intended to inform or instruct the reader on a particular topic

- **biography**—narrative nonfiction written about a person's life

- **autobiography**—narrative nonfiction that an author writes about his or her own life

- **personal essay**—a narrative about a certain topic, usually expressive of the author's feelings or opinions

- **persuasive essay**—a narrative intended to persuade the reader to a point of view either in favor of or against an idea or individual. Personal and persuasive essays may have first taken form as speeches, oral presentations that only later saw written publication, such as Abraham Lincoln's Gettysburg Address.

- **functional document**—a set of directions or other such guide to performing a specific task. They often contain diagrams, maps, or illustrations to supplement the text. Recipes, bus schedules,

Unit 4 Analyzing and Interpreting Nonfiction

assembly instructions, and annotated maps are a few of the many types of functional documents

- **advertisement**—persuasive writing intended to introduce and sell a product or idea

When distinguishing among different forms of nonfiction, it's helpful to think of these questions:

- What is the form of this work of literature?
- What is probably the purpose of this writing?
- What does the author want the reader to think or feel?
- How do the different characteristics of this form of writing support the author's purpose?

GUIDED PRACTICE

Read a passage and answer the questions.

This account is an official report made to the US House of Representatives in 1883, when Robert Smalls was a Member of Congress and a Captain in the United States Navy. At the time the incident described took place, Smalls had been a slave belonging to the Port of Charleston, South Carolina.

The Committee on Naval Affairs, to whom was referred the bill to retire Robert Smalls as captain of the Navy, beg leave to report as follows:

This claim is rested upon the very valuable services rendered by Robert Smalls to the country during the late war. The record of these has been very carefully investigated . . . They show a degree of courage, well directed by intelligence and patriotism, of which the nation may well be proud, but which for 20 years has been wholly unrecognized by it. The following is a succinct statement and outline of them:

On May 13, 1862, the Confederate steamboat *Planter*, the special dispatch boat of General Ripley, the Confederate post commander at Charleston, South Carolina, was taken by Robert Smalls under the following circumstances from the wharf at which she was lying, carried safely out of Charleston Harbor, and delivered to one of the vessels of the Federal fleet then blockading that port:

On the day previous, May 12, the *Planter*, which had for two weeks been engaged in removing guns from Cole's Island to James Island, returned to Charleston. That night all the officers went ashore and slept in the city, leaving on board a crew of eight men, all colored. Among them was Robert Smalls, who was virtually the pilot of the boat, although he was only called a wheelman, because at that time no colored man could have, in fact, been made a pilot. For some time previous he had been watching for an opportunity to carry into execution a plan he had conceived to take the *Planter* to the Federal fleet. This, he saw, was about as good a chance as he would ever have to do so, and therefore he determined not to lose it. . . . The design was hazardous in the extreme. The boat would have to pass beneath the guns of the forts in the harbor. Failure and detection would have been certain death. Fearful was the venture, but it was made. The daring resolution had been formed, and under command of Robert Smalls, wood was taken aboard, steam was put on, and with her valuable cargo of guns and ammunition, intended for Fort Ripley, a new fortification just constructed in the harbor, about two o'clock in the morning the *Planter* silently moved off from her dock, steamed up to North Atlantic wharf, where Smalls' wife and two children, together with four other women and one other child, and also three men, were waiting to embark. All these were taken on board, and then, at 3:25 a.m., May 13, the *Planter* started on her perilous adventure, carrying nine men, five women and three children. Passing Fort Johnson the *Planter's* steam-whistle blew the usual salute and she proceeded down the bay. Approaching Fort Sumter, Smalls stood in the pilot-house leaning out of the window with his arms folded across his breast, after the manner of Captain Relay, the commander of the boat, and his head covered with the huge straw hat which Captain Relay commonly wore on such occasions.

The signal required to be given by all steamers passing out, was blown as coolly as if General Ripley was on board, going out on a tour of inspection. Sumter answered by signal, "all right," and the *Planter* headed toward Morris Island, then occupied by Hatch's light artillery, and passed beyond the range of Sumter's guns before anybody suspected anything was wrong. When at last the *Planter* was obviously going toward the Federal fleet off the bar, Sumter signaled toward Morris Island to stop her. But it was too late. As the *Planter* approached the Federal fleet, a white flag was displayed, . . . [and] the ship *Onward* . . . opened her ports, and was about to fire into the *Planter*, when she noticed the flag of truce. As soon as the vessels came within hailing distance of each other, the *Planter's* errand was explained. Captain Nichols then boarded her, and Smalls delivered the *Planter* to him.

What characteristic of the passage **most** indicates to readers that it is nonfiction rather than fiction?

A the lack of dialogue

B the thematic message

C the setting of Charleston Harbor

D the mention of specific dates and times

A historical novelist would almost certainly have embellished an account of this event with whispered dialogue among Smalls and his family, and perhaps (if the point of view were third person) among the Confederate soldiers at the forts in the harbor. The message of courage, a setting in a real place, and a detailed chronology of the event could just as well be found in historical fiction, but the dry tone of this account and its record of facts without any attempt at characterization marks this selection as nonfiction. Choice A is the correct answer.

How does the author's use of affectless reporting influence the meaning of the passage?

A It requires the use of figurative language.

B It emphasizes the honor being conferred on Smalls.

C It suggests the focus on opinions supported by few facts.

D It highlights the details of the event without embellishing them.

This passage is a retelling of the key event of Congressman Smalls's life as an official report of the House of Representatives. There is no particular honor being conferred on Smalls. Figurative language is almost absent and indeed would be out of place in such a document. It characterizes the actions of Smalls and his family as "fearful" and "perilous," but these adjectives hardly represent opinion. It is a dry, factual account, with the only sense of excitement being conveyed by the facts themselves. Choice D is the correct answer.

GUIDED PRACTICE

Read a passage and answer the questions.

Emma Sansom, of Gadsden, Alabama, was 16 years old at the time this incident took place. Nathan Bedford Forrest was a Confederate general, known equally for his bravery in battle and his violent racism.

When the war came on, there were three children—a brother and sister older than I. In August, 1861, my brother enlisted in the second company that left Gadsden, and joined the 19th Alabama Infantry. My sister and I lived with our mother on the farm. We were at home on the morning of May 2, 1863, when about eight or nine o'clock a company of men wearing blue uniforms and riding mules and horses galloped past the house and went on towards the bridge.

Pretty soon a great crowd of them came along, and some of them stopped at the gate and asked us to bring them some water. Sister and I each took a bucket of water, and gave it to them at the gate. One of them asked me where my father was. I told him he was dead. He asked me if I had any brothers. I told him I had *six*. He asked where they were, and I said they were in the Confederate Army. "

"Do they think the South will whip [us]?"

"They do."

"What do you think about it?"

"I think God is on our side and we will win."'

"You do? Well, if you had seen us whip Colonel Roddey the other day and run him across the…river, you would have thought God was on the side of the best artillery."

By this time some of them began to dismount, and we went into the house. They came in and began to search for firearms and men's saddles. They did not find anything but a side-saddle, and one of them cut the skirts off that. Just then some one from the road said, in a loud tone: "You men bring a chunk of fire with you, and get out of that house." The men got the fire in the kitchen and started out, and an officer put a guard around the house, saying: "This guard is for your protection." They all soon hurried down to the bridge, and in a few minutes we saw the smoke rising and knew they were burning the bridge. As our fence extended up to the railing of the bridge, mother said: "Come with me and we will pull our rails away, so they will not be destroyed."

As we got to the top of the hill we saw the rails were already piled on the bridge and were on fire, and the Yankees were in line on the other side guarding it We turned back towards the house, and had not gone but a few steps before we saw a Yankee coming at full speed, and behind were some more men on horses. I heard them shout, "Halt! and surrender!" The man stopped, threw up his hand, and handed over his gun.

The officer to whom the soldier surrendered said, "Ladies, do not be alarmed, I am General Forrest; I and my men will protect you from harm." He inquired: "Where are the Yankees?" Mother said: "They have set the bridge on fire and are standing in line on the other side, and if you go down that hill they will kill the last one of you."

By this time our men had come up, and some went out in the field, and both sides commenced shooting. We ran to the house, and I got there ahead of all. General Forrest dashed up to the gate and said to me, "Can you tell me where I can get across that creek?" I told him there was an unsafe bridge two miles farther down the stream, but that I knew of a trail about two hundred yards above the bridge on our farm, where our cows used to cross in low water, and I believed he could get his men over there, and that if he would have my saddle put on a horse I would show him the way. He said, "There is no time to saddle a horse; get up here behind me." As he said this he rode close to the bank on the side of the road, and I jumped up behind him.

Just as we started off mother came up about out of breath and gasped out, "Emma,

what do you mean?"

General Forrest said: "She is going to show me a ford where I can get my men over in time to catch those Yankees…. Don't be uneasy; I will bring her back safe."

We rode out into a field through which ran a branch or small ravine and along which there was a thick undergrowth that protected us for a while from being seen by the Yankees at the bridge or on the other side of the creek. This branch emptied into the creek just above the ford. When we got close to the creek, I said, 'General Forrest, I think we had better get off the horse, as we are now where we may be seen.' We both got down and crept through the bushes, and when we were right at the ford I happened to be in front. He stepped quickly between me and the Yankees, saying, "I am glad to have you for a pilot, but I am not going to make breastworks[1] of you."

The cannon and the other guns were firing fast by this time, as I pointed out to him where to go into the water and out on the other bank, and then we went back towards the house. He asked me my name, and asked me to give him a lock of my hair. The cannonballs were screaming over us so loud that we were told to leave and hide in some place out of danger, which we did. Soon all the firing stopped, and I started back home. On the way I met General Forrest again, and he told me that he had written a note for me and left it on the bureau. He asked me again for a lock of my hair, and as we went into the house he said, "One of my bravest men has been killed, and he is laid out in the house. His name is Robert Turner. I want you to see that he is buried in some graveyard near here."

He then told me good-bye and got on his horse, and he and his men rode away and left us all alone. My sister and I sat up all night watching over the dead soldier, who had lost his life fighting for our rights, in which we were overpowered but never conquered….

---

[1] **breastworks:** temporary fortifications, chest high, to provide protection for soldiers firing over it from behind

Unit 4 Analyzing and Interpreting Nonfiction

In what way are the two passages **most** similar?

A   Each presents facts in an unembellished style.

B   Each is a personal account by an actual participant.

C   Each focuses on an act of bravery during the Civil War.

D   Each presents details about the later lives of the participants.

Emma Sansom describes an event that she actually participated in—the prevention of the capture of a Confederate general by Union forces. It is embellished with dialogue, descriptions of soldiers, and the dashing character she gives to General Forrest. The passage about Robert Smalls simply states facts. The tone of the two passages couldn't be more different, even though both describe incidents of personal heroism during the war, one on behalf of the North and one for the South. The correct answer is choice C.

What characteristic **most** clearly defines the passage as nonfiction rather than fiction?

A   the use of active verbs

B   the presence of a historical figure

C   the narration of rising action toward a climax

D   the inclusion of autobiographical details as exposition

Though the passage is written in an unliterary style, it *could* be a work of fiction. Historical fiction would include historical characters, active verbs, and rising action. But it would not likely begin with irrelevant details about the narrator's family. The correct answer is choice D.

How does the use of autobiographical memoir as a literary form influence the meaning of the passage?

- A   It emphasizes the drama of the event.

- B   It emphasizes the inclusion of facts and details.

- C   It emphasizes biographical information about General Forrest.

- D   It emphasizes the historical context to be explained to the reader.

Emma Sansom is describing an event in which she herself took part. Any account of an actual event would include facts and details. Emma assumes that her readers would know the relevant facts about the Civil War and any necessary particulars about General Forrest. She is describing a key event in what is probably an ordinary life, and she puts in as much drama as the incident merits for her, including her dialogue with the soldiers, her mother's fears for her, and her ride with General Forrest. Choice A is the correct answer.

IT'S YOUR TURN

Read two passages and answer the questions.

from The Journal of Madame Sarah Kemble Knight

Boston businesswoman Sarah Knight traveled to New York in 1704. She kept this account of her trip for the entertainment of her 15-year-old daughter. We join her in Connecticut, on her outward-bound journey.

Being at a merchants house, in comes a tall country fellow, with his [cheeks] full of tobacco; for they seldom loose their cud, but keep chewing and spitting as long as their eyes are open—he advanced to the middle of the room, makes an awkward nod, and spitting a large deal of aromatic tincture, he gave a scrape with his shovel-like shoe, leaving a small shovel full of dirt on the floor, made a full stop, hugging his own pretty body with his hands under his arms, stood staring round him, like a cat let out of a basket. At last, like the creature Balaam rode on[1], he opened his mouth and said: "Have you any ribbon for hatbands to sell I pray?" The questions and answers about the pay being past, the ribbon is brought and opened. Bumpkin simpers, cries "It's confounded gay I vow"; and beckoning to the door, in comes Joan Tawdry, dropping about 50 curtsies, and stands by him: he shows her the ribbon. "*Law, You,*" says she, "… take it, *tis dreadful pretty.*" Then

---

[1]**Balaam:** a figure from the Bible whose donkey speaks to him

174

Unit 4 Analyzing and Interpreting Nonfiction

she enquires, *"Have you any hood silk I pray?"* which being brought and bought, "Have you any *thread silk to sew it with*," says she, which being accommodated with they departed. They generally stand after they come in a great while speechless, and sometimes don't say a word till they are asked what they want, which I impute to the awe they stand in of the merchants, who they are constantly almost indebted to; and must take what they bring without liberty to choose for themselves; but they serve them as well, making the merchants stay long enough for their pay.

We may observe here the great necessity and benefit both of education and conversation; for these people have as large a portion of mother wit, and sometimes a larger, than those who have been brought up in cities; but for want of improvements, render themselves almost ridiculous, as above. I should be glad if they would leave such follies, and am sure all that love clean houses (at least) would be glad on't too....

December 6th. Being by this time well [rested], my business lying unfinished by some concerns at New York depending thereupon, my kinsman, Mr. Thomas Trowbridge of New Haven, must needs take a journey there before it could be accomplished, I resolved to go there in company with him, and a man of the town which I engaged to wait on me there. Accordingly, Dec. 6th we set out from New Haven, and about 1 the same [day] came to Stratford ferry; which crossing, about two miles on the other side baited our horses and would have eat a morsel ourselves, But the pumpkin and Indian mixed bread had such an aspect...that we left...and proceeded forward, and about seven at night come to Fairfield, where we met with good entertainment and lodged; and early next morning set forward to Norwalk... when about 12 at noon we arrived, and had a dinner of fried Venison, very savory. Landlady wanting some pepper in the seasoning, bid the girl hand her the spice in the little gay cup on the shelf. From hence we hastened towards Rye, walking and leading our horses near a mile together, up a prodigious high hill; and so riding till about nine at night, and there arrived and took up our lodgings at an ordinary[2], which a French family kept. Here being very hungry, I desired a fricasee, which the Frenchman undertaking, managed so contrary to my notion of cookery, that I hastened to bed supperless; and being showed the way up a pair of stairs which had such a narrow passage that I had almost stopped by the Bulk of my Body; but arriving at my apartment found it to be a little lean-to chamber furnished amongst other rubbish with a high Bed and a low one, a long table, a bench and a bottomless chair. Little Miss went to scratch up my kennel which rustled as if she'd bin in the barn amongst the husks, and suppose such was the contents of the ticking[3]. Nevertheless being exceeding weary, down I laid my poor carcass (never more tired) and found my covering as scanty as my bed was hard....

[2]**ordinary:** inn
[3]**ticking:** mattress stuffing

from The Autobiography of Benjamin Franklin

Franklin never completed his autobiography, which chronicles his life only as far as 1757, when he was 51 years old.

The precept of Order requiring that every part of my business should have its allotted time, one page in my little book contained [a] scheme of employment for the 24 hours of a natural day…. I entered upon the execution of this plan for self-examination, and continued it with occasional intermissions for some time. I was surprised to find myself so much fuller of faults than I had imagined; but I had the satisfaction of seeing them diminish. To avoid the trouble of renewing now and then my little book, which, by scraping out the marks on the paper of old faults to make room for new ones in a new course, became full of holes, I transferred my tables and precepts to the ivory leaves of a memorandum book, on which the lines were drawn with red ink, that made a durable stain, and on those lines I marked my faults with a black-lead pencil, which marks I could easily wipe out with a wet sponge. After a while I went through one course only in a year, and afterward only one in several years, till at length I omitted them entirely, being employed in voyages and business abroad, with a multiplicity of affairs that interfered; but I always carried my little book with me.

My scheme of ORDER gave me the most trouble; and I found that, though it might be practicable where a man's business was such as to leave him the disposition of his time, that of a journeyman printer, for instance, it was not possible to be exactly observed by a master, who must mix with the world, and often receive people of business at their own hours. Order, too, with regard to places for things, papers, etc., I found extremely difficult to acquire. I had not been early accustomed to it, and, having an exceeding good memory, I was not so sensible of the inconvenience attending want of method. This article, therefore, cost me so much

painful attention, and my faults in it vexed me so much, and I made so little progress in amendment, and had such frequent relapses, that I was almost ready to give up the attempt, and content myself with a faulty character in that respect, the man who, in buying an ax of a smith, my neighbor, desired to have the whole of its surface as bright as the edge. The smith consented to grind it bright for him if he would turn the wheel; he turned, while the smith pressed the broad face of the ax hard and heavily on the stone, which made the turning of it very fatiguing. The man came every now and then from the wheel to see how the work went on, and at length would take his ax as it was, without farther grinding. "No," said the smith, "turn on, turn on; we shall have it bright by-and-by; as yet, it is only speckled." "Yes," said the man, "but I think I like a speckled ax best." And I believe this may have been the case with many, who, having, for want of some such means as I employed, found the difficulty of obtaining good and breaking bad habits in other points of vice and virtue, have given up the struggle, and concluded that "a speckled ax was best"; for something, that pretended to be reason, was every now and then suggesting to me that such extreme nicety as I exacted of myself might be a kind of foppery in morals, which, if it were known, would make me ridiculous; that a perfect character might be attended with the inconvenience of being envied and hated; and that a benevolent man should allow a few faults in himself, to keep his friends in countenance.

In truth, I found myself incorrigible with respect to Order; and now I am grown old, and my memory bad, I feel very sensibly the want of it. But, on the whole, though I never arrived at the perfection I had been

Unit 4 Analyzing and Interpreting Nonfiction

so ambitious of obtaining, but fell far short of it, yet I was, by the endeavor, a better and a happier man than I otherwise should have been if I had not attempted it; as those who aim at perfect writing by imitating the engraved copies, though they never reach the wished-for excellence of those copies, their hand is mended by the endeavor, and is tolerable while it continues fair and legible.

It may be well my posterity should be informed that to this little artifice, with the blessing of God, their ancestor owed the constant felicity of his life, down to his 79th year, in which this is written. What reverses may attend the remainder is in the hand of Providence; but, if they arrive, the reflection on past happiness enjoyed ought to help his bearing them with more resignation. To Temperance he ascribes his long-continued health, and what is still left to him of a good constitution; to Industry and Frugality, the early easiness of his circumstances and acquisition of his fortune, with all that knowledge that enabled him to be a useful citizen, and obtained for him some degree of reputation among the learned; to Sincerity and Justice, the confidence of his country, and the honorable employs it conferred upon him; and to the joint influence of the whole mass of the virtues, even in the imperfect state he was able to acquire them, all that evenness of temper, and that cheerfulness in conversation, which makes his company still sought for, and agreeable even to his younger acquaintance. I hope, therefore, that some of my descendants may follow the example and reap the benefit.

1 In what way are the two passages **most** similar?

   A Each is written in a personal, conversational style.

   B Each presents challenges overcome during the course of a lifetime.

   C Each includes details about the author's personal experiences and observations.

   D Each is meant to instruct future generations about everyday life in colonial America.

2 What characteristic **most** identifies the excerpt from Sarah Knight's journal as nonfiction rather than fiction?

   A the mention of specific dates and places

   B the allusion to a character from the Bible

   C the relation of episodes without an apparent conflict

   D the author's sarcastic observations about the people she meets

3 How does Knight's use of a journal as a literary form influence the meaning of the passage?

    A It emphasizes the use of facts to support opinions.

    B It emphasizes the minute experiences of specific days.

    C It emphasizes the personal habits of people of different regions.

    D It emphasizes the historical context to be explained to the reader.

4 How does Franklin's use of autobiography as a literary form influence the meaning of the passage?

    A It allows the author to make vivid use of imagery.

    B It allows the author to use a folktale as a metaphor for a person's life.

    C It allows the author as an elderly man to reflect on the experiences of his youth.

    D It allows the author to use his life experiences as an example for others to follow.

5 Analyze how the similarities and differences between these two texts are reflective of the authors' respective purposes. Use information from both passages as evidence for your analysis.

_____

_____

_____

_____

_____

_____

_____

Unit 4 Analyzing and Interpreting Nonfiction

Elements of Nonfiction

L.N.2.3.1, L.N.2.3.2, L.N.2.3.3, L.N.2.3.4, L.N.2.3.5, L.N.2.3.6

Any written text tells a story, but what kinds of stories does nonfiction tell? Who are the characters in a set of instructions? What kind of plot does a political speech have? What is the setting of the description of a science experiment? How does tone affect the way you feel about the product in an advertisement? How does point of view condition the way you feel about the subject of a biography, as compared with the same subject's autobiography? When you read nonfiction, it's obvious that some of these elements are more important in some types of passages than in others, but it's useful to be able to compare, analyze, and evaluate them across all varieties of nonfiction.

Characters can be just as interesting in some nonfiction genres as they are in fiction. If you don't care about the subject of a biography, or about the people that informed and influenced his life and ideas, you won't be interested in reading very far. The same goes for historical writing—the interactions among people are often what drive events. Their actions, motivations, dialogue, individual traits, and the relationships among them can make a historical narrative as gripping as your favorite novel. An account of a scientific milestone, such as the discovery of the structure and significance of DNA, can involve a fascinating collection of complex characters whose interactions can affect not only who gets the Nobel Prize but the progress of science itself. Anything you read always has at least two characters, the **narrator** or **speaker** and yourself. How you feel about what you're reading depends to a great degree on how you respond to the narrator and to the silent dialogue between the two of you.

Setting also has a place in nonfiction narratives, though it's less obvious in some texts than in others. What's the setting in a set of instructions? That depends on where the reader is expected to follow them. Think of the recipe you read in Lesson 11. It's meaningless without the context of a kitchen—not one in a Pennsylvania Dutch farmhouse but the one in your home. You and the narrator are the characters in a familiar setting that includes the layout and fixtures, the stove and refrigerator, and the utensils and ingredients arrayed before you. What's the setting for a speech on an important national issue by the president of the United States? It's your own space, wherever you happen to be listening to the speech and how you feel about it, but it's also the setting we call "America" and everything that name connotes to you.

Plot is also more apparent in some types of nonfiction narratives than in others. When it's a historical account of, say, the early days of the US space program in Tom Wolfe's *The Right Stuff,* it's easy to discern the same elements of plot you're familiar with from fiction— **exposition, conflict, rising action, climax, falling action,** and/ or **resolution**. But even an advertisement can have these elements, though some are implicit rather than explicit. The exposition in a store ad, for example, can be entirely in your mind, such as "Mother's Day is approaching, and I can't think of what to get Mom for a present." The climax is the aspect of the ad that "closes" the deal—that makes up your mind to buy the product.

Theme is an element that may be easier to discern in some forms of nonfiction than character or conflict. An author of a biography, for example, may have any of a number of familiar themes in mind—how family shapes character, overcoming adversity, greatness lying in forging one's own path instead of following the herd. Where would you expect to find such themes as "The satisfaction of doing something yourself"? "The freedom to reinvent yourself"? "Innovation in conflict with tradition"? "The voice of the people is the voice of God"? These are universal themes that you might recognize in a variety of nonfiction genres, in contemporary writing and in the writing of centuries past.

Tone, style, and **mood** reflect the attitude of the author toward her subject, readers, and other characters in the narrative. The language, voice, and emotional content of a nonfiction text are usually conscious choices by an author to reflect the meaning she wishes to convey. For example, the author of an instructional text on a difficult subject may deliberately take a light, jocular tone to suggest to readers that they need not stress out as they approach it. A film critic reviewing a summer "blockbuster" movie with plenty of action would employ a different style to create a different mood than another critic reviewing a documentary about vanishing African wildlife. President Franklin D. Roosevelt, who pioneered the use of radio to reach a mass audience in the 1930s with his "fireside chats," would address his listeners as "My friends…." He took an entirely different tone in his speeches as our country's wartime leader after 1941.

Point of view in nonfiction as in fiction, may be **first person** or **third person,** and the narrator's point of view has a particular impact on the meaning of the text as a whole. But some nonfiction genres involve the point of view of the second person—you, the reader—to the point where the narrator effectively disappears, and the outcome of the conflict depends on the reader's thoughts and actions—as when you decide to spend the money you earned last summer on that Mother's Day present you saw in the advertisement.

Read a passage and answer the questions.

The author of this memoir, the Chevalier de Pontgibaud, was a French volunteer in America's war of independence. He joined General George Washington's troops in their winter quarters at Valley Forge, Pennsylvania, in November 1777.

Sand and forest, forest and sand, formed the whole way from Williamsburg to the camp at Valley Forge. I do not remember how many days I took to accomplish this difficult journey. Being badly fed, as a natural consequence I walked badly and passed at least six nights under the trees though not meeting with any habitation. Not knowing the language, I often strayed from the right road, which was so much time and labor lost. At last, early in November, I arrived at Valley Forge.

The American army was then encamped three or four leagues from Philadelphia, which city was then occupied by the British, who were rapidly fulfilling the prophecy of Dr. Franklin.

That celebrated man—an ambassador who amused himself with science, which he adroitly made to assist him in his diplomatic work—said, when some friends came to Passy to condole with him on the fall of Philadelphia: 'You are mistaken; it is not the British army that has taken Philadelphia, but Philadelphia that has taken the British army.' The cunning old diplomatist was right. The capital of Pennsylvania had already done for the British what Capua did in a few months for the soldiers of Hannibal. The Americans the 'insurgents' as they were called—camped at Valley Forge; the British officers, who were in the city, gave themselves up to pleasure; there were continual balls and other amusements; the troops were idle and enervated by inaction, and the generals undertook nothing all the winter.

Soon I came in sight of the camp. My imagination had pictured an army with uniforms, the glitter of arms, standards, etc., in short, military pomp of all sorts; Instead of the imposing spectacle I expected, I saw, grouped together or standing alone, a few militiamen, poorly clad, and for the most part without shoes—many of them badly armed, but all well supplied with provisions, and I noticed that tea and sugar formed part of their rations. I did not then know that this was not unusual, and I laughed, for it made me think of the recruiting sergeants on the Quai de la Ferraille at Paris, who say to the yokels, "You will want for nothing when you are in the regiment, but if bread should run short you must not mind eating cakes." Here the soldiers had tea and sugar.

In passing through the camp I also noticed soldiers wearing cotton nightcaps under their hats, and some having for cloaks or greatcoats coarse woolen blankets, exactly like those provided for the patients in our French hospitals. I learned afterwards that these were the officers and generals.

Such, in strict truth, was, at the time I came amongst them, the appearance of this armed mob, the leader of whom was the man who has rendered the name of Washington famous; such were the colonists—unskilled warriors who learned in a few years how to conquer the finest troops that England could send against them. Such also, at the beginning of the War of Independence, was the state of want in the insurgent army, and such was the scarcity of money, and the poverty of that government, now so rich, powerful, and prosperous, that its notes, called Continental paper money, were nearly valueless.

Which word **best** describes the author of this passage?

A naïve

B arrogant

C sympathetic

D contemptuous

Pontgibaud describes the soldiers of Washington's army as "an armed mob," poorly equipped. He is clearly dismayed at the sight of them, but his attitude toward the "insurgents" as a fighting force is not negative. Evidently, writing several years after independence was won, he marvels at how Americans created a new, ascendant country from such humble beginnings. Choice C is the correct answer.

Unit 4 Analyzing and Interpreting Nonfiction

Which sentence **best** describes the conflict of the events in the passage?

- A Pontgibaud wants to join the American forces, but the difficulty of travel in early America discourages him.

- B Pontgibaud wants to admire General Washington, but the condition of his men leaves him with little respect for him.

- C Pontgibaud observes the conditions of the troops at Valley Forge in contrast with what the American nation has become.

- D Pontgibaud disbelieves the predictions of Benjamin Franklin but admires the man's wisdom after he inspects the Continental troops.

The historic legend of the privations of "the winter at Valley Forge" comes largely from Pontgibaud's account. His description of the condition of the troops echoes his account of his journey through the wilderness: How can a nation arise from such as this? But a nation did arise, and therein lies the conflict of his narrative. The correct answer is choice C.

What is the relationship between the setting and the tone of the passage?

- A The bleakness of the setting parallels the bleakness of the tone.

- B The grandeur of the setting inspires the ironic humor of the tone.

- C The natural beauty of the setting is echoed by the expansiveness of the tone.

- D The military orderliness of the setting contributes to the bracing optimism of the tone.

A November journey through a wilderness. The ragged condition of the troops and their habitations. There is no grandeur in this setting, a singularly lack of military order, and if there is natural beauty, Pontgibaud doesn't see it that way after a six-day trek in which he kept getting lost. It adds up to a bleak setting, and the tone, except when the setting is briefly contrasted with Paris and Philadelphia, is equally bleak. The answer is choice A.

What is the effect of the first person point of view in the passage?

A It gives an objective description of General Washington and his troops.

B It provides a historical perspective of the encampment at Valley Forge.

C It offers a convincing explanation of how the Americans were able to defeat the British.

D It gives an entertaining account of a French officer's surprise at what he found in America.

Here is a foreign observer writing from the perspective of several years after the events he describes. He does not present a continuous narrative or a historical analysis but only a contrast between what he saw at Valley Forge and the young United States as a vigorous nation. He leaves it for others to analyze the process and the results; Pontgibaud is merely describing the "before" and "after." Choice B is the answer you want.

Read the passage and answer the questions.

www.nasa.gov

National Aeronautics and Space Administration

Lyndon B. Johnson Space Center
Houston, Texas 77058

Biographical Data

ELLEN OCHOA (PH.D)
DIRECTOR, LYNDON B. JOHNSON SPACE CENTER

PERSONAL DATA: Born in 1958 in Los Angeles, California, but considers La Mesa, California, to be her hometown. Married to Coe Fulmer Miles of Molalla, Oregon. They have two children. She is a classical flutist and private pilot, and also enjoys volleyball and bicycling. Ellen's mother, Rosanne Ochoa, is deceased. Coe's mother, Georgia Zak, is deceased. His stepfather, Louis Zak, resides in John Day, Oregon.

EDUCATION: Graduated from Grossmont High School, La Mesa, California, in 1975; received a Bachelor of Science degree in Physics from San Diego State University in 1980, and a Master of Science degree and Doctorate in Electrical Engineering from Stanford University in 1981 and 1985, respectively.

ORGANIZATIONS: Member of the Optical Society of America (OSA), the American Institute of Aeronautics and Astronautics (AIAA), Phi Beta Kappa and Sigma Xi honor societies.

SPECIAL HONORS: NASA awards include the Distinguished Service Medal, Exceptional Service Medal, Outstanding Leadership Medal, and four Space Flight Medals. Recipient of numerous other awards, including the Harvard Foundation Science Award, Women in Aerospace Outstanding Achievement Award, The Hispanic Engineer Albert Baez Award for Outstanding Technical Contribution to Humanity, the Hispanic Heritage Leadership Award, and San Diego State University Alumna of the Year. She also has two schools named after her: Ellen Ochoa Middle School in Pasco, Washington, and the Ellen Ochoa Learning Center in Cudahy, California.

EXPERIENCE: As a doctoral student at Stanford, and later as a researcher at Sandia National Laboratories and NASA Ames Research Center, Dr. Ochoa investigated optical systems for performing information processing. She is a co-inventor on three patents for an optical inspection system, an optical object recognition method, and a method for noise removal in images. As Chief of the Intelligent Systems Technology Branch at Ames, she supervised 35 engineers and scientists in the research and development of computational systems for aerospace missions. Dr. Ochoa has presented numerous papers at technical conferences and in scientific journals.

Selected by NASA in January 1990, Dr. Ochoa became an astronaut in July 1991. Her technical assignments in the Astronaut Office include serving as the Crew Representative for flight software, computer hardware and robotics, Assistant for Space Station to the Chief of the Astronaut Office, lead spacecraft communicator (CAPCOM) in Mission Control, Acting Deputy Chief of the Astronaut Office, Deputy Director of Flight Crew Operations, and Director, Flight Crew Operations, where she managed and directed the Astronaut Office and Aircraft Operations. A veteran of four space flights, Dr. Ochoa has logged over 978 hours in space. She was a mission specialist on STS-56 (1993), was the Payload Commander on STS-66 (1994), and was a mission specialist and flight engineer on STS-96 (1999) and STS-110 (2002). Dr. Ochoa currently serves as Director of the Lyndon B. Johnson Space Center in Houston, Texas.

SPACE FLIGHT EXPERIENCE: STS-56 ATLAS-2 Discovery (April 4–17, 1993) was a 9-day mission during which the crew conducted atmospheric and solar studies in order to better understand the effect of solar activity on the Earth's climate and environment. Dr. Ochoa used the Remote Manipulator System (RMS) robotic arm to deploy and capture the Spartan satellite, which studied the solar corona.

Dr. Ochoa was the Payload Commander on the STS-66 Atlantis Atmospheric Laboratory for Applications and Science-3 mission (November 3–14, 1994). ATLAS-3 continued the series of Spacelab flights to study the energy of the sun during an 11-year solar cycle and to learn how changes in the sun's irradiance affect the earth's climate and environment. Dr. Ochoa used the RMS to retrieve the CRISTA-SPAS atmospheric research satellite at the end of its 8-day free flight.

STS-96 Discovery (May 27 to June 6, 1999) was a 10-day mission during which the crew performed the first docking to the International Space Station, and delivered 4 tons of logistics and supplies in preparation for the arrival of the first crew to live on the station. Dr. Ochoa coordinated the transfer of supplies and also operated the RMS during the 8-hour spacewalk.

STS-110 Atlantis (April 8–19, 2002) was the 13th space shuttle mission to visit the International Space Station. Milestones during the 11-day mission included: the delivery and installation of the S0 (S-Zero) Truss; the first time the station's robotic arm was used to maneuver spacewalkers around the station; and the first time that all of a space shuttle crew's spacewalks were based from the station's Quest Airlock. Dr. Ochoa, along with Expedition 4 crewmembers Dan Bursch and Carl Walz, operated the station's robotic arm to install S0, and to move crewmembers during three of the four spacewalks.

Which sentence **best** states a theme in the passage?

A Success comes from a well-rounded life.

B Dedication and vision will overcome adversity.

C Exploring the unknown requires great courage.

D The support of family and friends leads to greatness.

All the answer choices are common themes in biographical literature. Which one best applies to Ellen Ochoa's story? There is no suggestion that she overcame adversity; there is little connection established between her family and her career, and while space flight certainly involves courage, the description of Ochoa's work aboard the space shuttle makes it sound less a brave adventure than a matter of competence and attention to detail. Yet here is a woman who is an astronaut, a director of the astronaut program, a flute-player, an athlete, an inventor, and a mother of two. There's a theme in these achievements, and choice A sums it up.

How does the author's style contribute to the tone of the passage?

A The author's use of objective language creates a dry tone.

B The author's use of technical language creates a scholarly tone.

C The author's use of positive language creates an admiring tone.

D The author's use of figurative language creates a celebratory tone.

This passage is NASA's official biography of Ochoa. The language used is neutral and factual. You'd be hard pressed to find any figurative language, and while there are some technical terms and acronyms, the passage is plainly written for the nonscientist. Ellen Ochoa is interesting; the style of this type of biography is characteristically not. Choice A is the answer you want.

Which word **best** describes Ellen Ochoa in the passage?

A modest

B brilliant

C outgoing

D accomplished

> The style and tone of the passage don't really give you an idea of what Ellen Ochoa is like as a person, do they? That's not the author's purpose; rather, it's to chronicle Ochoa's career as an astronaut and engineer. She may well be modest, brilliant, outgoing, or all three, but in this biography it's her accomplishments that the author wants to emphasize. Choice D is the correct answer.

What is the effect of the third-person point of view in the passage?

A It gives an objective summary of Ochoa's career.

B It gives an entertaining account of an unusual life.

C It provides an understanding of Ochoa's work in space.

D It provides an insightful analysis of what motivates Ochoa.

> A first-person account by Ochoa—an autobiography—might have provided a more entertaining account of her life and insights into what has driven her to achieve so much. A more detailed technical account might have given you a better idea of just what she did up there on the shuttle. What you get in this official biography is a summary of her life and work, choice A.

Read the passage. Then answer the questions.

> *Abraham Lincoln's "Gettysburg Address," delivered on November 19, 1863, at the dedication of a cemetery on the site of the Battle of Gettysburg, is the most famous speech in American history.*

Abraham Lincoln

The Gettysburg Address

Four score and seven years ago our fathers brought forth on this continent, a new nation, conceived in Liberty, and dedicated to the proposition that all men are created equal.

188

Unit 4 Analyzing and Interpreting Nonfiction

Now we are engaged in a great civil war, testing whether that nation, or any nation so conceived and so dedicated, can long endure. We are met on a great battlefield of that war. We have come to dedicate a portion of that field, as a final resting place for those who here gave their lives that that nation might live. It is altogether fitting and proper that we should do this.

But, in a larger sense, we can not dedicate—we can not consecrate—we can not hallow—this ground. The brave men, living and dead, who struggled here, have consecrated it, far above our poor power to add or detract. The world will little note, nor long remember what we say here, but it can never forget what they did here. It is for us the living, rather, to be dedicated here to the unfinished work which they who fought here have thus far so nobly advanced. It is rather for us to be here dedicated to the great task remaining before us—that from these honored dead we take increased devotion to that cause for which they gave the last full measure of devotion—that we here highly resolve that these dead shall not have died in vain—that this nation, under God, shall have a new birth of freedom—and that government of the people, by the people, for the people, shall not perish from the earth.

How does the setting contribute to the mood of the passage?

A The official setting suggests a stuffy mood.

B The battlefield setting leads to a sober mood.

C The outdoor setting predicates a peaceful mood.

D The autumnal setting contributes to a bleak mood.

The scene has been re-imagined many times, and as a Senator predicted at the time, the speech has become more important than the battle. It would truly be little noted if its mood were stuffy or bleak, but a peaceful mood would have been grotesquely out of place on a battlefield that had seen roughly 50,000 casualties. The setting was a serious one, sober but not somber, and Lincoln's speech reflects it to this day. Choice B is the correct answer.

Which phrase **best** states the narrative conflict implied in the address?

A   celebrating heroes or mourning the dead

B   finding the true significance of the occasion

C   struggling against the impulse toward violence

D   calling for a continuance of the war where so many died

What story is Lincoln telling with this speech? He is dedicating a battlefield cemetery, but he is saying that the soldiers who fought there have already done that better than he or anyone in his audience could. Their job—and ours, Lincoln suggests—is to honor the dead by doing their part to re-create and to preserve the best possible USA. The correct answer is choice B.

IT'S YOUR TURN

Read the passage. Then answer the questions.

What I Found in My Pocket

by G. K. Chesterton

Once when I was very young I met one of those men who have made the Empire what it is—a man in an astracan coat, with an astracan moustache—a tight, black, curly moustache. Whether he put on the moustache with the coat or whether his Napoleonic will enabled him not only to grow a moustache in the usual place, but also to grow little moustaches all over his clothes, I do not know. I only remember that he said to me the following words: "A man can't get on nowadays by hanging about with his hands in his pockets." I made reply with the quite obvious flippancy that perhaps a man got on by having his hands in other people's pockets; whereupon he began to argue about Moral Evolution, so I suppose what I said had some truth in it. But the incident now comes back to me, and connects itself with another incident—if you can call it an incident— which happened to me only the other day.

I have only once in my life picked a pocket, and then (perhaps through some absent-mindedness) I picked my own. My act can really with some reason be so described. For in taking things out of my own pocket I had at least one of the more tense and quivering emotions of the thief; I had a complete ignorance and a profound curiosity as to what I should find there. Perhaps it would be the exaggeration of eulogy to call me a tidy person. But I can always pretty satisfactorily account for all my possessions. I can always tell where they are, and what I have done with them, so long as I can keep them out of my pockets. If once anything slips into those unknown abysses, I wave it a sad Virgilian farewell. I suppose that the things that I have dropped into my pockets are still there; the same presumption applies to the things that I have dropped into the sea. But I regard the riches stored in both these bottomless chasms with the same reverent ignorance. They tell us that on the last day the sea will give up its dead; and I suppose that on the same occasion long strings of extraordinary things will come running out of my pockets. But I have quite forgotten what any of them are; and there is really nothing (excepting the money) that I shall be at all surprised at finding among them.

. . . . .

Such at least has hitherto been my state of innocence. I here only wish briefly to recall the special, extraordinary, and hitherto unprecedented circumstances which led me in cold blood, and being of sound mind, to turn out my pockets. I was locked up in a third-class carriage for a rather long journey. The time was towards evening, but it might have been anything, for everything resembling earth or sky or light or shade was painted out as if with a great wet brush by an unshifting sheet of quite colourless rain. I had no books or newspapers. I had not even a pencil and a scrap of paper with which to write a religious epic. There were no advertisements on the walls of the carriage, otherwise I could have plunged into the study, for any collection of printed words is quite enough to suggest infinite complexities of mental ingenuity. When I find myself opposite the words "Sunlight Soap" I can exhaust all the aspects of Sun Worship, Apollo, and Summer poetry before I go on to the less congenial subject of soap. But there was no printed word or picture anywhere; there was nothing but blank wood inside the carriage and blank wet without. Now I deny most energetically that anything is, or can be, uninteresting. So I stared at the joints of the walls and seats, and began thinking hard on the fascinating subject of wood. Just as I had begun to realise why, perhaps, it was that Christ was a carpenter, rather than a bricklayer, or a baker, or anything else, I suddenly started upright, and remembered my pockets. I was carrying about with me an unknown treasury. I had a British Museum and a South Kensington collection of unknown curios hung all over me in different places. I began to take the things out.

. . . . .

The first thing I came upon consisted of piles and heaps of Battersea tram tickets.

There were enough to equip a paper chase. They shook down in showers like confetti. Primarily, of course, they touched my patriotic emotions, and brought tears to my eyes; also they provided me with the printed matter I required, for I found on the back of them some short but striking little scientific essays about some kind of pill. Comparatively speaking, in my then destitution, those tickets might be regarded as a small but well-chosen scientific library. Should my railway journey continue (which seemed likely at the time) for a few months longer, I could imagine myself throwing myself into the controversial aspects of the pill, composing replies and rejoinders pro and con upon the data furnished to me. But after all it was the symbolic quality of the tickets that moved me most. For as certainly as the cross of St. George means English patriotism, those scraps of paper meant all that municipal patriotism which is now, perhaps, the greatest hope of England.

The next thing that I took out was a pocket-knife. A pocket-knife, I need hardly say, would require a thick book full of moral meditations all to itself. A knife typifies one of the most primary of those practical origins upon which as upon low, thick pillows all our human civilisation reposes. Metals, the mystery of the thing called iron and of the thing called steel, led me off half-dazed into a kind of dream. I saw into the intrails of dim, damp wood, where the first man among all the common stones found the strange stone. I saw a vague and violent battle, in which stone axes broke and stone knives were splintered against something shining and new in the hand of one desperate man. I heard all the hammers on all the anvils of the earth. I saw all the swords of Feudal and all the weals of Industrial war. For the knife is only a short sword; and the pocket-knife is a secret sword. I opened it and looked at that brilliant and terrible tongue which we call a blade; and I thought that perhaps it was the symbol of the oldest of the needs of man. The next moment I knew that I was wrong;

for the thing that came next out of my pocket was a box of matches. Then I saw fire, which is stronger even than steel, the old, fierce female thing, the thing we all love, but dare not touch.

The next thing I found was a piece of chalk; and I saw in it all the art and all the frescoes of the world. The next was a coin of a very modest value; and I saw in it not only the image and superscription of our own Caesar, but all government and order since the world began. But I have not space to say what were the items in the long and splendid procession of poetical symbols that came pouring out. I cannot tell you all the things that were in my pocket. I can tell you one thing, however, that I could not find in my pocket. I allude to my railway ticket.

1 Which word **best** describes the narrator of this passage?

   A distracted

   B bored

   C curious

   D thoughtful

2 What is the relationship between the setting and the narrator?

   A He is trapped on the train with nothing to do, which gives him time to think.

   B He is on a journey, which makes him think about the past.

   C He has nothing to look at, which makes him use his imagination to entertain himself.

   D He is excited to be on the train, which makes him eager to look at the items in his pocket.

3 Which sentence **best** describes the conflict of the events in the passage?

   A The narrator is looking for a way to pass the time on the train.

   B The narrator is searching for his lost train ticket.

   C The narrator is trying to understand himself through the items he carries.

   D The narrator is trying to find a deeper meaning in the items in his pocket.

Unit 4 Analyzing and Interpreting Nonfiction

4 Which sentence **best** states a theme in the passage?

    A It's best to be organized.

    B The things we carry can say a lot about us.

    C Small items can have a deeper meaning.

    D Most people have no idea what they carry around with them.

5 How does the style of the passage influence the tone?

    A The use of blunt language creates a stark tone.

    B The use of analytical language creates a critical tone.

    C The use of comical language creates a friendly tone.

    D The use of figurative language creates an expansive tone.

6 What is the effect of the first person point of view in the passage?

    A It gives an amusing account of an ordinary person's possessions.

    B It gives an impartial perspective on the items people carry.

    C It gives an objective account of traveling on a train.

    D It gives a critical account of everyday life.

When you read nonfiction, you take in meaning through more than just the words. How the ideas in a selection are organized advances the author's purpose and enhances the reader's understanding of the text. A well-organized text helps you locate and understand information and understand where the author is taking you. For example:

- A set of directions usually presents information as a **sequence** of steps: *First,* you do this, *next* you do that, and so on. A biography or historical narrative, will also describe events in **chronological order,** but not in every case. Often, a biography begins with the subject's death or with a key event in her life and then goes back and tells the story in chronological order, beginning with details about her family. Likewise a historical narrative may begin part way through the event it describes to focus on a dramatic climax and then go back and explain the events that led up to that climax. Watch for dates and other time clues that can help you mentally place events in the correct sequence.

- A passage that *analyzes* a historic event, or a science article, is often structured as a series of **causes and effects.** Such a passage will frequently contain words like *because, since, in order that, as a result, on account of,* and *therefore.* These are clues that can point to cause-and-effect relationships.

- Some passages may be structured in a way that lets you **compare and contrast** information. A newspaper or web feature on a political campaign may use such a structure to highlight the similarities (comparing) and differences (contrasting) about the two candidates.

- A traditionally structured news article usually presents information in **order of importance,** from greatest to least. Such a passage typically starts with the "five W's" (who, what, where, when, why) that give the reader the most important information and then continues following the "inverted pyramid" model, with supporting information given in descending order of importance.

- A how-to guide, such as a manual for home repairs, often structures information as a series of **problems and solutions.**

- An interview, or an informational text that responds to frequently asked questions about a topic, is usually structured as a series of **questions and answers.**

Unit 4 Analyzing and Interpreting Nonfiction

Read the passage and answer the questions.

Fix a Separated Zipper

Getting into your favorite outfit can be a problem when the bottom of a zipper becomes separated! Fortunately, you can usually fix it at home and be on your way to the party without much trouble.

Tools and Materials

- Needle-nose pliers
- Sewing needle and strong thread
- Scissors

Procedure

Using the needle-nose pliers, pry off the zipper's metal stop, the little band that stops the slider when you open the zipper. Move the slider all the way to the bottom, below the zipper's teeth. Realign the teeth so that they mesh smoothly. Now, zip the zipper up all the way to the top.

Make a new stop out of thread: Make six or seven stitches across the bottom of the zipper, where the metal stop was. Be sure you start and end on the back side of the zipper. Tie a knot in the thread and snip off the loose end with the scissors. Now, you're good to go!

What is the main organizational structure of the passage?

A cause and effect

B sequence of steps

C compare and contrast

D problem and solution

The passage does give a solution to a problem, but that does not describe how the passage is structured. To solve the problem, you need to follow a sequence of steps. The correct answer is choice B.

According to the passage, what should be done first when repairing a separated zipper?

A   Realign the teeth.

B   Thread the needle.

C   Remove the metal stop.

D   Move the slider to the bottom.

You follow a sequence of procedures any time you perform a science experiment, assemble an item, or install a new computer system. The *first* thing you should do when following any how-to sequence of steps is to make sure you have all your tools and equipment. Sometimes you have to mentally edit a set of instructions in order to complete the procedure. You also may have noticed, for example, that this passage assumes you know how to thread a needle, and there's no reason you can't do that step first. But according to the passage, your first step is to remove the metal stop at the bottom of the zipper, choice C.

Read the passage and answer the questions.

Genetics and Genomics

What are genetics and genomics?

Genetics is a term that refers to the study of genes and their roles in inheritance—in other words, the way that certain traits or conditions are passed down from one generation to another. Genetics involves scientific studies of genes and their effects. Genes (units of heredity) carry the instructions for making proteins, which direct the activities of cells and functions of the body.

Genomics is a more recent term that describes the study of all of a person's genes (the genome) including interactions of those genes with each other and with the person's environment. Genomics includes the scientific study of complex diseases such as heart disease, asthma, diabetes, and cancer because these diseases are typically caused more by a combination of genetic and environmental factors than by individual genes. Genomics is offering new possibilities for therapies and treatments for some complex diseases, as well as new diagnostic methods.

Why are genetics and genomics important to my health?

Genetics and genomics both play roles in health and disease. Genetics helps individuals and families learn about how conditions such as sickle cell anemia and cystic fibrosis are inherited in families, what screening and testing options are available, and, for some genetic conditions, what treatments are available.

Genomics is helping researchers discover why some people get sick from certain infections, environmental factors, and behaviors, while others do not. For example, there are some people who exercise their whole lives, eat a healthy diet, have regular medical checkups, and die of a heart attack at age 40. There are also people who smoke, never exercise, eat unhealthy foods, and live to be 100. Genomics may hold the key to understanding these differences.

Apart from accidents (such as falls, motor vehicle accidents, or poisoning), genomic factors play a role in nine of the ten leading causes of death in the United States (for example, heart disease, cancer, and diabetes. All human beings are 99.9 percent identical in their genetic makeup. Differences in the remaining 0.1 percent hold important clues about the causes of diseases. Gaining a better understanding of the interactions between genes and the environment by means of genomics is helping researchers find better ways to improve health and prevent disease....

What are some of the new genetic and genomic techniques and technologies?

Proteomics

The suffix -ome comes from the Greek for all, every, or complete.... Proteomics... is a...large-scale analysis of all the proteins in an organism, tissue type, or cell (called the proteome). Proteomics can be used to reveal specific, abnormal proteins that lead to diseases, such as certain forms of cancer.

Pharmacogenetics and Pharmacogenomics

The terms pharmacogenetics and pharmacogenomics are often used interchangeably in describing the intersection of pharmacology (the study of drugs, or pharmaceuticals) and genetic variability in determining an individual's response to particular drugs. The terms may be distinguished in the following way.

Pharmacogenetics is the field of study dealing with the variability of responses to medications due to variation in single genes. Pharmacogenetics takes into account a person's genetic information regarding specific drug receptors and how drugs are transported and metabolized by the body. The goal of pharmacogenetics is to create an individualized drug therapy that allows for the best choice and dose of drugs. One example is the breast cancer drug trastuzumab (Herceptin). This therapy works only for women whose tumors have a particular genetic profile that leads to overproduction of a protein called HER2....

Pharmacogenomics is similar to pharmacogenetics, except that it typically involves the search for variations in multiple genes that are associated with variability in drug response.... Pharmacogenomic studies may also examine genetic variation among large groups of people (populations), for example, in order to see how different drugs might affect different racial or ethnic groups.

Pharmacogenetic and pharmacogenomic studies are leading to drugs that can be tailor-made for individuals, and adapted to each person's particular genetic makeup. Although a person's environment, diet, age, lifestyle, and state of health can also influence that person's response to medicines, understanding an individual's genetic makeup is key to creating personalized drugs that work better and have fewer side effects than the one-size-fits-all drugs that are common today....

Stem Cell Therapy

Stem cells have two important characteristics. First, stem cells are unspecialized cells that can develop into various specialized body cells. Second, stem cells are able to stay in their unspecialized state and make copies of themselves. Embryonic stem cells come from the embryo at a very early stage in development (the blastocyst staqe). The stem cells in the blastocyst go on to develop all of the cells in the complete organism. Adult stem cells come from more fully developed tissues, like umbilical cord blood in newborns, circulating blood, bone marrow, or skin.

Medical researchers are investigating the use of stem cells to repair or replace damaged body tissues, similar to whole organ transplants. Embryonic stem cells from the blastocyst have the ability to develop into every type of tissue (skin, liver, kidney, blood, etc.) found in an adult human. Adult stem cells are more limited in their potential (for example, stem cells from the liver may only develop into more liver cells). In organ

Unit 4 Analyzing and Interpreting Nonfiction

197

transplants, when tissues from a donor are placed into the body of a patient, there is the possibility that the patient's immune system may react and reject the donated tissue as "foreign." However, by using stem cells, there may be less risk of this immune rejection, and the therapy may be more successful.

Stem cells have been used in experiments to form cells of the bone marrow, heart, blood vessels, and muscle. Since the 1990s, umbilical cord blood stem cells have been used to treat heart and other physical problems in children who have rare metabolic conditions, or to treat children with certain anemias and leukemias. For example, one of the treatment options for childhood acute lymphoblastic leukemia is stem cell transplantation therapy....

What is the main organizational structure of the passage?

A   cause and effect

B   sequence of events

C   order of importance

D   question and answer

This passage, adapted from a US government website, takes a form usually referred to by the acronym FAQ—"frequently asked questions." It's a way of organizing information that focuses on the topics that most people want to know about. Choice D is the correct answer.

What is the organizational structure of the subsection headed "**Why are genetics and genomics important to my health**"?

A   cause and effect

B   order of importance

C   compare and contrast

D   problem and solution

Very often part of a passage will have a different organizational structure than the passage as a whole. The clue to the structure of this section is the word "Why?" in the question. It tells you that the answer will address the *reasons* something happens. It gives several reasons why genetics and genomics are important to a person's health, the causes of the effect. Choice A is the answer you want.

Unit 4 Analyzing and Interpreting Nonfiction

What is the organizational structure of the subsection headed *"Pharmacogenetics and Pharmacogenomics"*?

A   sequence of events

B   order of importance

C   compare and contrast

D   problem and solution

Fortunately, you don't have to know how to pronounce or spell the Greek-derived names for these relatively new sciences. You just need to analyze how the information is structured. Read the first paragraph. It tells you that the two terms are "often interchangeably used" and signals that the following paragraphs will tell you the differences between them. Similarities and differences mean comparison and contrast, choice C.

IT'S YOUR TURN

Read two passages and answer the questions.

Driving Directions

The annual Senior Picnic and Awards Ceremony will be held Saturday, June 19 from 3 until 10 p.m. at Sage Hill State Park.

1. From Lafayette High School at **1200 Bedford Street,** head **southeast** on **Bedford St** toward **Bay St**   1.3 mi

2. Slight right onto **Bay St**   1.6 mi

3. Slight right to merge onto **US-219 S** toward **Dorset**   21.6 mi

4. Take the **State Route 281** exit toward **Salchow/Dorset**   0.2 mi

5. Turn right onto **Route 281 S/Salchow Rd**   1.7 mi

6. Turn left onto **N Mount Pleasant Ave**   0.3 mi

7. Turn right onto westbound **State Route 31.** Continue to follow State Route 31.   7.4 mi

8. Turn left onto **Trent Rd**   1.7 mi

9. Turn right onto **Sage Hill Park Rd**   0.3 mi

The picnic area is on the left, 0.4 mile from the park entrance.

Troubleshooting Your Smoke Detector

A smoke detector is a device you don't want to wait to troubleshoot until after it breaks down. If it fails to work when you need it, you could be in serious danger. Test your smoke alarms about once a month to make sure they're working:

- Press the test button to see if it sounds.

- Light a candle for about 10 seconds, then blow it out.

- Hold the smoking candle near the smoke detector. If the device is mounted on a wall instead of a ceiling, use a piece of paper to direct the smoke into the detector.

What happens?	Possible Cause	What to Do
Alarm chirps	• Weak battery • Loose electrical connections • Dust, cobwebs, or dead insects clogging sensors	• Replace battery. (This should be done every 6 months.) • Tighten connection. • Clean alarm with brush or with vacuum on low setting.
Alarm fails to sound during test	• Dead battery • Dust, cobwebs, or dead insects clogging sensors	• Replace battery. • Clean alarm as above.
Alarm fails to sound after cleaning	• Alarm mechanism is broken	• Get a new smoke detector.
Alarm sounds when no smoke is present	• Detector is poorly located • Dust from heating system is setting off alarm • Faulty wiring (on AC-powered devices) • Faulty wiring (on battery-powered devices)	• Install at least 20 feet (6 m) from heat sources such as ovens, and at least 10 feet (3 m) from sources of humidity such as bathrooms. Do not install in dusty locations such as garages. • This may happen when a furnace is turned on in the fall. Clean detector and install a new air filter in the furnace. • Do not attempt to repair yourself. Call an electrician. • Get a new smoke detector.

1   What is the overall structure of the passage "Driving Directions"?

A   cause and effect

B   sequence of steps

C   compare and contrast

D   problem and solution

2 According to the passage "Driving Directions," what should a driver look for after turning onto Bay Street?

A   the State Route 281 exit

B   a sign for State Route 31

C   a slight right to merge onto US 219

D   a left turn onto North Mount Pleasant Avenue

3 What is the main organizational structure of the passage "Troubleshooting Your Smoke Detector"?

A   cause and effect

B   question and answer

C   compare and contrast

D   problem and solution

4 According to the passage "Troubleshooting Your Smoke Detector," what is the first thing you should do to test whether a smoke detector is working?

A   check the wiring

B   replace the battery

C   press the test button

D   hold a source of smoke near it

5 You can infer from the passage that you don't have to run the candle test if

A   the smoke detector is chirping.

B   you have just cleaned the device.

C   you have tested it within the last 6 months.

D   the device is more than 20 feet from a heat source.

In the passage "Genetics and Genomics" in the last lesson, did you notice how helpful the headings and subheadings were? They organized the information on a difficult topic into sections and subsections so that you could more easily understand what you were reading. You probably also found the steps in the "Driving Directions" passage easier to follow than the ones in the selection about fixing a zipper. The driving directions were numbered, while the other passage gave the steps in paragraph form. And the instructions for troubleshooting a smoke detector were easy to follow because they were presented as a table.

In nonfiction writing, **organizational features** may provide a road map to help the reader follow the author's presentation. In a biography, for example, a time line of the subject's life can summarize the text and help the reader focus on key events. Maps can help you make sense of where events took place. Headings, illustrations, graphs, and charts may also enhance meaning. A well-organized text helps the reader locate and understand information and understand where the author is taking her. Here are some examples of organizational features that may help you find information or understand a passage:

- **titles**—usually tell the reader what a passage is about

- **headings** and **subheadings**—make it easier for the reader to find information

- **bulleted** or **numbered lists**—organize information and help the reader skim for specific information

- **boldface** or *italic* **print**—used to emphasize words or phrases and also to distinguish among different types of information

- **illustrations** and **photographs**—add interest or color and may support the reader's understanding of the passage

- **charts** and **graphs**—give new information or provide statistics or supporting information

- **diagrams**—show the reader how something works or is put together and help support the reader's understanding of a passage

- **maps**—give a visual image of a place that helps the reader's understanding of a passage

Read the passage and answer the questions.

What Is an Explanation-of-Benefits Statement?

If you're a member of a health plan, this information will help you read your Explanation of Benefits Statement, or EOB.

After you go to the doctor or hospital or purchase prescription drugs, you'll receive an EOB statement in the mail or by email. Your EOB shows you medical care the plan pays for, services it can't pay for and why, and any charges you may owe out of your own pocket.

What you'll find on your statement

Insurance providers' EOB statements may vary, but most include the following features:

Member contract information that includes your name, address, and the group and contract information that's listed on your insurance card. You'll also see the name of your family member who received the medical care.

Customer Service contacts. Your EOB has a toll-free phone number and address to contact the health plan with questions about your statement. You can also find this information on your plan's ID card.

Summary of Services lists the medical services you, or a family member, received since your last statement date. You'll see any savings you received through participating providers and any charges that you may owe. Match this information with your bills to make sure it's accurate.

Summary of Deductibles and Copayments shows you how much of your copays and deductibles you've paid to date.

Details of Services shows you what type of care you received, the date of your appointment and your doctor's name, and the charges your doctor submitted. Compare this information with what is on your health care bills.

Balance. Learn how we calculate payments and balances you may owe.

If you have further questions about your EOB, you'll find contact information on the form and on the back of your enrollee ID card.

CH Comprehensive Health

P.O. Box 999999
Harrisburg, PA 17103

Libby McCann, M.D.
101 Main Street
Excelsior, NJ 08324

Date Printed:	07/25/2013
Tax ID Number:	333-33-3333
Check Number:	74938-019
Check Amount:	**$150.00**

Patient Name: **DAVID PAULL**

Patient Account 824770273364   Patient ID # 777777777

Member ID: V10010001

Relation: Self	Member: David Paull	**Comprehensive Health**
Diag: 3638	Group Name: Victor's Coffee	**Insurance Company**
APC/DRG	Claim ID: FL6R6U36M00	Group Number: 771480-10-001
	Rec'd: 07/22/2013	

SERVICE DATES	SUBMITTED CHARGES	NEGOTIATED OR ALLOWED AMT	COPAY AMT	NOT PAYABLE	SEE REMARKS	DEDUCTIBLE	CO INSURANCE	PATIENT RESP.	PAYABLE AMOUNT
07/15/13	110.00			90.00			7.00	27.00	63.00
07/15/13	140.00			96.67			9.67	9.67	87.00
07/15/13	110.00			90.00	1			90.00	
TOTALS	360.00	276.67	20.00	90.00			16.67	126.67	150.00

ISSUED AMT: $150.00

Remarks:

1—We have paid the maximum allowed by your plan of benefits for this service. The balance is the member's responsibility.

For questions regarding this claim:

P.O. Box 3360, Anytown, USA 98765-4321

Call 1-800-888-8888 for Assistance

Note: All inquiries should reference the ID number above for prompt response.

Total Patient Responsibility:	$126.67
Claim Payment:	$150.00
Total Payment to Libby McCann, MD:	$150.00

What effect does the text organization have on the passage?

A It helps the reader to interpret the EOB form.

B It gives the reader a guide to the coded numbers on the EOB form.

C It guides the reader through the steps necessary to contact the insurance provider.

D It shows the reader how to contest a denial of payment from the insurance provider.

If the passage helps you make sense of the EOB form, it's probably because it organizes information in a bulleted list, with boldface type indicating the topics of each paragraph. It does not present information in steps or explain the coded numbers, and while it does include a note on contacting the provider, that is only one heading among several. Choice A is the correct answer.

Based on information in the form and in the passage, what conclusion can be made about the amount David Paull saved through his insurance plan with Comprehensive Health?

A He saved $90.00.

B He saved $126.67.

C He saved $233.33.

D He saved $360.00.

The passage helps you understand that the $360.00 figure under "Submitted Charges" is the amount Dr. McCann billed Comprehensive Health for her services to Mr. Paull, and that the health plan and other benefits are covering all but $126.67, indicated as "Patient Responsibility." Simple math shows you that the correct answer is choice C.

How does the EOB form help to clarify information in the passage?

A   It describes the services the patient received.

B   It gives tips on how to save money on medical bills.

C   It shows details of how payments due are calculated.

D   It includes a point-by-point explanation of each paragraph.

EOB statements vary, so you should not expect to find a point-by-point correlation between the form and the passage. If services are specified on an EOB, they are usually listed by code number, and it is not the business of the insurance provider to give money-saving information. What the form does is show the total charges, the specific amounts for each service, and details on the amounts allowed and disallowed by the plan. Choice C is the answer you want.

Read the passage and answer the questions.

US Naturalizations: 2012

JAMES LEE, US Department of Homeland Security

The naturalization process confers US citizenship upon foreign citizens or nationals who have fulfilled the requirements established by Congress in the Immigration and Nationality Act (INA). After naturalization, foreign-born citizens enjoy nearly all of the same benefits, rights, and responsibilities that the Constitution gives to native-born U.S. citizens, including the right to vote. This Office of Immigration Statistics *Annual Flow Report* presents data on the number and characteristics of foreign nationals aged 18 years and over who naturalized during 2012.

In 2012, a total of 757,434 persons naturalized (see Table 1 and Figure 1). The leading countries of birth of new citizens were Mexico (102,181), the Philippines (44,958), India (42,928), the Dominican Republic (33,351), and the People's Republic of China (31,868). The largest number of persons naturalizing lived in California (158,850), Florida (100,890), and New York (93,584).

THE NATURALIZATION PROCESS

An applicant for naturalization must fulfill certain requirements set forth in the INA concerning age, lawful admission and residence in the United States. These general naturalization provisions specify that a foreign national must be at least 18 years of age; be a US legal permanent resident (LPR); and have resided in the country continuously for at least five years. Additional requirements include the ability to speak, read, and write the English language; knowledge of the US government and history; and good moral character.

Special provisions of naturalization law exempt certain applicants from some of these general requirements. The primary types of applicants who may, under certain conditions, be eligible for specific exemptions include spouses and minor children of US citizens and persons with qualifying military service in the Armed Forces of the United States.

Every applicant for naturalization who is 18 years of age or older must file an N-400 Application for Naturalization. All applicants who meet the preliminary documentary requirements must be interviewed by officers from US Citizenship and Immigration Services (USCIS) to determine their eligibility to naturalize. In most cases, the officer verifies the applicant's knowledge and understanding of English and the history and government of the United States. Qualified applicants are then scheduled for an oath ceremony before a judge or before an officer with authority delegated by the Secretary of Homeland Security.

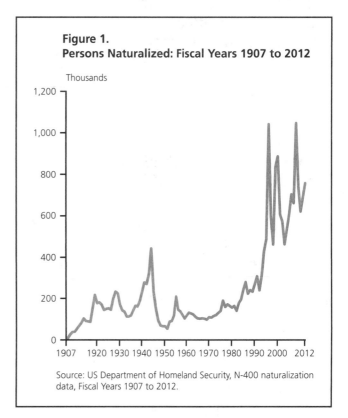

Figure 1.
Persons Naturalized: Fiscal Years 1907 to 2012

Source: US Department of Homeland Security, N-400 naturalization data, Fiscal Years 1907 to 2012.

DATA

This report uses data from administrative records of USCIS of the Department of Homeland Security. These records consist of information taken from N-400 applications, such as date and country of birth; sex; marital status; and state of residence. The Computer Linked Application Information Management System (CLAIMS) of USCIS provided nearly all of the data; a small number of records came from the Central Index System of USCIS.

Caution should be exercised in drawing conclusions from these data about trends in the demand to naturalize. Year-to-year fluctuations in the number of naturalizations are not uncommon and reflect volatility in the volume of applications filed with USCIS and related impacts on application processing. Annual averages of persons naturalizing over a period of years provide a more accurate indication of long-term trends in the propensity to naturalize.

Table 1.
Persons Naturalized by Region and Country of Birth: Fiscal Years 2010 to 2012

(Countries ranked by 2012 persons naturalized)

Region and country of birth	2012		2011		2010	
	Number	Percent	Number	Percent	Number	Percent
REGION						
Total	757,434	100.0	694,193	100.0	619,913	100.0
Africa	74,775	9.9	69,738	10.0	64,022	10.3
Asia	257,035	33.9	249,940	36.0	251,598	40.6
Europe	82,714	10.9	82,209	11.8	78,011	12.6
North America	261,673	34.5	217,750	31.4	163,836	26.4
Caribbean	109,762	14.5	79,820	11.5	62,483	10.1
Central America	40,592	5.4	33,784	4.9	25,706	4.1
Other North America	111,319	14.7	104,146	15.0	75,647	12.2
Oceania	3,886	0.5	3,734	0.5	3,646	0.6
South America	76,992	10.2	70,485	10.2	58,474	9.4
Unknown	359	—	337	—	326	0.1
COUNTRY						
Total	757,434	100.0	694,193	100.0	619,913	100.0
Mexico	102,181	13.5	94,783	13.7	67,062	10.8
Philippines	44,958	5.9	42,520	6.1	35,465	5.7
India	42,928	5.7	45,985	6.6	61,142	9.9
Dominican Republic	33,351	4.4	20,508	3.0	15,451	2.5
China, People's Republic	31,868	4.2	32,864	4.7	33,969	5.5
Cuba	31,244	4.1	21,071	3.0	14,050	2.3
Colombia	23,972	3.2	22,693	3.3	18,417	3.0
Vietnam	23,490	3.1	20,922	3.0	19,313	3.1
Haiti	19,114	2.5	14,191	2.0	12,291	2.0
El Salvador	16,685	2.2	13,834	2.0	10,343	1.7
Jamaica	15,531	2.1	14,591	2.1	12,070	1.9
Korea, South	13,790	1.8	12,664	1.8	11,170	1.8
Peru	11,814	1.6	10,266	1.5	8,551	1.4
Pakistan	11,150	1.5	10,655	1.5	11,601	1.9
Brazil	9,884	1.3	10,251	1.5	8,867	1.4
Iran	9,627	1.3	9,286	1.3	9,337	1.5
Ukraine	9,459	1.2	8,489	1.2	7,345	1.2
Nigeria	9,322	1.2	9,344	1.3	9,126	1.5
Somalia	9,286	1.2	7,971	1.1	5,728	0.9
United Kingdom	9,145	1.2	9,246	1.3	8,401	1.4
All other countries	278,635	36.8	262,059	37.8	240,214	38.7

—Figure rounds to 0.0.

Source: US Department of Homeland Security, N-400 naturalization data for persons aged 18 and over, Fiscal Years 2010 to 2012.

TRENDS AND CHARACTERISTICS OF PERSONS NATURALIZING

The number of US naturalizations increased to 757,434 in 2012 from 694,193 in 2011, and 619,913 in 2010. These increases were consistent with the growing number of naturalization applications filed and processed during 2010–2012.

Historical Trend

The average annual number of persons naturalizing increased from less than 120,000 during the 1950s and 1960s to 210,000 during the 1980s, 500,000 during the 1990s, and to 680,000 between 2000 and 2009 (see Figure 1). Until the 1970s, the majority of persons naturalizing were born in European countries. The regional origin of new citizens shifted from Europe to Asia due to increased legal immigration from Asian countries, the arrival of Indochinese refugees in the 1970s, and the historically higher naturalization rate of Asian immigrants. Consequently, Asia has been the leading region of origin of new citizens most years since 1976.

Region and Leading Countries of Birth

Thirty-five percent of persons naturalizing in 2012 were born in North America, followed by 34 percent from Asia and 11 percent from Europe (see Table 1).

Mexico was the leading country of birth of persons naturalizing in 2012 (14 percent). The next leading countries of origin of new citizens in 2012 were the Philippines (5.9 percent), India (5.7 percent), the Dominican Republic (4.4 percent), and the People's Republic of China (4.2 percent). The 10 countries with the largest number of naturalizations accounted for 49 percent of all new citizens in 2012.

From 2011 to 2012, the number of naturalizations increased the most for immigrants from North America. Among leading countries of origin, the largest increase in naturalizations during this period—in absolute and percentage terms—occurred among persons born in the Dominican Republic (12,843 or 63 percent) and Cuba (10,173 or 48 percent). In addition, the number of naturalizations of immigrants born in India and the People's Republic of China decreased for two consecutive years from 2010 to 2012 partly due to a decline in the number of naturalizations of persons from these countries who were granted LPR status under employment-based preference categories.

In the passage, what information is included under the first boldface head?

A   where most naturalized citizens come from

B   how immigrants become naturalized citizens

C   a comparison of legal and illegal immigration

D   how the number of applicants has changed over time

The text features give you a clue to this one even if you didn't read the passage! The first boldface head is "The Naturalization Process." That suggests that the information in this section deals with how people become naturalized. Where new citizens come from and how their numbers have changed would naturally be found under the second head, "Trends and Characteristics of Persons Naturalizing" and its subheads. The passage deals only with legal, not illegal, immigration. Choice B is the answer you want.

Based on the **graph** and the passage, what conclusion can be made about naturalization since 1990?

A It has come mostly from Asia and the Americas.

B It has fluctuated considerably from year to year.

C The English skills of most applicants have declined.

D Significantly more men than women have been naturalized.

The graph does not indicate where newly naturalized citizens come from or their gender, while the passage specifically states that knowing sufficient English is one of the requirements for naturalization. But the passage discusses the fluctuation of the number of naturalizations from year to year, and the graph supports that information. The correct answer is choice B.

Based on the **table** and the passage, what conclusion can be made about naturalization since fiscal year 2010?

A It has increased by less than 100,000 per year.

B It has increased by more than one million per year.

C The greatest increase has come from the region of Asia.

D The largest number of persons naturalizing live in California.

The table provides numerical data over a three-year period on where new citizens have come from. It contains considerably more detail than the passage, but only the passage tells you which states lead in the number of new naturalizations, and the passage also indicates that the greatest increase in naturalizations came from Asia during the 1970s, but no longer. The table is only concerned with the years since 2010, and both it and the passage indicate that the correct answer is choice A.

How does the **graph** help to clarify information in the passage?

A   It illustrates the process by which an applicant becomes naturalized.

B   It indicates how the Department of Homeland Security compiled the data.

C   It provides information on the changes over time in the numbers of naturalizations.

D   It explains why there was a steep drop in the number of naturalizations during the 1940s.

The graph does not include the kind of detailed data that the table does, nor does it interpret the data or indicate its source. It does one thing in support of the passage: It shows how the numbers of naturalizations have changed over the past century, illustrating the statement that a single year's statistics do not indicate a trend. Choice C is correct.

Read the passage and answer the questions.

Hurricane/Post-Tropical Cyclone Sandy, October 22–29, 2012
US DEPARTMENT OF COMMERCE
National Oceanic and Atmospheric Administration

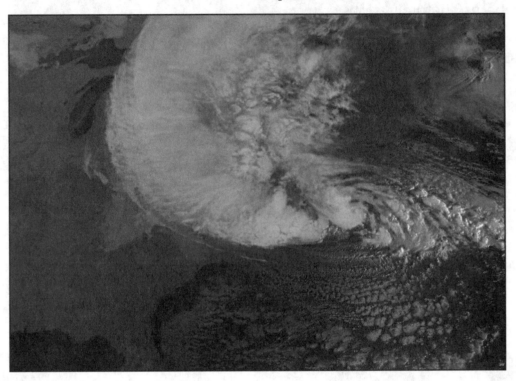

Hurricane/Post-tropical Cyclone Sandy1 was unique in many ways. Its historically unprecedented track approached New Jersey and New York from the east; storms typically approach from the south. Sandy also made an atypical transition to post-tropical status. The storm evolved when a tropical cyclone merged with an intense low-pressure system and dramatically increased in size before landfall.

Sandy made landfall along the southern New Jersey shore on October 29, 2012, causing historic devastation and substantial loss of life. The National Hurricane Center (NHC) Tropical Cyclone Report estimated the death count from Sandy at 147 direct deaths. In the United States, the storm was associated with 72 direct deaths in eight states: 48 in New York, 12 in New Jersey, 5 in Connecticut, 2 each in Virginia and Pennsylvania, and 1 each in New Hampshire, West Virginia, and Maryland. The storm also resulted in at least 75 indirect deaths (i.e., related to unsafe or unhealthy conditions that existed during the evacuation phase, occurrence of the hurricane, or during the post-hurricane/clean-up phase). These numbers make Sandy the deadliest hurricane to hit the US mainland since Hurricane Katrina in 2005....

Damage estimates from Sandy exceed $50 billion, with 24 states impacted by the storm. Sandy was so large that tropical storm force winds extended over an area about 1,000 miles in diameter. Sandy caused water levels to rise along the entire East Coast of the United States from Florida northward to Maine. The highest storm surges and greatest inundation, which reached record levels, occurred in New Jersey, New York,

Unit 4 Analyzing and Interpreting Nonfiction

and Connecticut, especially in and around the New York City metropolitan area. In many of these locations, especially along the coasts of central and northern New Jersey, Staten Island, and southward-facing shores of Long Island, the surge was accompanied by powerful, damaging waves. Storm surge caused flooding exceeding 8 feet above ground level in some locations. Power outages from the combined effects of wind and surge left some coastal communities in New Jersey without power for months. In addition, because of the storm's late October timing, it also generated heavy snows across portions of the central Appalachians, especially in West Virginia and the mountains of western North Carolina. Snowfall totals of up to 36 inches combined with strong winds to produce blizzard conditions. Closer to the coast, more than 12 inches of rainfall resulted in river, stream, and creek flooding over portions of the Mid-Atlantic.

Emergency Managers (EMs), media, and commercial weather service providers thought the National Weather Service (NWS) forecasted Sandy well. The NHC forecast track error at 3 and 5 days for the storm was well below the 5-year average. Hydrometeorological Prediction Center (HPC) day 6 and 7 forecasts were also highly accurate, giving the first indication that Sandy was a threat to the northeastern United States. EMs at the state and local level consistently stated they were well aware of the serious threat posed by Sandy several days in advance.... The early awareness for this significant storm provided lifesaving information to decision makers well in advance and resulted in declarations of several States of Emergency and activation of numerous Emergency Operations Centers (EOC) long before landfall.

Overall, the National Oceanic and Atmospheric Administration (NOAA) performed well in forecasting the impacts of this extremely large storm. NOAA issued high wind watches and warnings well in advance of their associated impact and

extended them well inland to include portions of the Ohio valley. NHC issued the initial storm surge inundation forecast of 4 to 8 feet above ground level for the New Jersey, New York, and Connecticut coastlines in its 1500 Coordinated Universal Time (UTC) 27 October public advisory, well over 2 days prior to landfall of the center of the cyclone. While surge forecasts were consistent with the observed conditions as the storm approached landfall, the amount of lead time for surge and the way it was communicated represent two areas the Sandy Assessment Team found to be most in need of improvement.

Storm Transition and Coordination: The unique evolution of Sandy from a Category 3 hurricane in the Caribbean to an intense post-tropical cyclone in the hours before landfall posed several operational challenges to NWS offices. A final decision was made on Friday, October 26, to have local NWS Weather Forecast Offices (WFO) issue non-tropical watches and warnings versus having NHC issue hurricane watches/warnings north of Duck, NC. NWS made this decision after extensive discussion between NHC, NWS Eastern Region Headquarters (ERH), the Ocean Prediction Center (OPC), and the HPC, as well as several WFOs. NWS needed to make this decision well before landfall because EMs and other public officials, including a governor, expressed a strong preference that the warning suite type (i.e., tropical or nontropical) not change once NWS initiated watches and warnings. NWS policy in place through 2012 required WFOs to issue nontropical watches and warnings for posttropical cyclones. The EMs and other officials were concerned with the potential for confusion and disruption during critical periods of preparation, including evacuations. Despite efforts to publicize this decision, the Service Assessment Team found that as Sandy approached the coast, not all EMs were aware of how the information flow would change once the storm became posttropical. Further, NWS did not consistently reflect this service approach across all its websites (e.g., NHC's highly trafficked website lacked WFO-issued coastal flood and high wind warnings). Given the unprecedented nature of Sandy, fully resolving all of these challenges beforehand may have been impossible. However, this Assessment identifies critical needs to improve service delivery for future storms.

Weather Forecast Watch and Warning Products: The Service Assessment Team found differences between many of the views of NOAA's partners and public opinion research on whether issuing nontropical watches and warnings for Sandy's landfall influenced perceptions of severity and response. A University of Pennsylvania Wharton School telephone survey of people along the Mid-Atlantic coast (Virginia to New York) conducted during the Sandy event revealed a majority thought they were under a hurricane watch on the day Sandy made landfall (even though they were under nontropical watches and warnings). A telephone survey of coastal residents conducted 5 months after the storm also found a significant proportion thought a hurricane watch or warning was in effect when Sandy made landfall…. This statistic is consistent with the views of EMs interviewed by the Team who thought the tone and urgency of information from NOAA/NWS offices and the media regarding Sandy's intensity was strong enough that people responded properly….

Communication and Information Dissemination: The Assessment Team found several issues with the ability of NWS users and constituents to find critical information easily among various NWS products and websites. This difficulty included finding needed information on a particular website as well as knowing which website to go to for information in general. *"Too many clicks"*

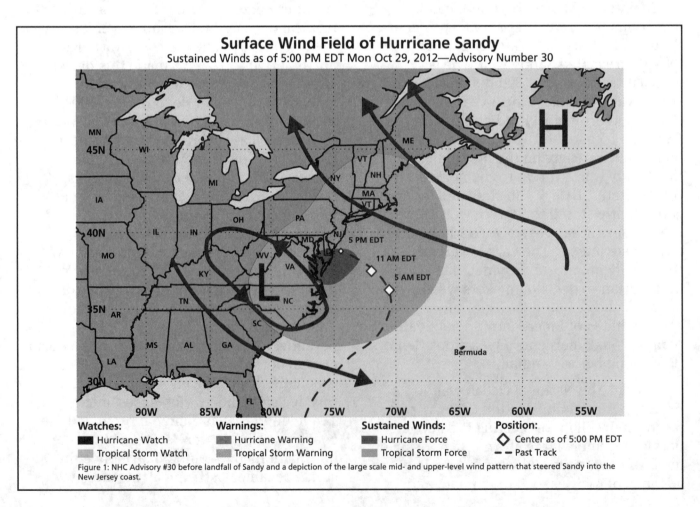

Figure 1: NHC Advisory #30 before landfall of Sandy and a depiction of the large scale mid- and upper-level wind pattern that steered Sandy into the New Jersey coast.

Unit 4 Analyzing and Interpreting Nonfiction

was a phrase often repeated with respect to the number of sites necessary to visit to get needed information. In contrast, there are examples of particular products that served customers well. Local and state EMs in New York and New Jersey praised briefing packages sent by WFOs Upton and Mt. Holly. NWSChat also received consistent praise. Nonetheless, the need for significant improvements to NWS communications and dissemination of information is a key theme of this assessment.

Social Media and Web Services: It was clear from interviews with media, EMs, and NOAA/NWS staff that social media played an important role in increasing awareness of Sandy's threats. Social media was an effective means of reaching the public…. WFOs, RFCs, and the National Centers for Environmental Prediction accrued 27,633 new Facebook likes during the event, providing the potential to reach millions of other Facebook users. In some cases, those interviewed stated more people sought storm information through a city or county

Facebook page or Twitter feed than from the city or county web pages. EMs stated their Facebook pages gained credibility by being associated with NOAA/NWS office Facebook pages and encouraged NWS to continue enhancements to its social media presence. Social media also played a key role in assessing impacts from the storm as it made landfall. Some local emergency officials noted they learned of the need for water rescues by monitoring social media feeds. Even with this increase in the use of social media, NOAA websites remained one of the most significant sources of information on Sandy, collectively receiving close to 1.3 billion hits during the storm.

Storm Surge: The highest priority need identified by NOAA/NWS customers and constituents is for improved high-resolution storm surge forecasting and communication. In particular, there is a crucial need for storm surge graphical inundation guidance. Seventy-nine percent of coastal residents surveyed in March 2013 said the impact of Sandy's surge in their area was "more than

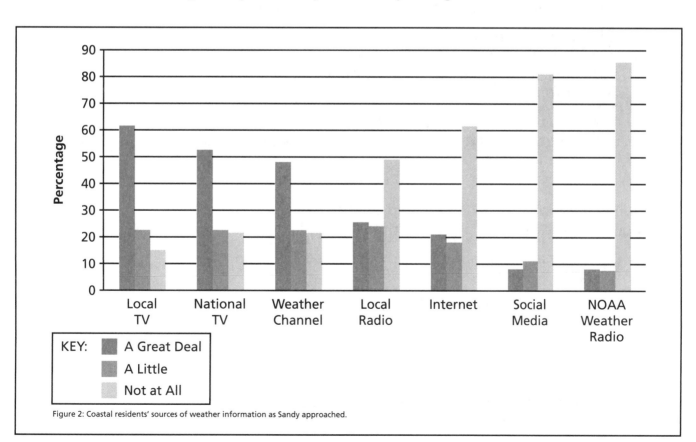

Figure 2: Coastal residents' sources of weather information as Sandy approached.

they expected."

There is widespread support for a storm surge warning product for coastal and tidally influenced waterways. NOAA has identified this need in previous service assessments. Improving inundation forecasting and communication of storm surge impacts should be a top priority for NOAA. To meet this need, NOAA needs to allocate additional resources to adequately support storm surge forecasting and software development for tropical and extra-tropical storms....

1 The headings in this passage show that information is **mainly** organized according to

A   sequence of events.

B   order of importance.

C   aspects of response to the storm.

D   states and regions affected by the storm.

2 Which sentence from the passage is **most** emphasized by the satellite photograph at the beginning of the passage?

A   "Sandy made landfall along the southern New Jersey shore on October 29, 2012, causing historic devastation and substantial loss of life."

B   "Sandy was so large that tropical storm force winds extended over an area about 1,000 miles in diameter."

C   "The highest storm surges and greatest inundation, which reached record levels, occurred in New Jersey, New York, and Connecticut, especially in and around the New York City metropolitan area."

D   "Closer to the coast, more than 12 inches of rainfall resulted in river, stream, and creek flooding over portions of the Mid-Atlantic."

3 Based on information from the **map** and the passage, what conclusion can be made about Hurricane Sandy?

A   Damage estimates from the storm exceeded $50 billion in 24 states.

B   The initial storm surge was forecast to be between four and eight feet.

C   Wind patterns drove the strongest force of the storm into the New Jersey coast.

D   A majority of people in the Mid-Atlantic states thought they were under a hurricane watch.

4 How does the map help to clarify information in the passage?

A It indicates the reasons Sandy grew so powerful.

B It shows the extent of snowfall in the Appalachian Mountains.

C It illustrates the path the storm took and the strength of the winds.

D It shows why flood damage was greatest in the New York City area.

5 Based on information from the **graph** and the passage, what conclusion can be drawn about public information about the storm?

A Most people heard about the approach of the storm from local TV.

B Information about the storm from the Internet was inaccurate and unreliable.

C Social media was a leading factor in spreading information about the storm.

D Most people heard about the approach of the storm from NOAA weather radio.

Fact and Opinion

L.N.2.5.1, L.N.2.5.2

There are certain passages that any thinking person will read with skepticism. When you read an advertisement, for example, you know that the author's purpose is to persuade you to spend money for something you don't necessarily need. Advertising is a part of commerce, but you understand that any facts you're reading are heavily laced with opinions. But that may be true of nonfiction written for any purpose, or even of fiction. An author may mix facts with opinions, or use opinions disguised as facts, to get you to believe or vote a certain way. To judge the validity and accuracy of what you are reading, you need to be able to:

- distinguish fact from opinion.

- analyze and explain the author's use of facts and opinions in a text.

- distinguish between essential and nonessential information in an author's argument.

Generally speaking, a **fact** is a statement that can be proven. An **opinion** is a statement that the author can't possibly know to be a fact. Here are some further criteria that may be used to identify opinions:

- **Judgments**—Some words are signals of opinions in and of themselves. Words like *think, feel, believe, best, worst, should* and *must* are often clues that the writer is stating something that he cannot prove is true.

- **Categorical generalizations**—Words such as *all, always, everyone, never, nobody, should, must* and *the people* should be examined critically. When an author begins a sentence with "As is well known…" or when a politician giving a speech asserts "The American people believe that…," ask yourself how he can know the statement is true in all cases, or for all Americans.

- **Subjective characterizations**—A statement such as "Mayor Ryan answered evasively when asked about city contracts being doled out to his supporters" should be taken as an opinion. The author hasn't proved that the mayor was evasive. What were the mayor's exact words? Is the author quoting them fully or taking a statement out of context?

- **Unverified statements**—Facts can be backed up with references to verifiable sources. How do you know that the author of an Internet blog is a qualified expert on health care? When an author is citing data, does she cite sources so that you can verify

Unit 4 Analyzing and Interpreting Nonfiction

her conclusions? If an ad cites statistics, how were the data compiled? If a politician blames "the media" for bias, what media is she talking about? And does "bias" amount to nothing more than reporting facts that conflict with the politician's prejudices?

GUIDED PRACTICE

Read the passage and answer the questions.

President Franklin D. Roosevelt gave this speech to Congress in response to the Japanese attack on Pearl Harbor. The attack killed 2,300 Americans, destroyed ships and planes, and brought the United States into World War II.

Franklin D. Roosevelt

War Message to Congress

Yesterday, December 7, 1941—a date which will live in infamy—the United States of America was suddenly and deliberately attacked by naval and air forces of the Empire of Japan.

The United States was at peace with that nation and, at the solicitation of Japan, was still in conversation with the government and its emperor looking toward the maintenance of peace in the Pacific.

Indeed, one hour after Japanese air squadrons had commenced bombing in Oahu, the Japanese ambassador to the United States and his colleagues delivered to the Secretary of State a formal reply to a recent American message. While this reply stated that it seemed useless to continue the existing diplomatic negotiations, it contained no threat or hint of war or armed attack.

It will be recorded that the distance of Hawaii from Japan makes it obvious that the attack was deliberately planned many days or even weeks ago. During the intervening time, the Japanese government has deliberately sought to deceive the United States by false statements and expressions of hope for continued peace.

The attack yesterday on the Hawaiian Islands has caused severe damage to American naval and military forces. Very many American lives have been lost. In addition, American ships have been reported torpedoed on the high seas between San Francisco and Honolulu.

Yesterday, the Japanese government also launched an attack against Malaya.

Last night, Japanese forces attacked Hong Kong.

Last night, Japanese forces attacked Guam.

Last night, Japanese forces attacked the Philippine Islands.

Last night, the Japanese attacked Wake Island.

This morning, the Japanese attacked Midway Island.

Japan has, therefore, undertaken a surprise offensive extending throughout the Pacific area. The facts of yesterday speak for themselves. The people of the United States have already formed their opinions and well understand the implications to the very life and safety of our nation.

As commander in chief of the Army and Navy, I have directed that all measures be taken for our defense.

Always will we remember the character of the onslaught against us.

No matter how long it may take us to overcome this premeditated invasion, the American people in their righteous might will win through to absolute victory.

I believe I interpret the will of the Congress and of the people when I assert that we will not only defend ourselves to the uttermost, but will make very certain that this form of treachery shall never endanger us again.

Hostilities exist. There is no blinking at the fact that our people, our territory and our interests are in grave danger.

With confidence in our armed forces— with the unbounding determination of our people—we will gain the inevitable triumph—so help us God.

I ask that the Congress declare that since the unprovoked and dastardly attack by Japan on Sunday, Dec. 7, a state of war has existed between the United States and the Japanese empire.

Which sentence from the passage contains an opinion?

A "The United States was at peace with that nation and, at the solicitation of Japan, was still in conversation with the government and its emperor looking toward the maintenance of peace in the Pacific."

B "The attack yesterday on the Hawaiian Islands has caused severe damage to American naval and military forces."

C "It will be recorded that the distance of Hawaii from Japan makes it obvious that the attack was deliberately planned many days or even weeks ago."

D "The people of the United States have already formed their opinions and well understand the implications to the very life and safety of our nation."

The United States had been attacked, people killed, and material destroyed, and although tensions had been building between the two nations for more than 20 years, it was a fact that Japanese diplomats were engaged in sham negotiations. But while "the people" did unite behind the war effort, it was by no means a provable fact on the day after the attack that Americans had fully formed their opinions, let alone understood their implications. Choice D is the correct answer.

Read this sentence from the passage.

"No matter how long it may take us to overcome this premeditated invasion, the American people in their righteous might will win through to absolute victory."

What does the opinion used in this sentence contribute to the passage?

A It rallies Americans to be strong and to persevere.

B It emphasizes that the Japanese attack was planned.

C It cuts off any possible argument against going to war.

D It assures Americans that victory will be achieved swiftly.

President Roosevelt uses facts to gather people to his opinions. After describing in as much detail as wartime secrecy would allow the extent of the Japanese attack (the true measure of the damage at Pearl Harbor would not be revealed for years), Roosevelt is telling Congress, and the American people, that we are at war. Phrases like "righteous might" and "absolute victory" appeal to Americans' sense of pride, while "No matter how long it takes" reminds the people that they will have to endure for a long time. The answer is choice A.

Which detail is **least** essential to the overall understanding of the passage?

A   Many American lives were lost and ships sunk.

B   The United States had been at peace with Japan.

C   The Japanese had obviously been planning the attack.

D   The Japanese offensive extended throughout the Pacific region.

Americans were outraged by the attack on Pearl Harbor because it appeared to be an unprovoked "sneak attack." In fact, the US and Japan had been spoiling for a fight, and both nations had been arming for war. It was enough that we had been attacked, that the attack had been planned for some time, and that it was part of a general Pacific offensive. We were already at war; that we had been at peace the day before was irrelevant to the message. Choice B is the answer you want.

Roosevelt's war message is an example of how an author will combine facts with opinions to persuade people to his point of view. Roosevelt needed little in the way of opinion to convince the American people that war had come. But authors may use any of a number of techniques to appeal to a reader's emotions or to create needs in the reader's mind, as most product advertising does. To judge the accuracy and truthfulness of what you are reading, you need to be able to identify such uses of **bias**—the presentation of opinions that are not supported by facts—and **propaganda**—the systematic spreading of beliefs through a combination of facts, opinions disguised as facts, deliberate distortion of the facts, and repetition.

Bias and propaganda in political writing and other forms of prose nonfiction involve the same persuasive techniques that advertisers use when they offer products or services for sale. In fact, some languages make no distinction between "advertising" and "propaganda," using the same word for both. Here are some common techniques of persuasion that may be hiding bias or propaganda:

- **Appeal to statistics**—Presenting data out of context in place of evidence. The results of a survey or opinion poll, for example, may represent what a certain group of people believes, but it should not be mistaken for fact.

- **Bandwagon**—influencing people by implying that "everyone" supports one's position. The bandwagon approach is all about peer pressure. The idea is that "everyone" is doing something, so you should do it, too.

- **Card-stacking**—offering only one side of an issue to support one's position.

- **Diversion**—focusing on trivial or side issues to divert attention from a central point. Calling fast-food consumption "a matter of personal choice," for example, is a diversion from the fact that it can be harmful to health.

- **Elitism**—linking a concept or product with high social standing, education, wealth, or fame. A product endorsement by a well-known sports figure or an endorsement of a political candidate by a popular rock star are examples of this technique.

- **Emotional appeal**—prodding people's feelings to distract them from unpleasant facts. A video clip of a political candidate leaving church with her family or relaxing with her dog may be an attempt to mask dishonesty or incompetence by appealing to religious believers and animal lovers.

- **Glittering generalities**—using words that produce a positive emotional response but that may mean different things to different people. A slogan such as "job creation" on a politician's bumper sticker, for example, carries a positive message without offering any specifics about the candidate's program. The word *natural* on a food product conveys an image of healthfulness without describing contents.

- **Name-calling** —also known as mud-slinging: pointing out negative qualities of the opposing position while ignoring any positive qualities. This is the opposite of the glittering generalities approach.

- **Plain folk**—the opposite of elitism: appealing to the common point of view or using language like "we, the people" that signals that product users or a candidate's backers are just like everyone else. The technique was used successfully to portray the affluent railroad lawyer Abraham Lincoln as "Honest Abe, the rail splitter," born in a log cabin.

- **Repetition**—saying the same message or using the same words or phrases more than once in order to make an impression on the reader or listener.

- **Stereotype**—ascribing characteristics to an individual based on the perceived characteristics of a group to which she belongs. Most people recognize the falseness in stereotypes based on race, religion, or ethnic group, but stereotyping of other groups—rich people, poor people, single mothers, overweight people, and many others—can be equally as false.

- **Testimonial**—using endorsements from celebrities or other people. A picture of a star athlete on a cereal box is a familiar example, as is your favorite rock star appearing in a commercial for a political candidate.

- **Transfer**—using a symbol to carry a message. A computer company, for example, might use an actor portraying scientist Albert Einstein in a commercial to convey the message that its product can make you smarter.

Read this sentence from President Roosevelt's war message.

> *"With confidence in our armed forces— with the unbounding determination of our people—we will gain the inevitable triumph—so help us God."*

What persuasive technique does Roosevelt use in this statement?

A diversion

B plain folk

C bandwagon

D emotional appeal

President Roosevelt uses several persuasive techniques in this historic speech—the "bandwagon" in phrases like "our whole nation," and "card-stacking" when he portrays the attack as "unprovoked" and "dastardly." In this sentence, he is clearly calling on the American people to be resolute by appealing to our feelings about ourselves and our fighting forces. Choice D is the correct answer.

Read these sentences from the speech.

> *"Yesterday, the Japanese government also launched an attack against Malaya."*
>
> *"Last night, Japanese forces attacked Hong Kong."*
>
> *"Last night, Japanese forces attacked Guam."*
>
> *"Last night, Japanese forces attacked the Philippine Islands."*
>
> *"Last night, the Japanese attacked Wake Island."*
>
> *"This morning, the Japanese attacked Midway Island."*

Unit 4 Analyzing and Interpreting Nonfiction

Why is the propaganda technique used in these sentences effective?

A   It persuades listeners that Americans are historically on the side of the powerless.

B   It emphasizes the apparent differences between the United States and its enemies.

C   It emphasizes that the attack on Pearl Harbor was part of a well-coordinated offensive.

D   It persuades listeners that the war effort is worth the sacrifices Americans will have to make.

Here the president uses repetition to emphasize that the attack was only part of a campaign of ruthless aggression. (Indeed, the Japanese aim was to conquer eastern and southern Asia, and Pearl Harbor was an attempt to knock out the American navy so that the United States could not stop them.) The sentences read like the drumbeat of an advancing army and are even more effective when you listen to a recording of the speech. Choice C is the correct answer.

Analyze how President Roosevelt constructs the argument in the passage. Use examples from the passage to support your analysis.

_____

_____

_____

_____

_____

_____

_____

_____

This constructed-response question calls on you to consider Roosevelt's speech as a whole—how he uses facts, opinions, and techniques of persuasion to rally Congress and the people to go to war. Here is one possible answer:

The American people probably didn't need much persuading after the attack on Pearl Harbor. Roosevelt was telling them what they already knew, that the country was at war and there would be major sacrifices ahead. His speech rallies the people for the struggle by combining facts and opinions to describe the nature of the enemy and appealing to the ways Americans like to think about themselves. He begins by naming the day of the attack as "a date which will live in infamy," and it has, just as we remember September 11, 2001. He uses words like "suddenly and deliberately" and emphasizes that up until the attack there had been no war to vilify the enemy and to imply that the Japanese were devious and sneaky, in implied contrast with Americans, who "fight fair." In fact in any fight someone has to throw the first punch, and this one had been brewing for some time, but that didn't much matter when our people had been killed and our ships and planes destroyed. The list of other places the Japanese had attacked further emphasized that they were trying to build an empire and had to be stopped. Roosevelt knows that American opinion will be overwhelmingly on his side, but he bolsters that opinion by appealing to "the people of the United States," "our whole nation," "the American people in their righteous might" and their "unbounding determination."

IT'S YOUR TURN

Read the passage and answer the questions.

This speech was given by another US president in a different kind of war. The "Cold War" (1947–1989) between the United States and the Soviet Union (Russia) was largely a war of propaganda between democratic capitalism and Soviet communism. Europe was divided between the two camps, with Germany straddling the line between them and the city of Berlin split into eastern and western sides. In 1961, the Russians built a wall across Berlin to prevent people from leaving the part of Europe they controlled for the freer West. President John F. Kennedy gave this speech at the Berlin wall on June 26, 1963.

I am proud to come to this city as the guest of your distinguished Mayor, who has symbolized throughout the world the fighting spirit of West Berlin.

And I am proud to visit the Federal Republic with your distinguished chancellor who for so many years has committed Germany to democracy and freedom and progress, and to come here in the company of my fellow American, General Clay, who has been in this city during its great moments of crisis and will come again if ever needed.

Two thousand years ago the proudest boast was "civis Romanus sum"[1]. Today, in the world of freedom, the proudest boast is "Ich bin ein Berliner"[2].

I appreciate my interpreter translating my German!

There are many people in the world who really don't understand, or say they don't, what is the great issue between the free world and the Communist world. Let them come to Berlin.

There are some who say that Communism is the wave of the future. Let them come to Berlin.

And there are some who say in Europe and elsewhere we can work with the Communists. Let them come to Berlin.

And there are even a few who say that it is true that Communism is an evil system, but it permits us to make economic progress. Lass' sie nach Berlin kommen. Let them come to Berlin.

Freedom has many difficulties and democracy is not perfect, but we have never had to put a wall up to keep our people in, to prevent them from leaving us.

I want to say, on behalf of my countrymen, who live many miles away on the other side of the Atlantic, who are far distant from you, that they take the greatest pride that they have been able to share with you, even from a distance, the story of the last 18 years.

I know of no town, no city, that has been besieged for 18 years that still lives with the vitality and the force, and the hope and the determination of the city of West Berlin.

While the wall is the most obvious and vivid demonstration of the failures of the Communist system, for all the world to see, we take no satisfaction in it, for it is, as your mayor has said, an offense not only against history but an offense against humanity, separating families, dividing husbands and wives and brothers and sisters, and dividing a people who wish to be joined together.

What is true of this city is true of Germany—real, lasting peace in Europe can never be assured as long as one German out of four is denied the elementary right of free men, and that is to make a free choice.

In 18 years of peace and good faith, this generation of Germans has earned the right to be free, including the right to unite their families and their nation in lasting peace, with good will to all people.

You live in a defended island of freedom, but your life is part of the main.

So let me ask you as I close, to lift your eyes beyond the dangers of today, to the hopes of tomorrow, beyond the freedom merely of this city of Berlin, or your country of Germany, to the advance of freedom everywhere, beyond the wall to the day of peace with justice, beyond yourselves and ourselves to all mankind.

Freedom is indivisible, and when one man is enslaved, all are not free.

When all are free, then we can look forward to that day when this city will be joined as one and this country and this great continent of Europe in a peaceful and hopeful globe.

When that day finally comes, as it will, the people of West Berlin can take sober satisfaction in the fact that they were in the front lines for almost two decades.

All free men, wherever they may live, are citizens of Berlin, and, therefore, as a free man, I take pride in the words "Ich bin ein Berliner."

---

[1] **Civis romanus sum:** Latin, "I am a Roman citizen"
[2] **Ich bin ein Berliner:** German, "I am a Berliner"

1 Which sentence from the passage contains an opinion?

   A "Today, in the world of freedom, the proudest boast is 'Ich bin ein Berliner.'"

   B "There are many people in the world who really don't understand, or say they don't, what is the great issue between the free world and the Communist world."

   C "Freedom has many difficulties and democracy is not perfect, but we have never had to put a wall up to keep our people in, to prevent them from leaving us."

   D "Freedom is indivisible, and when one man is enslaved, all are not free."

2 Read the sentence from the passage.

   "I want to say, on behalf of my countrymen, who live many miles away on the other side of the Atlantic, who are far distant from you, that they take the greatest pride that they have been able to share with you, even from a distance, the story of the last 18 years."

   What does the opinion used in this sentence contribute to the passage?

   A It declares that the American people stand with the people of Berlin.

   B It implies that the United States is willing to fight for the freedom of Berlin.

   C It suggests that Americans are impressed by the president's attempts to speak German.

   D It shows that the president is anxious to make a strong impression on the Soviet Union.

3 What detail is **least** essential to the overall understanding of the passage?

   A Kennedy's criticisms of the Communist system

   B Kennedy's praise of West Berlin as a symbol of freedom

   C Kennedy's comment about the interpreter translating his German

   D Kennedy's acknowledgment of the presence of the mayor of Berlin and the German chancellor

Unit 4 Analyzing and Interpreting Nonfiction

4 What persuasive technique does Kennedy use with the use of the phrase, "Let them come to Berlin"?

A transfer

B repetition

C emotional appeal

D glittering generalities

5 Read the sentence from the passage.

"Freedom has many difficulties and democracy is not perfect, but we have never had to put a wall up to keep our people in, to prevent them from leaving us."

Why is the propaganda technique used in this sentence effective?

A It compares the Communist system to a prison.

B It suggests that Berliners are protected by the wall.

C It makes apologies for the failures of the democratic system.

D It assures the people of Berlin that in time the wall will come down.

6 Why does Kennedy speak in German at various points in his speech?

A to prove a point about "the brotherhood of mankind"

B to demonstrate America's empathy for the people of Berlin

C to acknowledge differences between American and German cultures

D to warn the Soviet Union that the US is prepared to fight for the freedom of Berlin

7 Evaluate the argument President Kennedy presents in this speech. Explain why it is or why it is not a convincing argument.

_____

_____

_____

_____

_____

_____

_____

Unit 4 Analyzing and Interpreting Nonfiction

Read the passage and answer questions 1–11.

The Fallacy of Success

by G. K. Chesterton

> *English writer Gilbert Keith Chesterton is best remembered today for his mystery fiction featuring the priest-detective Father Brown. He also wrote poems, plays, essays, and criticism, both art and literary. This essay was published in 1909.*

There has appeared in our time a particular class of books and articles which I sincerely and solemnly think may be called the silliest ever known among men. They are much more wild than the wildest romances of chivalry and much more dull than the dullest religious tract. Moreover, the romances of chivalry were at least about chivalry; the religious tracts are about religion. But these things are about nothing; they are about what is called Success. On every bookstall, in every magazine, you may find works telling people how to succeed. They are books showing men how to succeed in everything; they are written by men who cannot even succeed in writing books. To begin with, of course, there is no such thing as Success. Or, if you like to put it so, there is nothing that is not successful. That a thing is successful merely means that it is; a millionaire is successful in being a millionaire and a donkey in being a donkey. Any live man has succeeded in living; any dead man may have succeeded in committing suicide. But, passing over the bad logic and bad philosophy in the phrase, we may take it, as these writers do, in the ordinary sense of success in obtaining money or worldly position. These writers profess to tell the ordinary man how he may succeed in his trade or speculation—how, if he is a builder, he may succeed as a builder; how, if he is a stockbroker, he may succeed as a stockbroker. They profess to show him how, if he is a grocer, he may become a sporting yachtsman [and] how, if he is a tenth-rate journalist, he may become a peer[1].... This is a definite and business-like proposal, and I really think that the people who buy these books (if any people do buy them) have a moral, if not a legal, right to ask for their money back. Nobody would dare to publish a book about electricity which literally told one nothing about electricity; no one would dare publish an article on botany which showed that the writer did not know which end of a plant grew in the earth. Yet our modern world is full of books about Success and successful people which literally contain no kind of idea, and scarcely any kind of verbal sense.

It is perfectly obvious that in any decent occupation (such as bricklaying or writing books) there are only two ways (in any special sense) of succeeding. One is by doing very good work, the other is by cheating. Both are much too simple to require any literary explanation. If you are in for the

---

[1]**peer:** titled nobleman

high jump, either jump higher than any one else, or manage somehow to pretend that you have done so. If you want to succeed at whist, either be a good whist-player, or play with marked cards. You may want a book about jumping; you may want a book about whist; you may want a book about cheating at whist. But you cannot want a book about Success. Especially you cannot want a book about Success such as those which you can now find scattered by the hundred about the book-market. You may want to jump or to play cards; but you do not want to read wandering statements to the effect that jumping is jumping, or that games are won by winners. If these writers, for instance, said anything about success in jumping it would be something like this: "The jumper must have a clear aim before him. He must desire definitely to jump higher than the other men who are in for the same competition. He must let no feeble feelings of mercy…prevent him from trying to *do his best*. He must remember that a competition in jumping is distinctly competitive, and that, as Darwin has gloriously demonstrated, THE WEAKEST GO TO THE WALL." That is the kind of thing the book would say, and very useful it would be, no doubt, if read out in a low and tense voice to a young man just about to take the high jump. Or suppose that in the course of his intellectual rambles the philosopher of Success dropped upon our other case, that of playing cards, his bracing advice would run— "In playing cards it is very necessary to avoid the mistake (commonly made by maudlin humanitarians and Free Traders) of permitting your opponent to win the game. You must have grit and snap and *go in to win*. The days of idealism and superstition are over. We live in a time of science and hard common sense, and it has now been definitely proved that in any game where two are playing IF ONE DOES NOT WIN THE OTHER WILL." It is all very stirring, of course; but I confess that if I were playing cards I would rather have some decent little book which told me the rules of the game. Beyond the rules of the game it is all a question either of talent or dishonesty; and I will undertake to provide either one or the other—which, it is not for me to say.

Turning over a popular magazine, I find a queer and amusing example. There is an article called "The Instinct that Makes People Rich." It is decorated in front with a formidable portrait of Lord Rothschild. There are many definite methods, honest and dishonest, which make people rich; the only "instinct" I know of which does it is that instinct which theological Christianity crudely describes as "the sin of avarice." That, however, is beside the present point. I wish to quote the following exquisite paragraphs as a piece of typical advice as to how to succeed. It is so practical; it leaves so little doubt about what should be our next step—

"The name of Vanderbilt is synonymous with wealth gained by modern enterprise. 'Cornelius,' the founder of the family, was the first of the great American magnates of commerce. He started as the son of a poor farmer; he ended as a millionaire 20 times over.

"He had the money-making instinct. He seized his opportunities, the opportunities that were given by the application of the steam-engine to ocean traffic, and by the birth of railway locomotion in the wealthy but underdeveloped United States of America, and consequently he amassed an immense fortune.

"Now it is, of course, obvious that we cannot all follow exactly in the footsteps of this great railway monarch. The precise opportunities that fell to him do not occur to us. Circumstances have changed. But, although this is so, still, in our own sphere and in our own circumstances, we *can* follow his general methods; we can seize those opportunities that are given us, and give ourselves a very fair chance of attaining riches."

In such strange utterances we see quite clearly what is really at the bottom of all these articles and books. It is not mere business; it is not even mere cynicism. It is mysticism; the horrible mysticism of money. The writer of that passage did not really have the remotest notion of how Vanderbilt made his money, or of how anybody else is to make his. He does, indeed, conclude his remarks by advocating some scheme; but it has nothing in the world to do with Vanderbilt. He merely wished to prostrate himself before the mystery of a millionaire. For when we really worship anything, we love not only its clearness but its obscurity. We exult in its very invisibility. Thus, for instance, when a man is in love with a woman he takes special pleasure in the fact that a woman is unreasonable. Thus, again, the very pious poet, celebrating his Creator, takes pleasure in saying that God moves in a mysterious way. Now, the writer of the paragraph which I have quoted does not seem to have had anything to do with a god and I should not think (judging by his extreme unpracticality) that he had ever been really in love with a woman. But the thing he does worship—Vanderbilt—he treats in exactly this mystical manner. He really revels in the fact his deity Vanderbilt is keeping a secret from him. And it fills his soul with a sort of transport of cunning, an ecstasy of priestcraft, that he should pretend to be telling to the multitude that terrible secret which he does not know.

Speaking about the instinct that makes people rich, the same writer remarks—

"In the olden days its existence was fully understood. The Greeks enshrined it in the story of Midas, of the 'Golden Touch.' Here was a man who turned everything he laid his hands upon into gold. His life was a progress amidst riches. Out of everything that came in his way he created the precious metal. 'A foolish legend,' said the wiseacres of the Victorian age. 'A truth,' say we of today. We all know of such men. We are ever meeting or reading about such persons who turn everything they touch into gold.

Success dogs their very footsteps. Their life's pathway leads unerringly upwards. They cannot fail."

Unfortunately, however, Midas could fail; he did. His path did not lead unerringly upward. He starved because whenever he touched a biscuit or a ham sandwich it turned to gold. That was the whole point of the story, though the writer has to suppress it delicately, writing so near to a portrait of Lord Rothschild. The old fables of mankind are, indeed, unfathomably wise; but we must not have them expurgated in the interests of Mr. Vanderbilt. We must not have King Midas represented as an example of success; he was a failure of an unusually painful kind. Also, he had the ears of an ass. Also (like most other prominent and wealthy persons) he endeavored to conceal the fact. It was his barber (if I remember right) who had to be treated on a confidential footing with regard to this peculiarity; and his barber, instead of behaving like a go-ahead person of the Succeed-at-all-costs school and trying to blackmail King Midas, went away and whispered this splendid piece of society scandal to the reeds, who enjoyed it enormously. It is said that they also whispered it as the winds swayed them to and fro. I look reverently at the portrait of Lord Rothschild; I read reverently about the exploits of Mr. Vanderbilt. I know that I cannot turn everything I touch to gold; but then I also know that I have never tried, having a preference for other substances, such as grass, and good wine. I know that these people have certainly succeeded in something; that they have certainly overcome somebody; I know that they are kings in a sense that no men were ever kings before; that they create markets and bestride continents. Yet it always seems to me that there is some small domestic fact that they are hiding, and I have sometimes thought I heard upon the wind the laughter and whisper of the reeds.

At least, let us hope that we shall all live to see these absurd books about Success covered with a proper derision and neglect. They do not teach people to be successful, but they do teach people to be snobbish; they do spread a sort of evil poetry of worldliness. The Puritans are always denouncing books that inflame lust; what shall we say of books that inflame the viler passions of avarice and pride? A hundred years ago we had the ideal of the Industrious Apprentice; boys were told that by thrift and work they would all become Lord Mayors. This was fallacious, but it was manly, and had a minimum of moral truth. In our society, temperance will not help a poor man to enrich himself, but it may help him to respect himself. Good work will not make him a rich man, but good work may make him a good workman. The Industrious Apprentice rose by virtues few and narrow indeed, but still virtues. But what shall we say of the gospel preached to the new Industrious Apprentice; the Apprentice who rises not by his virtues, but avowedly by his vices?

1 What is the author's purpose in writing the passage?

   A to compare various authors' ideas of success

   B to describe how Cornelius Vanderbilt achieved success

   C to advance the idea that success has nothing to do with money

   D to critique books that claim to teach the reader how to achieve success

2 Which word is a synonym for <u>avarice</u>?

   A greed

   B failure

   C wisdom

   D dishonesty

Unit 4 Analyzing and Interpreting Nonfiction

3 Read the sentence from the passage.

"You may want to jump or to play cards; but you do not want to read wandering statements to the effect that jumping is jumping, or that games are won by winners."

Which statement **best** describes how the author's use of this sentence influences the reader?

A The phrase suggests that you can't learn to do anything by reading.

B The phrase implies that sports and card games are a waste of time.

C The phrase shows that the author believes the pursuit of success to be an useless effort.

D The phrase emphasizes the author's point that books about "success" are really about nothing.

4 Based on information in the passage, what conclusion can be made about Lord Rothschild?

A He was a poor man who attained great wealth by dishonest means.

B He was a rich man who lost much of his fortune because of a scandal.

C He was a rich man who gave away much of his fortune to charitable enterprises.

D He was a poor man who attained great wealth through hard work and business sense.

5 How does the author's style influence the tone of the passage?

A The author's use of positive language creates a warm tone.

B The author's use of negative language creates a sarcastic tone.

C The author's use of informal language creates a conversational tone.

D The author's use of old-fashioned language creates a humorous tone.

6 Which sentence from the passage contains an opinion?

   A "That a thing is successful merely means that it is; a millionaire is successful in being a millionaire and a donkey in being a donkey."

   B "These writers profess to tell the ordinary man how he may succeed in his trade or speculation—how, if he is a builder, he may succeed as a builder; how, if he is a stockbroker, he may succeed as a stockbroker."

   C "Yet our modern world is full of books about Success and successful people which literally contain no kind of idea, and scarcely any kind of verbal sense."

   D "In our society, temperance will not help a poor man to enrich himself, but it may help him to respect himself."

7 What detail is **least** essential to the overall understanding of the passage?

   A the example of cheating at cards as a path to success

   B the mystical nature of the way authors write about success

   C the comparison of Lord Rothschild with the mythical King Midas

   D the quotations from the article "The Instinct that Makes People Rich"

8 Read these opening sentences from the passage.

   "There has appeared in our time a particular class of books and articles which I sincerely and solemnly think may be called the silliest ever known among men. They are much more wild than the wildest romances of chivalry and much more dull than the dullest religious tract."

   What persuasive technique does the author use by beginning his essay this way?

   A elitism

   B bandwagon

   C name-calling

   D emotional appeal

9 Which statement from the passage **best** supports the generalization that books about "success" are really about the worship of money?

A "They are books showing men how to succeed in everything; they are written by men who cannot even succeed in writing books."

B "They profess to show him how, if he is a grocer, he may become a sporting yachtsman [and] how, if he is a tenth-rate journalist, he may become a peer."

C "I know that I cannot turn everything I touch to gold; but then I also know that I have never tried, having a preference for other substances, such as grass, and good wine."

D "At least, let us hope that we shall all live to see these absurd books about Success covered with a proper derision and neglect."

10 Based on information in the passage, how does the myth of King Midas relate to Chesterton's argument about "the fallacy of success"?

_____

_____

_____

_____

_____

_____

_____

_____

11 Analyze how the author constructs the argument in the passage. Use examples from the passage to support your analysis.

_____

_____

_____

_____

_____

_____

_____

_____

Read the passage and answer questions 12–19.

Apollo 8: Christmas at the Moon

NASA

Christmas Eve, 1968. As one of the most turbulent, tragic years in American history drew to a close, millions around the world were watching and listening as the *Apollo 8* astronauts—Frank Borman, Jim Lovell, and Bill Anders—became the first humans to orbit another world.

As their command module floated above the lunar surface, the astronauts beamed back images of the moon and Earth and took turns reading from the book of Genesis, closing with a wish for everyone "on the good Earth."

"We were told that on Christmas Eve we would have the largest audience that had ever listened to a human voice," recalled Borman during 40th anniversary celebrations in 2008. "And the only instructions that we got from NASA was to do something appropriate."

"The first ten verses of Genesis is the foundation of many of the world's religions, not just the Christian religion," added Lovell. "There are more people in other religions than the Christian religion around the world, and so this would be appropriate to that and so that's how it came to pass."

The mission was also famous for the iconic "Earthrise" image, snapped by Anders, which would give humankind a new perspective on their home planet. Anders has said that despite all the training and preparation for an exploration of the moon, the astronauts ended up discovering Earth.

The *Apollo 8* astronauts got where they were that Christmas Eve because of a bold, improvisational call by NASA. With the clock ticking on President Kennedy's challenge to land on the moon by decade's end, delays with the lunar module were threatening to slow the Apollo program. So NASA decided to change mission plans and send the *Apollo 8* crew all the way to the moon without a lunar module on the first manned flight of the massive *Saturn V* rocket.

The crew rocketed into orbit on December 21, and after circling the moon 10 times on Christmas Eve, it was time to come home. On Christmas morning, mission control waited anxiously for word that *Apollo 8's* engine burn to leave lunar orbit had worked. They soon got confirmation when Lovell radioed, "Roger, please be informed there is a Santa Claus."

The crew splashed down in the Pacific on December 27. A lunar landing was still months away, but for the first time ever, men from Earth had visited the moon and returned home safely.

12 What is the main organizational structure of the passage?

A   cause and effect

B   order of importance

C   problem and solution

D   comparison and contrast

13 The word <u>improvisational</u> suggests that the decision to orbit the moon on Christmas eve

A   had not been planned.

B   involved a great degree of risk.

C   was meant to coincide with the holiday.

D   was made by the astronauts contrary to orders.

14 How does the photograph help to clarify information in the passage?

A   It shows that it was taken on Christmas Eve.

B   It shows Earth as a unified world isolated in space.

C   It shows Earth as viewed from the surface of the moon.

D   It shows that the *Apollo 8* astronauts were the first to orbit the moon.

15 What additional information would **best** support the author's purpose?

A   technical data about the *Saturn V* rocket

B   biographical information about the *Apollo 8* crew

C   details about how the astronauts celebrated Christmas in space

D   an explanation of why 1968 was "one of the most turbulent, tragic years in American history"

16 According to the passage, what was the significance of Astronaut Lovell's remark about Santa Claus?

 A   It was a joke aimed at skeptical scientists.

 B   It was a greeting meant for Lovell's children.

 C   It suggested that the astronauts were filled with childlike wonder.

 D   It implied that a potentially dangerous flight maneuver had proceeded safely.

17 Read the incomplete summary of the passage.

 • *On Christmas Eve, 1968, the* Apollo 8 *astronauts became the first people to orbit the moon.*

 • *The astronauts read selections from the Bible as a holiday greeting.*

 • *NASA had sent the crew to the moon in an attempt to speed up the Apollo program.*

 • _____

Which sentence **best** completes the summary?

 A   It was the first manned flight of the *Saturn V* rocket.

 B   The crew landed safely back on Earth on December 27.

 C   Seven months later, the first astronauts landed on the moon.

 D   The crew performed an engine burn to leave orbit on Christmas morning.

18 Which statement **best** states a theme in the passage?

 A   Space is "the last frontier."

 B   Holidays bring people together.

 C   All people on Earth are a single family.

 D   We remember events that made us feel good.

19 Read this sentence from the passage.

"Anders has said that despite all the training and preparation for an exploration of the moon, the astronauts ended up discovering Earth."

Analyze how the opinion used in this sentence contributes to the passage.

_____

_____

_____

_____

_____

_____

_____

Read the passage. Then answer questions 20–27.

from The Exploration of the Colorado River and its Canyons
by John Wesley Powell

In 1869, John Wesley Powell led a three-month expedition down the Green and Colorado rivers of the western United States that was highlighted by the first known passage through the Grand Canyon. Powell was a university professor and a former army officer who had lost his right arm in a battle during the Civil War. The Explorations of the Colorado River and its Canyons *was published in 1895.*

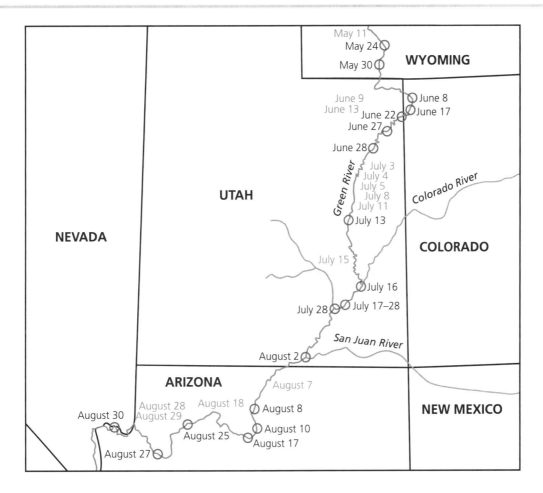

May 30. This morning we are ready to enter the mysterious canyon, and start with some anxiety. The old mountaineers tell us that it cannot be run; the Indians say, "Water heap catch 'em"; but all are eager for the trial, and off we go.

Entering Flaming Gorge, we quickly run through it on a swift current and emerge into a little park. Half a mile below, the river wheels sharply to the left and enters another canyon cut into the mountain. We enter the narrow passage. On either side the walls rapidly increase in altitude. On the left are overhanging ledges and cliffs, 500, 1,000, 1,500 feet high.

On the right the rocks are broken and ragged, and the water fills the channel from cliff to cliff. Now the river turns abruptly around a point to the right, and the waters plunge swiftly down among great rocks;

and here we have our first experience with canyon rapids. I stand up on the deck of my boat to seek a way among the wave-beaten rocks. All untried as we are with such waters, the moments are filled with intense anxiety. Soon our boats reach the swift current; a stroke or two, now on this side, now on that, and we thread the narrow passage with exhilarating velocity, mounting the high waves, whose foaming crests dash over us, and plunging into the troughs, until we reach the quiet water below. Then comes a feeling of great relief. Our first rapid is run. Another mile, and we come into the valley again.

Let me explain this canyon. Where the river turns to the left above, it takes a course directly into the mountain, penetrating to its very heart, then wheels back upon itself, and runs out into the valley from which it started only half a mile below the point at which it entered; so the canyon is in the form of an elongated letter U, with the apex in the center of the mountain. We name it Horseshoe Canyon.

Soon we leave the valley and enter another short canyon, very narrow at first, but widening below as the canyon walls increase in height. Here we discover the mouth of a beautiful little creek coming down through its narrow water-worn cleft. Just at its entrance there is a park of two or three hundred acres, walled on every side by almost vertical cliffs hundreds of feet in altitude, with three gateways through the walls—one up the river, another down, and a third through which the creek comes in. The river is broad, deep, and quiet, and its waters mirror towering rocks…. At night we camp at the foot of this canyon.

Our general course this day has been south, but here the river turns to the east around a point which is rounded to the shape of a dome. On its sides little cells have been carved by the action of the water, and in these pits, which cover the face of the dome, hundreds of swallows have built their nests. As they flit about the cliffs, they look like swarms of bees, giving to the whole the appearance of a colossal beehive of the old-time form, and so we name it Beehive Point.

The opposite wall is a vast amphitheater, rising in a succession of terraces to a height of 1,200 or 1,500 feet. Each step is built of red sandstone, with a face of naked red rock and a glacis clothed with verdure. So the amphitheater seems banded red and green, and the evening sun is playing with roseate flashes on the rocks, with shimmering green on the cedars' spray, and with iridescent gleams on the dancing waves. The landscape revels in the sunshine.

May 31. We start down another canyon and reach rapids made dangerous by high rocks lying in the channel; so we run ashore and let our boats down with lines. In the afternoon we come to more dangerous rapids and stop to examine them. I find we must do the same work again, but, being on the wrong side of the river to obtain a foothold, must first cross over—no very easy matter in such a current, with rapids and rocks below. We take the pioneer boat, "Emma Dean," over, and unload her on the bank; then she returns and takes another load. Running back and forth, she soon has half our cargo over. Then one of the larger boats is manned and taken across, but is carried down almost to the rocks in spite of hard rowing. The other boats follow and make the landing, and we go into camp for the night. At the foot of the cliff on this side there is a long slope covered with pines; under these we make our beds, and soon after sunset are seeking rest and sleep. The cliffs on either side are of red sandstone and stretch toward the heavens 2,500 feet. On this side the long, pine-clad slope is surmounted by perpendicular cliffs, with pines on their summits. The wall on the other side is bare rock from the water's edge up 2,000 feet, then slopes back, giving footing to pines and cedars.

As the twilight deepens, the rocks grow dark and somber; the threatening roar of the water is loud and constant, and I lie awake with thoughts of the morrow and the canyons to come, interrupted now and then by characteristics of the scenery that attract my attention. And here I make a discovery. On looking at the mountain directly in front, the steepness of the slope is greatly exaggerated, while the distance to its summit and its true altitude are correspondingly diminished. I have heretofore found that to judge properly of the slope of a mountain side, one must see it in profile. In coming down the river this afternoon, I observed the slope of a particular part of the wall and made an estimate of its altitude. While at supper, I noticed the same cliff from a position facing it, and it seemed steeper, but not half so high. Now lying on my side and looking at it, the true proportions appear. This seems a wonder, and I rise to take a view of it standing. It is the same cliff as at supper time. Lying down again, it is the cliff as seen in profile, with a long slope and distant summit…. I have found a way to estimate the altitude and slope of an inclination, in like manner as I can judge of distance along the horizon….

June 1. Today we have an exciting ride. The river rolls down the canyon at a wonderful rate, and, with no rocks in the way, we make almost railroad speed. Here and there the water rushes into a narrow gorge; the rocks on the side roll it into the center in great waves, and the boats go leaping and bounding over these like things of life, reminding me of…herds of startled deer bounding through forests beset with fallen timber…. At times the waves break and roll over the boats, which necessitates much

bailing and obliges us to stop occasionally for that purpose. At one time we run twelve miles in an hour, stoppages included….

At last we come to calm water, and a threatening roar is heard in the distance. Slowly approaching the point whence the sound issues, we come near to falls, and tie up just above them on the left. Here we shall be compelled to make a portage; so we unload the boats, and fasten a long line to the bow of the smaller one, and another to the stern, and moor her close to the brink of the fall. Then the bowline is taken below and made fast; the stern line is held by five or six men, and the boat let down as long as they can hold her against the rushing waters; then, letting go one end of the line, it runs through the ring; the boat leaps over the fall and is caught by the lower rope.

Now we rest for the night.

June 2. This morning we make a trail among the rocks, transport the cargoes to a point below the fall, let the remaining boats over, and are ready to start before noon.

On a high rock by which the trail passes we find the inscription: "Ashley 18-5." The third figure is obscure—some of the party reading it 1835, some 1855. James Baker, an old-time mountaineer, once told me about a party of men starting down the river, and Ashley was named as one. The story runs that the boat was swamped, and some of the party drowned in one of the canyons below. The word "Ashley" is a warning to us, and we resolve on great caution. Ashley Falls is the name we give to the cataract.

20 In what way is this passage most similar to "*Apollo 8: Christmas on the Moon*"?

A Each focuses on an exploratory expedition.

B Each focuses on the beauty of scenery, on Earth or in space.

C Each presents details about how people cooperate in stressful conditions.

D Each presents details about celebrating a holiday under unusual circumstances.

21 Read the sentence from the passage.

"So the amphitheater seems banded red and green, and the evening sun is playing with roseate flashes on the rocks, with <u>shimmering</u> green on the cedars' spray, and with iridescent gleams on the dancing waves."

What is being suggested by the use of the word <u>shimmering</u>?

A speed

B beauty

C danger

D mystery

22 How does the author's use of a journal as a literary form influence the meaning of the passage?

A The journal form suggests the use of facts to support opinions.

B The journal form obliges the author to be accurate and truthful.

C The journal form organizes information as a series of causes and effects.

D The journal form allows for a focus on the author's thoughts and observations.

Unit 4 Analyzing and Interpreting Nonfiction

23 Which sentence **best** describes the conflict of the events in the passage?

    A Powell is commanding a crew that mistrusts him and the mission he is leading them on.

    B Powell is leading his men through little-known territory with the potential of life-threatening danger.

    C Powell wants to observe and record the geography and wildlife, but his first duty is the safety of his crew.

    D Powell means to proceed on but hesitates at the warnings of more experienced mountain men and Native Americans.

24 What effect does the text organization have on the passage?

    A It helps the reader to understand the sequence of events on the expedition.

    B It allows the reader to understand the problems that Powell and his crew need to solve.

    C It helps the reader to visualize the setting by comparing it with other places Powell has been.

    D It allows the reader to understand the dual nature of Powell's role as scientist and commander.

25 Which sentence **best** describes the relationship between the map and the text?

    A The passage allows the reader to visualize the appearance of specific locations on the map.

    B The map helps the reader to appreciate how the land has changed since Powell's expedition.

    C The map allows the reader to see approximately where the expedition was on any given date.

    D The passage helps the reader to understand the difficulty of traversing the canyon country without a map.

26 What is the effect of the first-person point of view in the passage?

   A   It gives an objective description of the expedition's progress.

   B   It provides rich sensory details about the river and its canyons.

   C   It highlights the individual personalities of Powell and his crew.

   D   It places the expedition within the broader perspective of United States history.

27 What is the relationship between the setting and the characterization of John Wesley Powell as presented in the passage? Use examples from the passage to support your answer.

_____

_____

_____

_____

_____

_____

_____

_____

Unit 4 Analyzing and Interpreting Nonfiction

Glossary

A

act	a division of a play
allegory	metaphor in which objects, persons, and objects in a narrative have meanings that lie outside the narrative (e.g. *The Pilgrim's Progress* by John Bunyan; *Animal Farm* by George Orwell)
alliteration	repetition of initial sounds in neighboring words
allusion	reference, either direct or implied, to a familiar event, place, or person
antonyms	words with an opposite meaning
argument	a claim or position that the author makes
aside	short speech directed at the audience in a play
assonance	repetition of vowel sounds in neighboring words
autobiography	story of person's life written by that subject

B

ballad	narrative poem originally written to be sung
bias	a positive or negative approach towards a claim
biography	story of a person's life written by someone other than the subject

C

cast	a list of the characters in a drama or play
characters	the people in a story or play; character can also be the narrator or speaker
climax	the high point or turning point of the story
conflict	the struggle in a story; can be man versus man, man versus nature, man versus society, or man versus himself
couplet	two lines that rhyme in a poem

D

dialect	a particular way of speaking that varies from the standard in vocabulary, pronunciation, and grammar; often tied to a particular area or locale
dialogue	what the characters say in a story or play
diction	author's choice of words, phrases, sentence structure, and figurative language to create tone and meaning
dramatic literature	playing with facts to make a more interesting story, not sticking to the facts in a story

E

editorial	article that gives someone's opinion
exposition	usually the beginning of a work where the characters, conflict, and setting are introduced

F

fable	short story in which characters may be animals portrayed as human types; teaches a lesson
fact	statement supported by evidence
falling action	the events that follow the climax of a story
fantasy	story that takes place in an unreal setting or features unreal events; features characters with superhuman powers, magical worlds, or fantastic creatures
fiction	any imaginary work such as a story or play
figurative language	language used to create a special effect or feeling; language that is not meant literally
flashback	events that happened at an earlier time
folktale	story about ordinary people that contains a lesson about human nature
foreshadowing	suggestion that some event is to occur in the future
free verse	poem that does not rhyme or have a rhythm

G

generalization   a broad statement about a topic or person drawn from specific information about a topic or person

genre   type of literature

H

haiku   Japanese 17-syllable poem; usually written in three lines

historical fiction   stories set in a different time period from the past

homographs   words that are spelled the same but that have different meanings

hyperbole   exaggerated statement for effect

I

idiom   phrase that means something other than the literal meaning

imagery   language used to create an impression that appeals to senses

inciting incident   the event in a story which sets the conflict in motion

inference   judgment made by reading between the lines rather than through an explicit or direct statement

irony   use of a word or phrase to mean the opposite of its usual meaning; difference between the actual result of actions and the expected result

L

legend   tale from the past about people and events, usually connected to a specific place or time

limerick   humorous rhyming five-line poem

literary device   technique (e.g., alliteration, dialect, dialogue) used by the author to provide voice to a text

literary element   literature techniques such as characterization, setting, plot

literary form   the overall structure of the work whether type such as a play or poem or patterns of meter, rhyme, and lines (stanza, verse)

literary nonfiction   nonfiction that uses literary elements like character and setting to report on actual persons, places, or events (e.g., travel writing, biography)

lyric poem   a poem that expresses the poet's feelings

M

main idea   what the story, article, or paragraph is about

metaphor   type of figurative language that compares two unlike things but does not use *like* or *as*

monologue   a speech delivered in a play to other characters

mood   the atmosphere or prevailing emotions of a work

myth   explains something about nature or a people's customs or beliefs

N

narrative poem   a poem that tells a story

narrator   the person who tells the story or describes the events to an audience

nonfiction   a story that is true

O

onomatopoeia   words that sound like what they are describing

opinion   judgment not supported by evidence; what someone thinks or believes

P

personal essay   person describes and reflects upon something important in that person's life

personification   giving human characteristics to animals, objects, or ideas

plot   the sequence of events in a story

point of view   who is telling the story

first-person   the main character is telling the story; uses first person pronouns *I* and *we*

third-person limited omniscient   narrator is limited to knowledge of the thoughts and feelings of only one of the characters; uses third-person pronouns *he, she,* and *they*

third-person omniscient   outside character is all-knowing and can reveal the thoughts and feelings of more than one of the characters; uses third-person pronouns *he, she,* and *they*

prediction   what you think the outcome will be

prefix	part of a word added to the beginning of another word that changes the meaning of the word
propaganda	information skewed to influence opinion or behavior (e.g., name calling, bandwagon, emotional appeal, testimonial, circular argument, repetition, sweeping generalizations, appeal to facts or statistics)

R

realistic fiction	story dealing with contemporary issues and setting
reasoned judgment	conclusion based on evidence
resolution	follows the climax; the explanation of what happens to the characters
rhyme	repeated sounds at the ends of words
rhythm	pattern of stressed and unstressed beats in a line of poetry
rising action	the events that build to the climax in a story or play

S

satire	work that ridicules or looks at human weakness or vice
scene	a division of an act of a play
scenery	the background and props that create the setting of a play
science fiction	story that takes place in an unreal setting or features an unreal event; some element of science fact forms the story background
script	the printed version of a play
sequence	the order in which actions occur
setting	the time and place in which a story or play takes place
simile	type of figurative language that compares two unlike things using *as* or *like*
soliloquy	a monologue spoken by a character alone on a stage; the speech reveals the character's inner thoughts and feelings
sonnet	a 14-line poem that follows a formal rhyme scheme
sound devices	elements of literature that use sound (e.g., onomatopoeia, rhyme, alliteration)
stage directions	advice on how actors should move or speak in a play
stanza	group of lines within a poem, similar to a chapter within a book

suffix	part of a word added to the end of another word that changes the meaning of the word
summary	short restatement of the ideas in a passage
symbolism	a symbol that stands for something else
synonyms	words that have a similar meaning
syntax	how words are ordered in phrases, clauses, and sentences

T

theme	the message or main idea of narrative text
tone	the feeling of a story; the author's attitude toward the characters and audience (e.g., serious, humorous)

V

voice	the author's unique way of creating a work (e.g., fluency, rhythm, and liveliness of the writing)